SAPPHIRE PROMISE

BASED ON THE TRUE STORY OF LOYALTY, TRUST, AND UNFAILING LOVE

SALLY BRANDLE

Dear Dr. Lum—
Life is full of surprises!
(Iris)
Thank you for the reviews!
Sally Brandle

CHP

CONTENTS

"Don't Despair" Batavia Coat of Arms

"Sally Brandle carries us into Batavia's pre-war daily life and into its architectural beauty. However, she also carries us, with Annika, into the darkness of Batavia's Tjideng Ghetto, a Japanese internment camp. This loss of her idyllic life caused despair but also hope." Dirk Teeuwen MSc, Nieuwpoort, The Netherlands

"The words take you there. *Sapphire Promise* is truly a gem that will transport you through time, to a place from long ago. The details honor the wonder of the Dutch East Indies -- a place where European structure and grace met the natural beauty and warmth of the Tropics. These vivid details captured the essence of what my dear Oma deeply yearned to return to, but never could. This coming-of-age story occurs during a time of great turbulence. The author takes such care in reminding the reader about what it means to be human, love, care, survive, and heal." Jamie Stern, Member at Large, Director of Research, The Indo Project   Trauma Therapist, Doctoral Candidate

"*Sapphire Promise* adds needed balance to all the somber recollections—as there were also fond memories of their youth in DEI that have returned to the survivors during the dwindling sunset of their remaining years, including the thrill of falling in a forever love, a hope that can sustain one during the most dire and trying times." Eric Morgan, Member at Large, The Indo Project

"I'm excited to share the compelling story of *Sapphire Promise* with my book group! The study questions at the end will ensure a lively, thoughtful discussion of this fascinating memoir." Pat H.

.

"I remember having a lovely conversation with Iris at a past museum holiday luncheon, hearing just a bit about her work during the war years, and recognizing what a unique life she had led. The determination, grace, and positive outlook of the heroine, Annika, surely reflect the character's inspiration. This book is a fitting tribute to a woman who led a remarkable life and triumphed in challenging circumstances." Kathleen Maki, Director of Human Resources, Seattle Art Museum

SAPPHIRE PROMISE

Copyright © 2021

SALLY BRANDLE

Cover Design by Michelle McDowell

This book is based on many interviews with a Dutch American woman born in 1923 who experienced most of these events, as well as research in various archives, diaries, articles, letters, and other material. Memory and history are subjective, and this work of literary fiction has an element of subjectivity as well. I have done my best to adhere to the truth as I and my sources believe it to be throughout this book, based on the information I have. However, there may be details others might interpret or have experienced differently. In addition, in places I have filled in sensory details of scenes, grounded in the historical material available to me, in the service of narrative interest.

For book club appearance information, please visit www. sallybrandle.com

ISBN: 978-1-944232-00-9

Audio book ISBN: 978-1-944232-02-3

eBook ISBN: 978-1-944232-03-0

Large Print Edition ISBN: 978-1-944232-01-6

*This book is dedicated to my little buddy, Iris,
and other strong, compassionate women
who believe in themselves and believe in love.*

ACKNOWLEDGMENTS

To write this story, it was necessary for my dear friend Iris to recall heart-wrenching occurrences from over eighty years ago. Her willingness to revisit these memories and trust in my ability to accurately pen her story is a treasured gift. Dirk Teeuwen, residing in Holland, provided countless photos, historical data, and even scene ideas in an accurate and often humorous manner. His knowledge of Batavia proved invaluable. Michelle McDowell show-cased her creativity and photography skills when she created the cover collage and prepared the book's accompanying photos.

Beta readers provided honest and insightful comments. My thanks to Nada Hughes, Jennifer Clukey, Mike Elliott, Kathleen Ekstrand, Kaylie Murphy, Pat Hodges, Pat Coonan, Viola Karsten, Susan McDonough Wachtman, Michelle and Steve

McDowell, Christine Lamb, Genie McFate, Jodi Ashland, Valerie Weston, Hope Malory, and bug authority James Anderson.

Special gratitude to the sensitivity readers from The Indo Project who helped me navigate historically complex and currently challenging issues: Priscilla Kluge McMullen, Jamie Stern, and Eric Morgan.

My husband, Brian, offered behind the scenes support in countless ways. His patience and perseverance amaze me. And a round of applause is due to editors Sharon Murray Roe and CJ Obray who provided their expertise on this project.

A NOTE FROM THE AUTHOR

Volunteering at the Seattle Art Museum connected me with Iris. An age difference of over thirty years never mattered, nor did it matter that her lineage included a French countess and mine a poor Irish immigrant grandmother. Our friendship grew from respect, common interests, and fun adventures.

Over time, Iris shared bits of her childhood growing up as a Dutch citizen in the city of Batavia in the Dutch East Indies (present day Jakarta, Indonesia*). Her poignant, exciting, and romantic story needed to be written. I began to take notes to create a timeline, from her birth in 1923 to her coming of age just prior to World War II. Iris's Dutch family descended from generations of colonists who profited from business on Java and then lost everything after the Japanese invasion. Her haunting experiences of being interned by the Japanese at eighteen while training to be a nurse did not deter her from going on to become a respected RN in Seattle.

I completed a biography of Iris's life as a gift to her for her ninety-sixth birthday. Shortly thereafter came the fictionalized version containing a minimum of fabricated scenes. This is the story that you are about to read. Names of her living family members have been changed to protect their privacy, while most historical names are accurate. The thoughts and emotions of our protagonist—now named Annika Wolter—are quoted verbatim, during real events she survived showing determination, grit, and enduring love. Although the novel takes place in a time of political and social upheaval, the intent is to portray the story of a young woman growing up in colonial society and the impact of war. Because Annika's life was multi-cultural and multilingual, many languages are routinely spoken and included in the story dialogue. Consult the Word Translation Table for easy reference. Here are examples:

- kleuter: (Dutch) toddler
- zakenman: (Dutch) older businessman
- verdorie: (Dutch) damn
- Mevrouw: (Dutch) Mrs.
- Juffrouw: (Dutch) Miss
- Nonna: (Malayan) Miss

*From 1619, the year the Netherlands founded Batavia on Java as their port and administrative center, the Malay Archipelago (over 6000 inhabited islands) became colonized by the Dutch as they began a lucrative trade in spices and sugar. Slavery was outlawed in 1860, followed by substantial taxes levied on the Indonesian "subjects." In 1901, the colonial government began pursuing their Dutch Ethical Policy, intended to benefit the indigenous population by improving their material living conditions through irrigation, transmigration from over-populated Java to other islands, and education. The policy suffered from underfunding, inflated expectations, and lack of acceptance in the Dutch colonial establishment. Little remained of it by the onset of the worldwide Great Depression in 1930. Iris's father had started a successful Dutch East Indies commodities brokerage in the early 1920s, then saw it also fail during the Great Depression. A rare, 1938 colorized silent film shows Dutch, Indonesian, and Indos (people of mixed Indonesian and European ancestry) in Batavia and Bandoeng near the time the book opens. A digital version of the film can be viewed online here: https://www.youtube.com/watch?v=3vtOdImMfLA (viewers may hit Skip Ads button to bypass commercials)

On September 27, 1940, one year after the start of World War II, Germany, Italy, and Japan signed the Tripartite (or Berlin) Pact. It was designed to create a defense alliance between the participating countries and deter neutral America from entering the conflict. This delay tactic worked for over a year. On December 7, 1941 Japan staged a simultaneous attack on Thailand, Pearl Harbor, and the U.S. protectorates of Guam, Wake Island, and the Philippine Islands, and on the British Empire colonies in Malaysia, Hong Kong, and Singapore. In an act of alliance with the U.S. and Great Britain, Queen Wilhelmina of the Netherlands declared war against Japan on December 8, 1941. The Japanese invaded Java early in 1942 to secure a strategic location and gain control of precious oil resources. They put the Dutch colonists in POW camps, enslaved and forced the Indonesian and Indo men into their army, and caused a famine. After the Allies defeated the Japanese in World War II, the Dutch and Indonesians fought each other for control of the islands until Indonesia gained independence in 1949. For further reading, please download the free historically accurate continuation of this story via a timeline at http://www.sallybrandle.com or refer to the sources listed in the References section of this book.

PROLOGUE

CALIFORNIA 2021

Annika dropped a bag of Earl Grey tea into the porcelain teacup—her wrinkled, sun-spotted hand showing evidence of her earliest decades spent in the tropics. The sapphire ring on her right hand still glowed deep, deep blue, and without thinking, she pressed it to her heart. A lock of silvery hair fell across her forehead. She brushed it back, and touched the bumpy scar at her hairline, vaulting an eighty-year-old memory into play.

Her body tensed while she relived the horrible moment of the noontime heat, the smell of petrol on the street, but worst of all, the crisp vision—a jeep full of Japanese enemies slowing as it drove by her, the passenger soldier glaring, the brake lights flashing a warning. The driver veered in front of her bicycle and stopped. She swung the handlebar to the right, parked on the shoulder, pulled out her Mobile Nurse card, and then bowed. One soldier jumped out and walked around her while another one stepped to her side and yelled an angry order in Japanese. She remained bowed and prayed for God to protect her and Mamma from harm.

A rifle barrel whacked her knee from behind, pitching her forward until her kneecaps hit gravel. She thrust her hands out before face-planting. Keeping her head lowered and bare shins on the rough ground, she pressed her chest to her thighs. Was this enough groveling to stay alive?

"Bow!" the ugly voice shouted. A saber rattled.

Please Lord, help me. She dropped her brow to the ground and stretched her shaking arms out ahead, palms down, as if prostrated in prayer.

"Bow!" he shouted again, and the sole of a boot pushed onto the back of her head and drove her forehead into sharp stones.

A whistling tea kettle jarred Annika back to the present. She slowly inhaled and exhaled and then poured steaming water over the teabag. The robust scent of the first brew brought a comfortable, calming warmth to her face.

Suffering brought enlightenment—a truth she'd read somewhere.

After sipping her tea and nibbling a cookie or two, she'd think back to the beginning—to the life she'd loved, the lessons she'd learned, and the wonderful people who had helped her through the toughest years of her life.

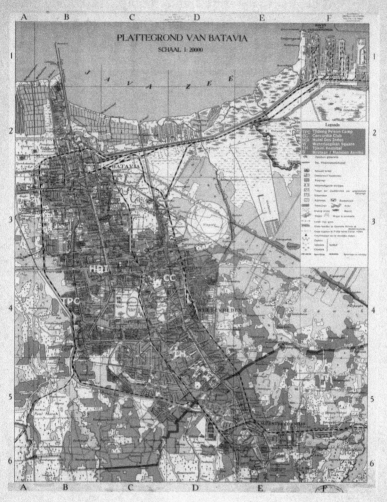

Locations of Annika's destinations
throughout Batavia

https://esdac.jrc.ec.europa.eu/content/plattegrond-van-battavia
(Specific area labels were added)

CHAPTER 1

APRIL 1939

- Hitler's Panzer tanks invade Czechoslovakia.
- Italy and Germany finalize a military alliance.
- Japanese Emperor Hirohito amasses a powerful Navy and Air Force. He uses poison gas against China.

BATAVIA, JAVA

When would Pappie get home to break up her quarantine exile with stories from the barn about her mare and her monkey? Annika Wolter paced another circuit between the Victrola record player that sat on her dresser and the armoire across the room. Two more days of seclusion upstairs and she'd be on horseback again instead of merely imagining rides on the hibiscus-filled trails. Thank the Lord her father's daily report through the closed bedroom door brightened the endless hours of reading and practicing her ballet performance for Mamma's fiftieth birthday. What if she wasn't over the mumps by her mother's party, like the doctor had promised?

Annika pressed her finger under her right ear and found the receding, yet tender, swollen gland. "Little kleuters needing highchairs get mumps, not young ladies of fifteen and a half," she mumbled to herself, and leaned onto the windowsill. Apricot-scents from oleander flowers drifted into her second-floor bedroom from the hedge below, planted along the circular driveway which led to Mansion Annika. She bit her lip. A grand house named in your honor mattered little when you were stuck in one of the seven bedrooms.

At any moment, Pappie and the chauffeur should be rounding the bend of the road that led onto Boxlaan. She looked past the rows of flowers which lined their driveway. Wait. Who was that crossing their grass? A stranger approached from the far corner of the acre of lawn. Shades of copper shone in his dark brown hair. She stood on tip toes and leaned close to the glass in the upper part of the window.

His stride proclaimed athlete, not the stiff walk of an old zakenman who might be headed here to visit Pappie on business.

He marched into full view, dressed in the white Dutch uniform of an officer. The hip-length coat fitted perfectly across his broad shoulders. Freshly pressed trousers covered his long legs and a small leather suitcase swung with each stride.

"Hmm." Annika tapped her cheek. Was this tall, mysterious guest a new boarder? If a herd of young soldiers preceded war, maybe war wouldn't be as horrible as Mamma and Pappie whispered. And no war had better start before she finished high school and completed nursing training, and certainly not before she had her first boyfriend. She moved to the side, lest the visitor catch her staring, and tucked her sleeveless blouse inside the waistband of her wide-legged trousers.

He continued toward their front door and for a moment tilted his head to study the lone wrought iron balcony which jutted out from the bedroom to Annika's right. Her pulse thrummed. No man should be so dashingly handsome as to compete with Errol Flynn. He swung his head to take in the tennis courts on the property next door, then looked over his shoulder at the cricket fields across the street, as if trying to determine a connection to the view from the balcony. The handsome stranger turned back toward Annika and rubbed his chin. His curiosity upped her admiration even further. "I'm going to marry him," she whispered.

At the veranda overhang, he disappeared. She groaned. His footsteps sounded on the flight of stairs.

Verdorie! Damn, she hated this blasted room! Annika thumped her hand against her dresser. The turntable shook on the Victrola. "My song for Saturday's performance!" she cried, and examined the brittle, 78 rpm shellac record. Whew, no scratched grooves. Her fingers relaxed and she slid the twelve-inch disc into its paper sleeve.

The mysterious stranger's suitcase suggested an overnight stay. Mamma hadn't mentioned him when she'd deposited today's lunch outside her door. She batted aside the billowing white mosquito netting which surrounded her bed, then opened her door, and leaned into the hallway. Two more days of exile would kill her! He might be gone by then!

In the distance, protective barks grew louder from Foxy, the family's wire fox terrier. If her furry little friend could talk, he'd quiz the stranger for details. A firm rap sounded from the wooden front door on the main level.

How unfair that her dog got to meet their visitor days before she would. Annika left the door open but retreated into the bedroom. Her future husband's hair shone like the russet brown Djati wood of her furniture.

In her room, a pink scarf fluttered, one filmy end tucked under the thin ribbon of spiraling teak wood that decorated the top of the mirror on her vanity. Annika caught sight of her reflection. Mamma said she had a heart-shaped face, and fashion magazines noted that as a plus. She laid her fingers alongside her chin. What demeanor would impress the dashing officer? Solemn and brooding, à la Greta Garbo? She posed. Or flirty like Janet Gaynor, her favorite American Hollywood star? She lifted one eyebrow and widened her hazel eyes, turned sideways, and looked over her shoulder into the mirror.

Posing was a useless waste of energy. She blew a wisp of light brown, wavy hair from her forehead. He'd never consider her. She was ugly. That's what Pappie's friend, Herman, had told her on his visits when she was a little girl. "Annika," he'd say in his soothing tone, "you're so smart. You're from such a good family. Tsk, tsk. Too bad you're so ugly." Many times, she'd heard him repeat that horrible observation.

Another knock sounded from below. Where were Luther and Ahmad, their servants who ushered guests into their home?

Mamma called out, "I'll greet our new lodger." Her pumps clicked on the white marble floor as she approached the entry from the living room. The heavy door creaked open.

Lodger. How exciting. Not a curmudgeon like

the other paid boarders they sometimes hosted for extra money. Did she dare step out to peek? Her bare feet made no noise as she crept out of her bedroom and across the polished stone hallway. A few feet back from the row of carved staircase balusters, she crouched with her fingertips on the floor for balance. If she tipped her head, she could look between the wooden spindles to see the tall stranger who stood at attention in the open doorway. He towered above Annika's barely five-foot tall Mamma. When he smiled, his angular face lost any formality, making him impossibly handsome. Annika's breath hitched in her throat.

"Thank you for accommodating me on short notice, Mevrouw Wolter." The rich, deep timbre of his voice stirred unfamiliar feelings in Annika. He defined her vision of a Hollywood leading-man. A sigh escaped, piercing the quiet of the empty hall.

The stranger bent and stroked Foxy's head. "I hope a two-week stay isn't an inconvenience." His gaze flicked toward Annika's perch.

She jerked backward, tipped onto her heels, and thrust her hands to the floor to keep her butt from smacking the marble. That was close. Too close. Rising slowly, keeping her back to the wall, she slipped inside her bedroom. Warmth rose in her cheeks. Had he seen her? She continued to eavesdrop, her hand gripping the door frame.

"Foxy, you furry pest. Go visit Annika." Mamma ordered. "Sorry, he's really no bother."

"The pup's an unexpected bonus," his friendly voice assured her mother.

"Good. We're happy to accommodate you, Lieutenant Van Hoven," Mamma said. "I understood from Marta's phone call that the steamship carrying her relatives from Holland arrived early, putting you out of a guest room."

Annika blew out her breath. Close call. Marta's twin daughters were her friends, both of them cute, and both of them currently without a boyfriend.

"That's correct," the lieutenant replied. "I appreciate staying next door to family friends. My quarters on base aren't quite ready. War preparations are slow and steady."

"So we've heard," Mamma agreed. "We feel fortunate to have Marta and her family as close neighbors. Please come inside. Tea is served at four and dinner at seven. In the meantime, I set out a pitcher of fresh lemonade on the shady veranda. I'll ask Emily to point out your room and give you a house tour."

Not Emily! Annika pushed her forehead into the wall. Her lips puckered as if she'd bitten into one of the blasted lemons. Mamma often voiced a saying: "Bitter in de mond maakt het hart gezond," *Bitter in the mouth makes the heart healthy*. Hers ached in pain. She clasped her hands in prayer and whispered, "Please don't let him meet Emily. Please let her be out on an errand." Her older cousin had glossy brown hair, alabaster skin, and elegant manners.

The distinctive clicks of doggy toenails sounded on the marble stairs. Foxy nosed open Annika's door. He'd been the runt of the litter and weighed under fifteen pounds, but his curiosity and energy were boundless.

Annika knelt and stroked down her dog's white neck, black shoulder, and tan back. Her own muscled forearms were brown as a bridle from hours spent riding her horse, Maggy. She hadn't paled a fraction in the five days since she'd come down with mumps, even though she had been sealed off to prevent the horrible virus she'd caught at school from infecting her family and servants. Foxy nudged her and she buried her head in his rough, wiry fur. The scent of freshly mown grass tugged at her restless soul. She should've been out on their lawn to meet their guest. She slumped against her dresser and pulled Foxy onto her lap.

"Emily," Mamma called from downstairs.

Demure footsteps pattered on the hallway floor outside Annika's room. Her worst nightmare continued. She listened intently.

"Yes, ma'am?" Sweet, refined Emily replied from the top of the stairs.

"Please meet Lieutenant Van Hoven. He's the new boarder I mentioned. I'd appreciate you showing him around."

Mamma spoke often of finding a suitor for Emily, and the young lieutenant fit the bill. Annika clutched her blouse at heart level. How could any man not fall for nineteen-year-old Emily, a not-so-poor orphan, and the epitome of a fashionable young lady? "Verdorie," she hissed again, and set Foxy on the floor.

Why did she have the cousin who looked every bit as much like a movie star as he did? Annika rose and looked out the window. Tears wet her eyes. Why couldn't Emily have stayed in Holland with her uncle after her parents died a few years ago? Why had she decided, out of all her Dutch relatives, to join their family in Batavia? And why, for heaven sakes, had Emily been available today as tour guide for the handsome lieutenant? Annika Wolter's handsome lieutenant!

Why? Because life wasn't fair.

Annika tapped her foot on the floor. Where was her father? Shouldn't Pappie be the one showing the new boarder around and learning the important facts about him?

"Ladies. Please, call me Phillip," his smooth voice drifted to Annika, the deep tone sending longing into her chest, soothing her frustration.

Emily murmured something, then the clipped military footsteps faded as the pair must've entered the long hallway below, flanked at the far end by the two bedrooms reserved for boarders. They'd be halfway to the altar by the time Annika got released from her prison.

She crossed her arms over her chest. Movement caught her eye above a framed picture on the far wall. She dashed across the room and glimpsed the disappearing tip of a house gecko's tail. "If you're smart, you'll let me catch you," she advised the tiny intruder as she unhooked the watercolor painting of her horse. Cupping her hand, she gauged the spotted gecko's path and trapped it against the wall. "Gotcha." She gently carried it to the window, pushed her hand outside, and opened her fingers. The gecko stayed in her palm. She ran her finger over the gray body, spotted in black and white. "No hurry to leave? At least you have a choice." In an effortless leap, the gecko landed on the outside wall to her left. "The servants aren't as forgiving," she warned it before she pulled her arm in and drummed her fingers on the windowsill. Every other creature but Annika was headed somewhere today.

The gecko climbed up white stucco, past the small window of the storage room to her left, and then headed toward the red tile roof. Annika looked to the right. Only on the roof would the gecko have a better view than from her mother's private balcony. If the lieutenant asked, would Emily tell him how that balcony had been purposely positioned for Mamma to watch Pappie play tennis next door or cricket at The English Club fields on the other side of Boxlaan? Or that her parents had ordered the workers to chisel "Annika" into the cement floor of the balcony when they'd built here the year after her birth? That should be shared, too.

Pappie needed to get home to give out those details. She glanced at the English Sports Club on the corner a half block away. Overlooking the outdoor pool in the rear, a handful of businessmen in beige-colored suits sat at wicker patio tables. She frowned. If Pappie had stopped there first for his afternoon glass of whiskey, she wouldn't spot him without field glasses.

On the street outside the pool's fence, a horse pulled a two-wheeled buggy, or sado. Sunshine glinted off its metal roof. One passenger faced backward in the seat at the rear. The driver up front steered alongside a row of trees which kept the hot sun off the street vendors. Their tables would be loaded with fresh picked cucumbers, papaya, mango, and pineapple. Annika licked her lips and imagined the taste of ripe, sweet pineapple dipped in shaved coconut.

The sado stopped near the club's covered entry. A uniformed Indonesian doorman in a white turban assisted a stoop-shouldered man out of the rig. He shuffled inside and would probably spend the next few hours enjoying tea and pound cake while talking to his cronies in a cool corner and waiting for the dining room to open at seven. She'd often seen elderly men seated in rocking chairs on the veranda after she'd done laps in the club's swimming pool. Each time she'd passed them in the last few months they'd been arguing in Dutch about the Nazis.

Annika rubbed her temple. Could Hitler's plans of domination really stretch to peaceful Batavia, her home in the Dutch East Indies? No. Her fists clenched. She looked toward the horizon. Ninety miles to the west the peaceful Indian Ocean rippled onto their island's white sandy beaches, with Europe and Hitler thousands of miles beyond. Surely none of his tanks or planes could travel that far. She squinted. Right now, something was flying her way. Not a soaring falcon native to Java, but two biplanes that dipped and dodged one another high up in the blue sky. They circled and vanished, no doubt headed back to the military base before sunset at five-thirty. How did a soldier fill the twelve hours of daylight they received on Java year-round? Did they rise with the sun every morning between five and six, then get off duty at sunset between the same hours in the evening? She should ask Rudy, her oldest brother.

At this very moment, Rudy could be practicing in one of those biplanes. Annika pretended to be him by moving an imaginary center stick, adjusting goggles, and checking the gauges, exactly as Pappie and his friend had shown her when they'd taken her flying in a Piper Cub. Even by handling the controls for a few minutes, she'd felt the strange freedom

Rudy often described he felt in a Koolhoven FK 51 aircraft, which the Royal Dutch Military had brought to Java for pilot training. If Rudy succeeded in joining the RAF out of England, where would he be sent to fight?

Goosebumps rose on her forearms. News clips at Batavia's movie theater warned of Hitler's threats. She closed her eyes and said a prayer for the German monster's swift defeat. Did she have the courage to confront an enemy, given the chance? She stared out the window again. Past the English Club's cricket fields sat The Batavia Civil Hospital for the poor. Since she'd been old enough to know what went on inside, she'd wanted to help sick people. That took plenty of courage, and medical knowledge helped in wartime.

In a metal case on her dresser sat the stethoscope Pappie had presented to her on her twelfth birthday. He'd known precisely what her dreams were, as always. Years of practice on tolerant pets and relatives had honed her skill in locating a heartbeat. Now she needed to practice patience. She wouldn't childishly pester any of the family with questions about Phillip. Instead, she'd show ladylike restraint. She straightened her spine and formed the slight suggestion of a reserved but approachable smile in the manner Oma Elodie had drummed into her.

What was she thinking? Pursuing someone so handsome was surely a lost cause. Annika dropped her chin to her chest. The boxy, stiff fronts of her pink ballet shoes caught her eye. She snatched them from beside her armoire, shoved in her feet, and tied the ribbons. The doctor had guaranteed that by Mamma's birthday celebration on Saturday night, her glands would be normal, and she wouldn't be contagious.

Only forty-eight hours remained for her to perfect the final pirouette of her Chopin piece and impress Phillip with her one talent. As she moved her body to balance en pointe, more than her toes ached.

CHAPTER 2

Saturday at last, and finally free from quarantine! Annika parked her bicycle beside Pappie's ten-stall barn and lifted Foxy from the bike's basket. A horse bugled in the distance. Her trusted steed, Maggy, always announced her arrival. Next came the little-horse whinny of her old pony, Penny, who shared the pasture. Annika grinned and pulled her thin cotton blouse away from her skin, damp from the heat of Saturday's noon sun and the several mile bike ride to their stables on the outskirts of town. Swimming in the pool at The English Sports Club would've been smarter.

Not to her pets, though. Foxy circled and yipped. He wiggled with anticipation for their jaunt in the woods to search for wonderful scentograms, no doubt inspired by tidbits from the table he'd receive after they left the barn and headed home for high tea.

Home, where Annika had completed her share of party preparations this morning in record time. She had been shooed out of the house without even a glimpse of the new boarder. Her own tingling anticipation for tonight rippled from her feet to her ponytail. Thank goodness her mother understood her need for a ride, so getting away wasn't a problem. What Mamma didn't understand, though, was her daughter's intense desire to impress Lieutenant Phillip van Hoven. Annika patted her heart. She'd kept that information safely hidden.

Luckily for her, Pappie had started to teach his jumping lessons earlier today, and he'd cancelled their father and daughter ride. He could read her like a book. She knew that too many exclamation points marked her thoughts about meeting handsome Phillip for the first time tonight and she didn't want Pappie to suspect anything. Tomorrow, she'd happily ride alongside Pappie and fulfill her treasured role of the family member carrying his equestrian gene. Her brothers, Rudy and Claude, now preferred airplanes or motor bikes and Mamma feared horses. How lovely it would be if Phillip rode!

Annika dusted off her tan jodhpurs and placed the toe of her black leather riding boot on the lowest rail of the fence attached to the barn's outside wall. She scanned the spacious arena. Pappie stood in the center with his back to her. An unfamiliar man stood outside the fence on the opposite side. Both seemed focused on a middle-aged woman who stepped off the mounting block and awkwardly swung her thigh onto Pappie's saddled jumper. She wore a white, long-sleeved blouse and a striped vest in shades of blue.

Only a twit would roast in two layers today. Annika leaned on the rail, balanced on her elbows. Hold on—this rider was also one of Mamma's tailoring customers; Annika recognized the striped vest as one Mamma had gone to great pains to design. Its heavy material contained a band of cerulean blue, and that precise shade needed to lay along the neckline to accentuate the customer's eyes. Annika shook her head. None of that mattered to the horse, of course.

Noir, a powerfully built, coal-black gelding, shifted under the woman's weight. Henri, Pappie's compact and strong Indonesian groom kept a calming hand on the horse's bridle. The woman glanced down at Henri, scowled, and said something which caused him to quit smiling. Annika clenched the rail. Had Pappie heard the woman's rude comment to Henri? If he did, it wouldn't matter how fancy the rider was dressed, her father would still voice his disapproval. He did not tolerate rudeness to one of their staff. Other Dutch on the island didn't treat their Indonesian servants as well as Pappie cared for theirs. Some staff lived away from the families they worked for, but not the Wolters' servants. Henri and Kokkie's family chose to live in the pavilion attached to Mansion Annika by a covered walkway, as did their chauffeur and their huisknecht, or butlers. Their staff had their own bedrooms, a communal kitchen, and a bathroom. Even when money was tight, Mamma made certain their help ate the same food Kokkie prepared for Annika's family.

Pappie must not have heard his student's remark, as he remained standing in the middle of the arena with his hands clasped behind his back in his thinking posture. The shining gold signet ring he wore with pride bore an inscribed crest of his French ancestors. Her father lived and breathed the family philosophy of noblesse oblige, that if you are of nobility, you have an obligation to behave accordingly. In Pappie's terms it meant that everyone was taken care of before you. Over and over, he'd coached her and her brothers in how to honor the family's noblesse oblige mantra. Today, her tall, slim father concentrated on his student. As he assessed her seat, his dark brows wrinkled. "Heels down, please," he instructed. He unconsciously smoothed his wavy hair with one hand, and smiled at Henri, who dipped his head in acknowledgement and released the bridle. "Circle the arena twice at a walk, then trot to warm him up," Pappie called to the woman.

Fortunately for their budget, if you wanted people to think you came from an old Dutch family of wealth, you had to know - or learn - how to sit a horse. So, even in difficult financial times, Pappie had plenty of paying customers eager to cement their reputations as members of the elite class.

Annika dropped her foot from the rail and thought of how Oma Elodie would've reprimanded her for this unladylike demeanor—a lady does not cling to or prop her feet on fence rails. Luckily, Pappie's French mother, Countess Elodie de Fisicat Wolter, preferred the piano to horses and never came to the barn. Oma Elodie's titled family had fled Marseille when the poor rose up against Marie Antoinette to fight the greedy French aristocracy.

When Pappie was sixteen, his father had died, yet somehow, despite being raised by his aristocratic mother, Pappie had developed a realistic attitude about finances. He knew everything to do with horses cost dearly and made certain that the money he earned for teaching riding lessons paid household bills and expenses for Maggy, Penny, and his own five horses.

While the expensively dressed rider trotted Noir on the outside rail of the arena, Annika recalled a time she'd been scared as a little girl, worrying that her pony, Penny, might be sold. She'd been no more than eight or nine and had been clueless that the world had suffered from a severe financial depression beginning in the 1930s. During the only time her parents had let their money worries slip, Pappie had asked Mamma to sit down in the dining room. "I'm totally ruined," he'd begun.

Her mother had stared at him. "Why do you say that?"

"I've lost nearly all my capital in this godforsaken depression. My export business is kapot."

Mamma had placed a hand on Pappie's shoulder and stayed silent for a moment. "Well. . . you can get paid for the riding lessons you now offer for free," she'd said, "and I suppose I can design couture clothes. I know wonderful Indonesian seamstresses who can sew them." She'd smiled and fingered the scalloped neckline of her own dress. "There will always be wealthy women needing new wardrobes." Pappie had paced the floor as Mamma continued, "We have no debt and could rent out the extra bedrooms in the house, too."

"I don't want you to work!" He'd thumped his hand on the table. It was the only disagreement Annika recalled hearing between her parents.

"There's nothing wrong with me." Mamma stood, her chin in the air. "I can work. I have my brain and plenty of servants." She'd kissed him. "I've been trained in dress design and went to fashion shows in Paris before we met. Don't worry about me."

And work they both had ever since that day, just

like right now, as her father coached the rider who was wearing Mamma's custom-made riding togs. The woman's rouged cheeks grew darker from exertion. "Take her over the green jump, Mevrouw," Pappie instructed. "Remember to lift your hips from the seat as he rises."

Dust rose as the imported English jumper trotted toward a low cross rail. The gelding stopped for an instant, gathered energy, and sailed over, carrying the upright woman. Noir's skills compensated for what his inconsiderate rider lacked in proper form. She'd not even raised her butt a fraction off the saddle or assisted him by leaning over his neck.

"Bravo," the bystander cheered, dressed in a cream-colored linen jacket more suited for a croquet party.

He must be a well-paid government worker because he obviously wasn't a horseman. The jump his friend had cleared barely reached Annika's knee, and clearly Noir did all the work. She turned her head and rolled her eyes. Mevrouw Cerulean Blue should consider bicycling if she didn't want to partner with her mount. Pappie could diplomatically point that out because Annika had better things to do. "Newt-newt!" she called, then removed a treat wrapped in her hankie from the bicycle basket.

Her pet monkey scampered out of the barn and made the friendly chatter which echoed his name. He climbed Annika's outstretched arm and swung onto her shoulder. His hair tickled her ear and his tail draped to her waist. He tugged her braid, then patted the top of her head.

Sunlight shone off the golden tips of his fur, his coat the color of a walnut shell. He smelled of the fresh straw he slept in, thanks to Henri having built the perfect macaque-sized wooden box. From her pocket she removed a handful of Kenari nuts. She ate a couple of the creamy tasting nuts and offered one to Newt-newt. "Want a treat?"

His warm, slate gray fingers plucked the nut, and he popped it into his mouth. He screeched in glee, his cheek whiskers spiked out from his grayish pink muzzle. The comical expression made Annika laugh. "Silly monkey." She unfolded her handkerchief. A fragrant, yeasty aroma from Kokki's freshly baked bread filled the air. "You're getting better at our racing-home game. A favorite snack if you win today." The monkey's bright, amber-colored eyes followed her movement while she placed the chunk of bread atop a gate post. He leapt to the ground and jumped up and down, ready to get the game started. "First, we go for a walk in the shady woods. Let's find Maggy and begin our trail ride."

At the sound of her name, the copper-colored mare whinnied from the nearby pasture, then trotted to meet them. She flipped her head, which rippled her long, flaxen mane. Penny, her brown and white pinto pony, trailed behind and favored her left hind leg. "Poor old girl, your hoof is still tender, even walking on grass."

Foxy dove under the gate and met the horses. Maggy and Penny lowered their heads to sniff him and complete their routine of friendly nose bumps. Foxy wagged his tail and then darted around the pasture barking at bugs, leaves, and who knew what else.

Annika laughed at Foxy, grabbed a hoof pick hanging on the post, and began the routine task of using the hoof pick to remove debris from each of her horse's hooves. "Yes, he's energetic and you're my pretty girls." She finished the chore and fed Penny a piece of carrot. "I'll bring you along in a few days. Rest that stone-bruised hoof, sweet girl." She buckled on Maggy's halter and swung open the pasture gate. "Tonight, I'm meeting the man I'm going to marry," she whispered into the big horse's velvety, russet-colored ear. "I'll give you details once we reach the woods." She closed the gate and patted sad-eyed Penny. "We'll be back soon."

On the walk to the barn, Maggy bumped her shoulder, as if she were anxious to hear Annika's plan. In a few moments, Maggy was groomed, her English saddle cinched in place, and her bridle properly fitted. Annika mounted and tapped the seat.

Newt-newt bounded off the ground. Using his wiry fingers, he gripped Annika's ankle, swung himself up with one arm, and plopped on the saddle in front of her with a furry leg on either side of Maggy's shoulders. He intertwined his slim, wrinkled fingers in strands of her shiny mane.

"Smart monkey." Annika stroked the little ridge of reddish hairs on the crown of his head, then scratched below the white spots on his ears. He made a soft gibber of satisfaction and patted her thigh. "Okay, we don't have much time today. Hold on."

"Foxy, time to hit the trail." The little dog dashed to Maggy's side and pranced along beside them. Annika steered Maggy to where two trees, spaced four feet apart, created the entrance to their favorite trek. Kembang sepatu, the shoe flower, grew from bushy evergreen shrubs along the shaded path. English travelers called these plate-sized blossoms hibiscus. Whatever the real name, she loved smelling the cranberry flavored tea made from the flowers their servants steeped and drank. Her family only used the black tea once traded by her father's commodities company.

Maggy stepped smoothly over a shin-high fallen log. "Good girl," Annika praised.

Away from the barn and people, frogs and birds trilled in the still air. Butterflies floated between plants. Her favorite, a Sulawesi striped blue crow, landed ahead, and stretched its wings to show bright cobalt patches dotted in white. A canopy of trees in full leaf provided cooling shade. Foxy crisscrossed in front of them, his white paws now dusty brown from searching for bugs and other forest creatures on the trail.

Annika relaxed into the saddle as Maggy settled into a comfortable walk. Rabbits and stray chickens darted after bugs in the underbrush, some pursued by Foxy. Newt-newt's head bounced from side to side, following the movements around them. Annika rubbed his light gray chest. "Glad you don't have to scramble for food?"

He leaned his back against her tummy, his little body relaxed.

They'd reached her thinking place. Annika took a deep breath of sweet, clean forest air and pictured the handsome lieutenant. She stroked her horse's neck and rode on to an old, gnarled Mimosa tree bearing upright, pink flowers shaped like round make-up brushes. "In four hours, I perform. Then I'll finally be introduced to Phillip. I'll dance the night away in his arms and he'll fall head over heels for me."

Newt-newt turned, a curious stare on his face.

"Silly monkey. He's the new boarder who's plenty rugged, and I'm dizzy about him already." She fanned her face. "Those are terms I heard during the last American movie we saw at the cinema. Translated, it means he's big and strong, and I'm very much in love."

Maggy's ears twitched. Newt-newt chattered

before he climbed onto Annika's shoulder. Typically when they reached the Mimosa tree landmark, they turned around to return to the barn. Newt-newt put his little paw on her head and waited for her to signal him to take the shortcut.

"I get it, fresh bread trumps knowing about my love life." She lifted her arm to bridge the gap for his jump to a nearby limb. "Go on. Beat me back!" Given the order to depart, he skipped onto her forearm, then swung from tree to tree as he raced to the stable.

Above the disappearing Newt-newt, a dark, foreboding cloud hung low in the sky. It would be better to have the rain now rather than later when guests arrived for the party.

"Foxy, time to head back." No sooner had she spoken when the dog dashed by, chasing a plantain squirrel until it jumped to a tree trunk. Annika pivoted Maggy and urged her to lope. "The race is on to beat the rain!" A small deer bounded across their path. Foxy barked but continued running at full speed and disappeared around a bend. "Every critter's looking for shelter." The mare's agile canter could never beat Newt-newt's leaping capability. Her little monkey earned the bread treat by cutting his return time after each try.

If trying worked, she'd earn Phillip's affection soon. Every waking hour since he'd crossed their lawn, she'd practiced her ballet moves.

They'd reached the barn. Big drops fell on her shoulder, followed by a sheet of rain. She walked Maggy to a stall, and her hand tightened on the reins. In the last two days, had Phillip become besotted by sweet, beautiful Emily?

Annika took a deep breath. The air held the fresh scent of the earlier rain they'd felt at the barn. She stood on tiptoes beside her bedroom window to get the full view of their circular driveway. An array of vehicles was lined up to deposit guests for Mamma's birthday. True to Dutch custom, no one arrived late. And they'd be happy to be on time. Mamma had spared no expense on her fiftieth birthday plans, intending to keep her reputation as the hostess who served the best food in Batavia. Still, how many guests were invited to the celebration? A sado driver stopped his dark gray horse at the front steps, which brought to a halt two gleaming black roadsters and a taxi. A couple she didn't recognize got out of the buggy. The neighboring family came into view, striding across the lawn in a colorful group. Marta's green gown blew in the breeze. Their twin daughters, classmates of Annika, wore matching yellow flapper dresses. Their exuberant walking caused silky white fringe to swing from the garments' cap sleeves and above-the-knee hems. Annika giggled. The invitation to Mamma's birthday celebration had suggested smoking attire for the men and free-style evening dress for the women. Thankfully, acceptable fashion for younger women included shorter dresses. The Roaring '20s style remained popular, especially on Java during warm, tropical evenings.

"Welkom," Pappie's deep voice rose from the entry below. He'd be standing in position to greet party guests. "High tea awaits you on our shady veranda," he announced. "Kokkie prepared her famous galantine of veal, cinnamon biscuits, Scotch Lawn Tennis Cake, and other delicacies." Annika heard a woman's French accent, followed by Pappie's deep laugh. "Yes, I requested the Tennis Cake," he continued. "The entertainment won't begin for an hour. Relax and enjoy refreshments."

Relax? Hardly. Annika's stomach knotted. One hour to do a warmup, shower, and dress. She left the window, turned on the gramophone, and carefully settled the needle on the grooved black record. She began her dance, trying to push everything from her brain except the choreography she'd created. Her body moved freely, interpreting Chopin's emotion-filled work. The last note sounded, and dull, measured clicks filled the room. A sense of finality hung in the air. She mentally pushed her nerves away, carefully lifted off the needle, and returned it to the cradle. Clanks and thumps from below told her the musicians had begun to set up on the corner of the veranda. Her body hummed in anticipation while she showered. Upon returning, the clock in her bedroom showed four forty-five.

Verdorie! The dance performance of her life would soon be announced by chimes sounding from the entry, delivered by a six-foot-tall grandfather clock topped by gilded trumpeting angels. Right now, Pappie would be encouraging guests to move into the living room to watch her dance. A wave of jitters struck. She'd reached the precise moment to put on her costume. Annika removed it from the hanger, stuck her feet through the leg holes, and slid it up over her hips. Below the stretchy leotard bodice, a bell-shaped tutu displayed multiple shades of rose-colored tule. Its pale pink top layer perfectly matched her satin en pointe shoes.

She stood straight, fluffed the five-inch ruff above the round neckline of her fuchsia leotard, then relaxed. Mamma's well-placed fabric covered her swimsuit strap lines and hid how unfashionably brown she'd become.

Her mother's other crafty idea had been to gather fist-sized sections of the filmy tutu material and stitch them to mimic flowers at the mid-thigh hemline. She pirouetted in front of the mirror, used her knee to flounce the front flower and smiled. Movement revealed darker, ruby shades in the under layers of the tulle, which accented her long, muscular legs. Phillip couldn't help but notice parts of her.

A knock sounded on her bedroom door. "How's your costume fitting?" Mamma stepped inside, the flowing skirt of her midnight-blue gown rustling at each step. The gown was styled to accent her Mae West hourglass shape.

Annika's girlfriends at school stuffed nylons in their bras and wore girdles to achieve the curvy look to impress boys. Until this week, she'd thought them silly. She'd been whistled at while wearing her swimsuit, and that had been more than enough attention at the time. After seeing Phillip, she wondered if maybe she was the nincompoop; not her friends. She spun again. "Your design is divine, Mamma. I hope it's enough to catch the attention of our new boarder."

"Tsk, tsk," Mamma scolded. "Don't be foolish, my schatje."

Annika didn't feel like Mamma's little treasure, a suitable endearment for a child of ten, not an almost sixteen-year-old. "What do you mean?" She grabbed the fingernail file and did a smoothing round on her spotless nails.

"The lieutenant's been chatting with Emily since he arrived. I caught the distinct scent of English Yardley aftershave on him tonight, the choice of a mature man. You're only a kid to him."

The words stung. Annika stretched to her full

height of five foot, seven inches, and glowered at her petite mother.

"Your height's irrelevant," Mamma stated. "He's twenty-three and a military officer. Emily's nineteen and a lovely, refined, young lady. They suit one another." She pointed her finger at Annika. "If you flirt with him, I'll break your legs," she pretended to threaten.

Annika bit back an angry retort. Countless times she'd been complimented on her maturity. "You advanced me two years in school."

"Speaking five languages fluently at thirteen impressed the school. The principal suggested your advancement. Don't have any illusions about Lieutenant Van Hoven." Mamma patted Annika's shoulder. "I'm excited to watch your ballet performance. There are plenty of boys your age, schatje. Pappie and I agree that Lieutenant Van Hoven is perfect for Emily." She crossed her arms and smiled, as if the matter were settled. "I'll tell Oma Elodie to be seated at the piano. I personally readied the Chopin sheet music. Join us in five minutes?"

She'd be doing more than joining them. A slight age difference wasn't going to ruin her plans for Phillip. "Yes, I only need to pin my hair." Annika grabbed a handful of bobby pins from the small drawer in her vanity. She flipped the rear of her tutu out of the way so she wouldn't crush it and plopped on the chair in front of the large mirror.

Mamma stood behind Annika and wiggled the fingers of her outstretched hand. "Allow me to get my prima ballerina's hair in place. The usual coiled braids?"

Braided coils were for schatjes. "A loose chignon at my neck, please, to balance the flouncy collar. And the tulle roses are beautiful."

"And you are my beautiful girl." She twisted Annika's thick hair and tucked under the bundle. "I've seen boys turn their heads your way."

Hair pins slid against Annika's scalp. She squelched the urge to divulge her impatience at teen-aged boys who gawked. Instead, she held her head steady, imitating a refined lady.

Mamma pushed in the final pins and kissed her cheek. "I thought you might want to borrow some jewelry for tonight." She pulled from her pocket an oval watch decorated by three diamonds on each side. Thin black cord formed the band, elegantly secured by a gold clasp.

Very adult and very precious. Annika fastened the delicate timepiece onto her wrist. "I know this is your favorite dress watch. I'll be careful."

"I trust your good judgement." Her mother opened a velvet pouch and lifted a necklace over Annika's head. "For you to wear after you dance. A young lady should accent her outfits by simple, elegant jewelry."

The emerald-cut diamond set in platinum felt

heavy against the hollow of Annika's neck. She swallowed. "Oma Elodie's diamond?"

"Yes. Someday these and other family heirlooms will be passed on to you and, God willing, your daughters." Mamma's voice held a wistful edge. "You may wear them on special occasions until all talk of war blows over." Her brow wrinkled in concern for a moment. "Enough of grownup worries," she scoffed.

Annika clasped the diamond setting and returned it to the pouch. She felt more grown-up than ever before. "It will be lovely with my dress. Thank you."

"And my thanks to you for performing on my special birthday."

"You are very welcome."

The first of five chimes struck below from the old Dutch clock.

"Merdi!" Mamma quoted the French version of wishing a dancer luck on a ballet performance. "It will be a highlight of my celebration." She blew her a kiss and left.

Annika tied her satin pointe shoes on, walked the hallway, and then slid the leather soles onto each polished stair. The evening should be a highlight of her life, too, if things went as planned.

The broad, tall grandfather clock hid Annika in the entry. Laughter and bits of conversation drifted to her from Mamma's birthday party crowd, who mingled in groups throughout the forty-foot-long living room. Earlier in the day, the servants had moved the furniture off one end of the smooth marble floor and onto the veranda to allow plenty of space for couples to dance after her ballet performance. On the opposite end of the room, a short half-wall separated the bigger space from the adjacent dining room, where the staff had pushed the large dinner table against the wall.

Pappie stepped into the center of the living room, caught Annika's eye, and winked at her. "Please direct your attention to our ballerina," his deep voice announced. Conversations ended.

Annika quietly walked to reach her starting position on the empty dance area. Her heart pounded as she tilted her chin and raised her left hand toward the crystal chandelier. Oma Elodie, seated at the piano and backed by the musicians on the veranda, took the cue and began to play the Chopin selection. Swirling music surrounded Annika. The emphatic notes pushed her to leap high and energized her throughout the dance. For her closing move, she spun the final pirouette, crossed her ankles, and curved her right arm overhead into the fourth ballet position. Pride welled in her chest. She'd performed flawlessly.

Applause erupted from the thirty or so guests. "Bravo!" several shouted. Emily stood in front and discreetly gave her the thumbs up gesture.

Annika flashed her a quick grin. The one person she needed a sign from was easy to locate in his spot near the wall on the right. Phillip stood a head above most of the crowd and his lively brown eyes still studied her. She'd been certain to glance his way during her dance routine, and he'd seemed riveted. Had she misread his attention? She dropped her arms and bowed, then popped up and blew kisses— one aimed purposely up and to the right.

Crinkles of tan skin reached Phillip's eyes from his beaming smile of approval. Tremors of excitement rushed through Annika. Thunderation! He'd noticed her all right. Her pulse raced, and not from the ballet performance.

Claude's loud wolf whistle sounded from the back of the room. Such a loyal brother. Verdorie! The musicians needed to be thanked! She blew a kiss to Oma Elodie and waved at the band. They'd played perfectly. She'd danced perfectly. Everything had gone perfectly!

Oma Elodie smiled back from behind the piano. Her long fingers rested on the ivory keys. At the base of her slender neck, silver hair glistened in a chignon, styled like Annika's. Her gold gown fanned out on the bench in perfect folds, countess style. How elegant she always looked. Annika touched the delicate watch on her wrist. Maybe someday, she too, would be a lady. Positioned a few feet from Oma, the five members of the Indonesian Batavia Rhythm and Jazz Band grinned and whooped, closer to what she felt inside right now.

Mamma stepped to her side. "Her dancing never ceases to amaze me." She kissed Annika's cheek. "I'm so proud of the accomplishments for her age."

For her age! As if she was a little kleuter of five. Where was a carpet to crawl under when you needed one? Annika forced a stiff smile as her mother squeezed her hand during the second round of applause.

"Now, dear family and friends, please enjoy the buffet, refresh your drinks, and save room for a slice of Kokkie's famous chocolate birthday cake. And I hope you're wearing your dance shoes. Dear Frederick procured sheet music for a recent Bing Crosby love song as a special birthday present. Our band members assured him they've practiced it." She glanced at Emily, then across the room to Phillip, and a pleased expression flashed on her face.

Thank the Lord, Phillip had lifted Foxy into his arms. Emily avoided anything furry, so Annika still might have a chance to win him over. She cleared her throat. "Thank you, everyone, and please excuse me to change into my other dancing shoes." She raised an eyebrow at Phillip, and he nodded. So regal, in his white dress uniform jacket with a stand-up collar and gold buttons. Mamma's plan to unite Phillip and Emily wouldn't work. Couldn't work. He'd nodded back, for heaven's sake. Annika rushed upstairs, trying to banish her worried thoughts of Emily.

Even wearing pointe shoes, she took the steps two at a time and charged into her bedroom. No time to waste, the band might play dance music any moment. Emily's aqua, sleeveless dress beautifully accentuated her thin arms and creamy white skin and would make her an appealing dance partner.

Annika's skin would never be pale—heredity dictated the fact. On Mamma's side, a long-ago Dutch grandfather Nolten became the chief commander of a Surakarta Indonesian sultan's small army. That grandfather had married a relative of the sultan, creating her Indo lineage. The link was so far back, her family was known as one of the premier Dutch families of Batavia. Regardless, Mamma, Annika, and her oldest brother, Rudy, carried those genes for skin which didn't burn in the sun. She'd considered it a blessing until tonight. Her pressed, sleeveless flapper dress lay on the bed. She fingered the iridescent, white fabric. Her bronzed fingers seemed even darker in contrast.

Claude and Rudy chided her that she preferred monkeys and horses to humans. "Tomboy," they'd teasingly yell, then point at her dirty fingernails and muddy boots. Well, tonight she'd do her darndest to lose their nickname. She slipped out of her leotard and stepped into the cool silk of her party dress, its color reminiscent of the inside of a seashell. She found the armholes and pulled it on. An attached stole of sorts, made from sheer white fabric draped the tops of her arms and fastened with a pearl button atop the V-necked bodice. It camouflaged her square swimmer's shoulders. Beginning at the dress's fitted waist and ending above her knees hung scalloped tiers of gathered strips of the same pearlized material.

Kokkie would say she resembled a fancy iced cake. Thanks to Mamma and her seamstresses, she might be called a real looker dressed like this.

"Annika," came Oudje's kind voice from the hallway.

Oudje, her beloved baboe, had raised her from an infant. She'd probably learned to pronounce her name as "ow-cha" along with learning Mamma and Pappie. Annika pushed open the door. "Thank you for leaving the party to help me dress. Can you button the back?"

Oudje's sandals pattered on the marble. Ornate, gilded hairpins held her gray hair in place, carefully done in a bun at the nape of her neck. All their staff were helping tonight, as they routinely did for parties.

Annika cocked her head. Overnight, it seemed Oudje had become so tiny, so thin, so old.

"Of course," Oudje said. "But not if you grow much taller." She wore a silk sarong and matching short jacket in forest green, a color she'd often said complemented her dark skin. "I buttoned your baby clothes, your frocks, and now the fancy dress of a young woman." Oudje kissed her cheek, her wrinkled skin soft and warm against Annika's. "You danced better than ever before. Now you'll reign as the belle of the ball. Should we loosen your hair?" She grasped Annika's hand and led her to the dressing table, as if she were still a wayward toddler.

Oudje's steady nature soothed her nerves. "Please. Maybe drawn off my face using the seed-pearl beaded combs? And you look splendid tonight."

"Why thank you," Oudje said. She slipped the combs against Annika's scalp, leaving a soft wave at the crown of her head and her loose, light brown hair cascading over the white fabric. "You could be a movie star from the Roaring 20s photos you've shown me, Annika."

"You honestly think so? As a child, one of Pappie's friends from work told me I looked ugly." Her chin fell to her chest.

"No! He was wrong and not a friend. Only a horrible person told such lies to my sweet girl." She stroked one of Annika's wavy locks. "You are uniquely beautiful. Kokkie, Budi, and Luther say you'll marry a rich merchant and travel the world. Ahmad thinks a prince will choose you." Oudje leaned in close and kissed her cheek again. "I don't care who you marry as long as you marry for love."

If all went well, that's exactly what Annika intended to do. She released a long breath. The other servants never gossiped in front of her family. Each group maintained a respectful rapport. "Thank you. Your advice has always steered me correctly." Nanny Oudje treated her more like a cherished daughter. "I'll tell you my secret. I hope Lieutenant Van Hoven asks me to dance. Has he been attentive to Emily?"

Oudje shook her head. "Not that I've seen. They greet one another politely. He leaves each morning on his motorbike for the military base and doesn't return until evening. Don't worry, your gifts are more than fragile beauty. He will see that."

Annika straightened in her chair, ready for any challenge, and more than ready to use the art of flirting she'd read about in novels and witnessed in movies. "Mamma gave me a special gift tonight. I can wear the French diamonds." She removed the necklace from the pouch, fastened the clasp, and squeezed Oudje's hand. "You worked magic on my hair and on my confidence." She rose from the vanity chair. "Now I need to remember how to walk gracefully, as Oma Elodie instructed." She exaggerated the flowing style she'd been taught, opened the door, and giggled. "Pray for me."

"You don't need prayers tonight." Oudje closed the door behind them. "Go have fun."

Annika's T-strap, heeled sandals barely touched the stairs in her hurry to reach the birthday party. At the landing she slowed for a graceful entrance into the room where the man she'd marry waited. Groups of two or three stood in the living room or the adjoining dining room. The party was in full swing—an array of empty cocktail glasses already sat on the half-wall which jutted out a few feet into the room. Beyond it was the table laden with hors d'oeuvres. The spicy, meaty scent of saucijsjes wafted to her. Bless Kokkie and her culinary magic! She could almost taste the little sausages wrapped in strips of pie dough. Had Phillip tried one?

She scanned the area for him and ignored men in smoking outfits, their white jackets and black pants contrasting with the jewel-colored silk cocktail dresses worn by women with upswept hairdos. They balanced champagne flutes and cocktail glasses in manicured hands.

There he was! And not with Emily. Phillip and Uncle Bajetto stood on the far end of the veranda, both attired in formal military dress. By their solemn faces, they'd been speaking of war.

That's all the adults spoke of, usually in hushed tones. Annika sighed, then lifted a plate from the end of the table and proceeded to fill it with golden crusted sausages. Next to their tray sat a shallow Delft bowl which held thin slices of pickled cucumbers, grown behind the house in their vegetable patch. She filled out the plate with Gruyere cheese, pâté grandmère, and fruit. Dancing made her hungry, and she'd be less nervous to approach her future husband on a full stomach. Later, she'd gorge on the roast beef, steamed vegetables, and fresh breads the staff would set out soon.

The first notes of Strauss's "The Blue Danube Waltz" rang out. Her parents' favorite piece typically opened the dancing at parties. Strict rules dictated the type of songs military men wearing formal Dutch uniforms were allowed to dance.

Mamma led Emily into the room, bee-lined to Phillip, and plucked his sleeve to interrupt his conversation. Graceful Emily took his arm and glided beside him to the dance area.

A bit of sausage stuck in Annika's throat. She turned toward the wall and blinked her damp lashes.

CHAPTER 3

Chatter from the birthday guests grew louder and more animated, a sign the liquor and champagne flowed freely—the usual at Mamma and Pappie's parties. Her parents returned to the dance floor and smiled from love and from their delight at another successful celebration.

At least in their eyes. Annika spread her napkin on her barely touched hors d'oeuvres and set her cocktail plate beside empty glasses on a tray. Eating brought no joy with all her plans kapot. No way she'd turn to see if Emily and Phillip had continued to dance to the second song. Maybe he was what Americans called a cement mixer, someone whose feet appeared cemented to the floor. She hadn't checked, but if he was, Emily could dodge shoes tonight.

The opening chords of an unfamiliar tune rang

out from the musicians on the veranda. She tilted her head. Must be the new song Pappie had requested they learn to play for Mamma's birthday. Soon enough, she'd be asked to dance by some old codger who took pity on her. Again. A nearby table held a punch bowl and various bottles of wine and liquor. She'd eaten enough to enjoy a flute of sweet Riesling. Mamma couldn't nix that, at fourteen she'd been allowed one glass of wine per party.

A finger pressed gently into her shoulder. "Please allow me to introduce myself," requested the deep, smooth, and very recognizable male voice from two days ago.

Phillip had found her! Annika's heart skipped several beats. He sounded even better this close. "Of course." She turned and lost herself in the dreamiest chocolate brown eyes on earth.

"I'm Lieutenant Phillip van Hoven, renting a room for a few weeks in this home. At your service and pleased to meet you, Juffrouw?" He'd changed from his military uniform to a white linen jacket and black trousers, fashionable, debonair, and without the restrictions on which dances he could enjoy.

"I'm Annika." She blinked to bring her brain back to reality. "Juffrouw Annika Wolter, upstairs prisoner until today, due to the mumps."

"And what a spectacular escape you made to freedom. The jailers didn't stand a chance." His eyes flicked to the hem of her short dress, then back to her face. "You danced superbly and interpreted each note with flowing movements. I'd have thought you were on break from the Amsterdam Ballet company."

The blush began at her chest and rose to her hairline. "Thank you. I appreciate your review." She fanned her face. "Should we get a cocktail?"

"First, I'd prefer a more casual mode of dance if you'd do me the honor. Bring on a jive, samba, or even a cha-cha." He winked and she felt her blush darken.

Cement mixer or not, when he held out his arm, she placed her fingers on his sleeve with conviction.

"I'm falling in love with someone," crooned the voice of a band member in Bing Crosby's mellow style.

Annika's eyes widened at the irony. They'd reached the edge of the cleared area and Phillip put one hand at her waist and lifted her palm with his other warm hand. She'd remember this moment forever. She inhaled his tangy citrus and bergamot scent and tilted her chin in the proper dance pose taught to her by Oma Elodie.

But this wasn't the same as dancing with her brothers. Phillip guided her in the steps of a foxtrot —long walking movements followed by a subtle rise and fall to their bodies to mimic the two slow beats and one quick step. They flowed together as if they'd been partnered for twenty-five years. Annika grinned. His light footwork was definitely not from a cement mixer. Her body relaxed into his strong arms, and she felt a connection unlike any other. The song ended.

"Another?" he asked, one dark eyebrow raised in anticipation.

She nodded, unwilling to break the spell. Two more dances with him cinched her notion that she'd found "the one." Keeping him presented a challenge she'd embrace.

And maybe, just maybe, it wouldn't be so difficult. They'd been perfectly synchronized during the sweeping, graceful turns of a Viennese waltz. After the music had ended, she caught his content, far-off look. His right palm still remained at her waist.

"We're going to liven things up," the drummer announced, and the horn player tooted the dant-dant, dant-dant, dant-dant ta da dant-dant Charleston beat. Annika's toes tapped the rhythm.

"I guess I'm game if you are," Phillip replied hesitantly. "Not my specialty. But, I'll attempt to muddle through."

If he needed courage, she'd lend some. "I'll show you. I learned the Charleston for a theater performance. Let's get this wingding hopping." Annika grabbed his hand and took him to the center of the floor.

Marta's daughters and other guests joined them. The band belted out the tune, as if they dared the dancers to keep up. The twins swished their fringed dresses from side to side as they stepped back and swung the opposite leg in a half-kick position, and then reversed the move.

Annika stood beside Philip and repeated the simple step. He followed her footwork to the beat. In no time they mirrored each other at a swift pace. Annika upped the ante by incorporating the Bee's Knee's. The showy hand-to-hand across-the-knees move brought cheers. Phillip flashed a shy grin. Their next rock steps and kicks perfectly matched. The rhythm increased as all the dancers performed tricky steps.

The song ended to hearty applause. Phillip grabbed her hand and raised it. Annika threw her head back and laughed. She caught a glimpse of her father in the crowd. His stern face wouldn't sober her gaiety. She'd dance all night if given the chance. "Muddle through my eye," she declared.

"I took basic dance lessons at seventeen," Phillip confided. "The Charleston wasn't on the agenda. A great instructor makes the difference. Thank you." He executed a crisp bow and flashed a smile she'd dream about tonight.

The lights blinked and Pappie tapped a fork against a crystal flute. "Our fabulous band deserves a break." He nodded to the smiling drummer. "Please enjoy refreshments gentlemen, and we'll all be ready for your second set. Now, dear guests, it's time for dessert, prepared by our talented cook, Kokkie."

Kokkie entered from the annex beside the dining room. Her black hair shone, restrained in a bun at the base of her neck by pins studded in colored stones. They matched the indigo and caramel colors which outlined peacocks at the hemline of her batik sarong. Henri handed her a round layer cake, nearly as large as a steering wheel, resplendent with piped white and yellow roses atop chocolate ganache frosting. Kokkie set her creation on the table and lit its array of slender candles. Pappie kissed Mamma and sang a beautiful rendition of the Dutch birthday song, "Lang Zal Ze Leven." *Long shall she live*. His deep baritone filled the room. After the last line, the crowd cheered and shouted their good wishes to Mamma while she blew out the candles.

Annika clapped and whistled. The man who she hoped would satisfy her own wish for many birthdays to come stood beside her and gave a deep-voiced, "And many more!"

Mamma cut into the cake. The chocolate aroma released into the air and teased Annika's taste buds. Her mouth watered at the thought of rich, moist cake and ganache—made from imported Dutch chocolate melted into heavy cream. She really hadn't eaten much supper.

Phillip squeezed her hand. "You're a cake lover, too?"

"I'll do about anything for chocolate." Annika cleared her throat and prepared to clarify the unlady-like statement. "Like the time I agreed to keep a secret. My parents went out on a rainy night. My two older brothers, Rudy and Claude, wanted to play soccer in this room."

"Here? Amongst all this expensive Delft china?" His hand motioned to the blue and white plates that hung on the wall. Their center sections depicted windmills and village scenes from Holland. On end tables sat Mamma's collection of cut-glass vases, holding sweetly scented, white oleander flowers.

"My brothers instructed our servants, Luther and Ahmad, to push the furniture aside. Worse, they forced them to be their goalies. The two men were scared to death one of Mamma's antiques would be broken to smithereens."

Phillip shook his head. "I wasn't raised with so many servants. We would've been spanked or told we'd be stuffed in the bag of Sint Nikolaas if we'd pulled a stunt which humiliated any staff."

"I felt bad for sweet Ahmad, and kind Luther, but Pappie had left my brothers in charge. We were way too old for a Sint Nikolaas threat, and my parents never knew. Pappie would've been furious," she confided. "I made Claude and Rudy turn over their monthly allowance to Ahmad and Luther the next day."

"A worthy gesture considering the scenario. How did they keep you quiet? A new tutu?" he teased.

"Very funny. They bribed me using three chocolate bars. I stipulated it equaled a down payment. I'm keeping that story tucked away until I need a big favor from them."

Phillip let loose a deep, hearty laugh. "You're going to keep me on my toes, Annika."

Her whole being radiated sparks of brilliant light. Oh, she'd keep him on his toes, alright. She blinked her lashes à la Janet Gaynor in her recent movie portrayal of a forlorn heroine. "I think you're quite tall enough as you stand." The mischievous twinkle in his eyes gave her courage. Maybe she wasn't ugly. Maybe being a muscled, tanned, tomboy hadn't ruined her chances.

Emily, the very picture of a refined and elegant officer's wife, approached the two of them. She smiled timidly and daintily balanced three pieces of cake on dessert plates between her manicured fingers.

Annika held her breath. Could she compete with her cousin?

"Thank you, Emily," Phillip said. He took two pieces of cake and returned his attention to Annika, then pretended to weigh each slice before he handed her the corner slice with the thickest frosting.

He'd chosen her! "An officer and a gentleman, as the British say," Annika teased him as she watched

Emily return to where Mamma filled more dessert plates.

"I do my best," he said in his low, rich voice.

Oh, she'd done her best and won round one. Annika forked a bite of thick ganache into her mouth. "Mmm." She licked her lips. "Wait until you try it."

Phillip's eyes traveled from her lips to her eyes. "I'm certain it will be delightful."

Flutters sent a vibrato pulse through Annika. He was flirting with her, if the romance novels she read were accurate. Now to keep things light and not appear too eager, or this effort entailed a trip for biscuits, the American term she'd read for an endeavor yielding no results.

They polished off their cake in comfortable silence. Conversations buzzed around them. Ahmad and Luther passed through the revelers bearing trays of highballs, Manhattans, champagne, and other spirits. Both men wore their finest white dress clothes. Ahmad wore his white turban and Luther a navy batik blangkon cap embroidered with gold thread. By the number of drinks they served, Pappie would need to secure a dozen sados and taxis for his guests to travel home safely tonight. Her lieutenant had declined the last few rounds of liquor, adding another plus to his attributes.

"Delicious cake," Phillip said, and set their empty plates on a tray behind him.

"Kokkie's a marvelous baker." Annika scanned the room to see if Mamma planned to push Emily his way again. No scheming mother in sight. Time to move discreetly forward on her life-changing, till-death-do-us-part goal. Her body thrummed at the thought of another dance with her beau. "I see Pappie whispering to the band leader. After the rich cake, he'll likely request a slower tempo pas de deux."

"Pardon? I'm not fluent in French."

"Oh, it means step of two," she said.

"You speak French?"

"Yes. Besides Dutch and Malay, Pappie insisted my brothers and I learn French, German, and English. Maybe he thought one day we'd work in his commodities business." She mustn't bore him. A lady listened. "What division did you choose in the Royal Dutch Army?"

"You speak five languages. Wow." He blinked. "Ah, my university studies focused on the sciences and mathematics. Flying utilizes those concepts, so I'm leaning in that direction." He tilted in an exaggerated Tower of Pisa stance. For a moment, their shoulders touched with their faces inches apart.

A leather pilot's cap would accent his dark eyes. The ones so close to hers now that she could see the gold flecks around his pupils. She clasped the side seams of her dress and forced herself to remain cool and collected, even though she was a mere hairsbreadth from his mesmerizing eyes. "Rudy, my brother, has always dreamt of flying." She looked away before she succumbed to the urge to lean into his solid shoulder. "Father bartered for flight lessons when he turned sixteen, so Rudy may be training in the new Koolhovens."

"Impressive you know the plane." Phillip straightened. "I met Rudy earlier tonight and learned of his aspirations to fly for the RAF. The British are very particular on who represents their elite squads. What are your plans?"

If he knew how he fit into her marriage plans, he might run out the door and test his luck in the jungle. "I take the high school graduation test in June." He didn't need to know she'd been moved ahead two years in school. "I qualified for gymnasium, the university preparation courses. The tests are administered throughout Java all at one time, so there's no chance of shenanigans. Writing, history, and foreign languages interest me. I plan a career in nursing, so I also need to excel at math and science."

"Nursing. Not the easiest vocation. What influenced your decision?"

"The options of teacher, seamstress, or secretary don't really suit my personality. And, as children, my brothers and I played hospital. They were questionable doctors, but I excelled at being the nurse. I've always been curious about sicknesses."

"Interesting. You'll need scientific curiosity and

good grades." He rubbed the subtle cleft in his chin. "I remember the pressure to attain a top rank on gymnasium tests. I had a university in mind and needed to excel. I can spare a few hours each week while I'm stationed here, so why don't I ask your father if my coaching you on math or science might improve your odds at entering the nursing program?"

Oh, she liked her future husband more by each passing moment. Her mind raced as she attempted to casually consider his offer and glanced at the chandelier off to her right. Had she successfully imitated the coy demeanor of women in the movies?

Luther came to the rescue. He approached, bearing a tray full of drinks, and stopped between them. "A cool refreshment, Meneer?"

"Thank you," Phillip said, and lifted a Manhattan in a cocktail glass, garnished by the requisite Maraschino cherry. "And for the lady?"

Lady. He must assume her to be eighteen, the typical age of a graduate. "White wine, please." Her hand brushed his wrist as she took the glass from him. Tingles shot up her arm. She sipped the cool, sweet Riesling, then placed her goblet on the little half-wall in front of the dining area. She drummed three fingers on her cheek. "About your offer to tutor me. I could use help in chemistry, physics, and calculus."

He straightened his wide shoulders and threw

her a mock salute. "I'll do my best to convince your father I'm the recruit for the job. Wouldn't want you to fail an exam if we can help it."

Failing would never happen, an irrelevant detail. Pappie must agree, he simply must. She'd prove to Phillip she could be more than his student. "I'd be forever grateful," she said quietly. For an instant, her world contained only the two of them, even while surrounded by family and friends. Ice clinked in cocktail glasses and laughter punctuated conversations.

Quick notes of a Samba rang out from the veranda. The trumpet player waved his hand to invite the dancers back to the floor. Phillip's focus shifted to the musicians for a moment. "Ready to cut the rug?"

"I believe so," she tried to sound nonchalant, but grinned while he led her to the dance area. After a samba, they glided through a foxtrot, and then a wild sort of cake walk in a tapioca. After a fun mambo and a cha-cha, the guitar player strummed the first chords of a tango. Yes! Sparks shot through Annika's body at the thought. Nothing could top the night like the most passionate and sensual dance partnered with Phillip. She stepped to a vase of flowers, broke the stem of a white chrysanthemum, and stuck it purposely behind her left ear to show she was not available.

Phillip led her to the edge of the marble area and

stared straight into her eyes. Was this part of the Tango stance, or did he believe they belonged together? Annika kept her gaze locked on his, as the romantic dance required. They spun and dipped through the complicated steps. She arched her back and swished past him. No one else joined them on the floor, and Phillip utilized the entire area by swooping and twirling her. At the final chord, he dipped her low, her hair sweeping an inch from the floor. Annika's chest heaved. She'd never danced romantically before.

His firm grip brought her upright. "My instructor from long ago lived for the tango," he disclosed. Guests smiled and clapped from the edge of the dance area. Off to their left stood her frowning mother. Emily stood solemnly beside her.

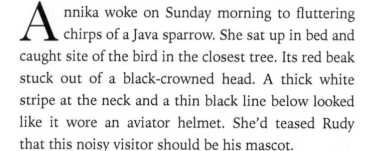

Annika woke on Sunday morning to fluttering chirps of a Java sparrow. She sat up in bed and caught site of the bird in the closest tree. Its red beak stuck out of a black-crowned head. A thick white stripe at the neck and a thin black line below looked like it wore an aviator helmet. She'd teased Rudy that this noisy visitor should be his mascot.

Verdorie! Phillip, her very own almost-pilot, could be at breakfast. If Annika's mother had anything to say about it, seated across from him would be Emily the early riser. As she parted the sheer mosquito net, she almost pulled it from the oval bamboo frame attached to the ceiling. The sense of urgency pressed into her as she scrambled off the mattress.

Foxy yipped from his spot on the other pillow.

"Scoot your bones. Time's a wasting." He trotted to the edge of the mattress and she set him on the floor. A moment couldn't be spared to wash up. She pulled on her red, high-waisted culottes and a blue and white striped top, then slipped her feet into sandals. Today held fabulous possibilities for further contact with Phillip, hopefully as his student. Luckily, Emily had graduated from high school last year and planned to be a primary school teacher. She wouldn't be a participant in the tutoring sessions.

Oudje met her in the hallway, pride and love in her smile. "Good morning. Your feet must be tired." She raised an eyebrow. "Should I get a bath started, Annika?"

"Not yet, thank you. I'll bathe after breakfast." Sliding downstairs on the bannister – a handy trick Claude had taught her to get to dinner quicker, Annika hopped off in time to avoid flying into the entry.

Voices sounded from the dining area. Phillip's appealing baritone sent her spirits to the roof. She walked in, stopped at the half wall, and scanned the oblong table built to seat twelve, now centered in the room again and surrounded by dining chairs. Pappie and Mamma sat at the closest end in their customary positions, their backs to her. Emily sat on Mamma's left. Phillip had taken a seat on the opposite side, near the middle, and held a teacup above his saucer. Luther filled it from a steaming silver pot. Phillip glanced at her, then returned his attention to Pappie.

No smile, no cheerful greeting? Had they been too showy on the dance floor? Annika inhaled and caught the fragrance of something sweet. "Goede morgen," she said, and gave each parent a kiss on the cheek. "Are you enjoying a slice of birthday cake for breakfast, Mamma?"

"I have, dear, and left a sliver for you to enjoy with our afternoon tea." Her pursed lips set Annika on edge.

Mamma narrowed her eyes and continued. "Seems you and Lieutenant Van Hoven engaged in interesting conversation last night." Not accusatory, or angry. Possibly concerned. No one else batted an eye at her warning tone.

Phillip cleared his throat. "Yes, Annika. Your parents and I discussed my tutoring offer to help you attain the highest marks at graduation." He stirred his tea. "Your mother mentioned how Marta's twin daughters struggle to master the same subjects. Your father suggested hiring me to oversee twice weekly sessions to assist you ladies."

Great, she'd be sharing him with her chatty and

available older friends. "The assistance would be appreciated," she remarked casually, and turned to Ahmad, standing at the far end of their typical Sunday buffet. "Breakfast smells divine." She slowly walked toward Ahmad and contemplated fresh sliced brown bread, boiled eggs, Gouda cheese, vegetables simmered in coconut milk, white rice, mango, and pawpaw, her favorite fruit. Did she act unconcerned enough? "Please, Ahmad, may I have a slice of bread and both cheeses, a bit of the vegetables with rice, and a selection of fruits? Thank you." She slid onto the chair opposite Phillip and unfolded her napkin.

Discussions between her father and Phillip continued about the tutoring sessions. Pappie suggested days for classes, and Phillip seemed agreeable to any.

Ahmad placed her filled plate in front of her and pointed to a fresh crepe de raisin, her Oma Elodie's favorite breakfast sweet, which she'd enjoyed as a girl in France. "You know me so well. Tell Kokkie thanks," she whispered.

Choosing pawpaw compote as her first bite brought an exotic flavor resembling mango into her mouth. Chewing slowly settled her stomach. Conversation moved to the previous evening's successful party, and Annika nodded and smiled as appropriate. She finished by eating tiny bites of the raisin-filled crepe. The sweetness coated her tongue almost as well as chocolate. She dabbed her mouth with her napkin and held her excitement at Phillip's upcoming tutoring. Her foot bounced on the thick Persian rug under the table.

After Ahmad cleared their empty plates, Pappie turned to Annika. "I've been summoned to a meeting at the English Club, so we won't be able to ride together today. Please continue jumping Maggy on the course. Cool her down in the woods and walk her over any logs you see. That'll strengthen her hindquarters." He aimed his attention on Phillip. "We took this Sunday off from church. Maybe next week you can join us at our worship service. Any plans for today?"

"I'd enjoy attending church next week. As for today, I thought about sightseeing or spending time exploring the woods. I trekked the hills in Bandoeng, my hometown," Phillip said, and held out his empty cup when Ahmad walked by with the silver teapot.

Bandoeng. Annika had heard that city called "the Paris of Java" for the landscape and architecture. How to show him the beauty of Batavia or do something more exciting? "Pappie, might Phillip ride Noir this afternoon? We could do a round of jumping, and then walk the horses in the woods," she asked cordially, and restrained herself from clapping in glee at a possible opportunity to spend time with him again. Certainly, he rode. She turned to Phillip. "Noir is a sixteen-hand warmblood. His name is French for black. He's not mysterious, but well-mannered."

Phillip raised his palm in the stop position. "Nope, not horseback for me, no matter how polite they are. But after a week of studying manuals and engineering details, being outdoors sounds appealing." His serious tone inferred her company wasn't necessary. He took a long draw of their favorite Javan black tea. "Delightfully strong brew does my soul good. I can put off the sightseeing. Might I observe the jumping and then walk alongside while Annika cools her horse? Hopping over downed logs would do me good."

He could've asked for a map of trails. Annika dribbled orange juice on the white tablecloth. She moved her saucer to cover the stain, not before Pappie raised an eyebrow.

"Annika won't ride today until after high tea. Cooler weather then. There are unappealing areas in Batavia, like any other city. It's a good idea to have a local show you our downtown. I'll see if Claude's available. He should be up shortly." Pappie smiled at Phillip, before he turned stern eyes to her. "Annika, I need to speak to you in my office."

Phillip rose from his chair. "Another delectable meal, Mevrouw Wolter. Thank you. Meneer Wolter, I'd appreciate a guide for Batavia but don't go to undue trouble."

Annika clenched her napkin under the table. That job belonged to her, not Claude, who denounced her at every opportunity as his tomboy sister. After a long swallow of tea, she rose and followed Pappie into his office. She chose the maroon velvet wing-back chair. Pappie faced her and leaned against his Djati wood desk. Behind him sat a Tiffany desk lamp, an antique ship's brass bell clock, and an open brief-case on the desk blotter.

"I'll only say this once, Annika," her father spoke in his take-notice tone. "Lieutenant Van Hoven is eight years your senior and an officer. I'd thought of hiring a tutor to ensure your graduation success and he presented his offer at the right time. However, you will not be getting any romantic ideas or casting goo-goo eyes at him."

That monkey left the tree last night. Was her age secret out? "Yes, Pappie." She lowered her voice.

"Fine. In any conversation you will call him Meneer. Not his first name, but Meneer. Do you understand?"

"Yes, Pappie. Might I call him Lieutenant Van Hoven in a crowd of people?" Pappie gave her a tight smile. He hadn't caught the cynical edge to her voice.

"That's appropriate. Mind my words, Annika." He turned and closed his briefcase. "I'm off to a long meeting at the English Club. Maggy needs a good workout today over the jumps. I trust you won't let her exercise routine lapse."

"Of course not." She cleared her throat. "Pappie, I believe I heard Claude mention plans for today.

Would you approve of me hiring a sado to tour Lieutenant Van Hoven? I could show him the main streets of Batavia and familiarize him with the government buildings. I'd act in my most formal and ladylike manner."

"He should know the lay of the land." Pappie's face transitioned to what Claude called his French Inquisition stare. "You may escort him on one condition. Lieutenant Van Hoven must wear his uniform."

Meaning absolute propriety. "Of course, Pappie. I can apprise him of your request." If she showed an iota of the enthusiasm bubbling in her chest, Pappie might cancel the tutoring, today's outing, and her life. "I'll give Maggy a good workout session afterward. I hope your meeting goes well." She did her best to glide out of the room as she'd been taught by Pappie's mother, Oma Elodie.

Minding his words and putting her plan in action were not mutually exclusive. The patient frog caught the fly. Time to hop on her lily pad, or buggy seat in this instance.

Annika stood on the front steps and watched the horse and buggy trot toward their house. A slightly curved piece of sheet metal served as a roof for the open-air sado, where the passenger seat faced backward. The light carriage was driven by a younger Indonesian man dressed in a colorful boxy shirt and shorts. She patted her jacket pocket where she'd stashed her page of notes. Pappie's book on Batavia history had given her the details she'd need to sound like an official guide, if they didn't pass an unfamiliar building. But had she dressed appropriately? Her hand went to her throat and pressed into the heirloom diamond she'd retrieved from the wall safe. A touch of elegance, or an ostentatious display for a casual ride?

"You look refined in your suit, Annika," Phillip said from beside her. "The pale aqua color casts a green shade to your hazel eyes."

Refined inferred grown-up. And he'd noticed her eye color! She took a slow, calming breath. "Thank you, Meneer."

He skipped down the veranda steps and approached the rear of the buggy. His pressed white uniform couldn't hide his trim but muscular physique. "May I help you in?"

She descended the stairs. "Yes please." If she bent forward, she'd see her grin reflected from his polished black shoes. His firm, warm grip steadied her on the metal step while she climbed onto the rear facing wooden seat. She placed her sun hat in her lap and crossed her ankles in an Oma Elodie approved pose. The hem of her straight skirt now hit above her knees.

"Please call me Phillip." He tugged down the sides of his coat and his finger brushed her skirt.

"Pappie prefers I address you formally."

"Oh." His surprise told her he probably didn't know her age. He slid his hips into his side of the seat frame. "So be it." For a second his lips thinned, then he turned to the driver. "We're ready. Please take Jakarta Weg into old VOC town."

The driver clicked his teeth and the horse trotted from their driveway onto Boxlaan. They went past The English Club's patio, which surrounded the side and back of the building. Annika kept her face forward. No way she'd chance seeing Pappie. "Sounds as if you know Batavia," she said, and laid out the route in her head. So far, so good.

"I've lived my entire life a few hours away, in Bandoeng," Phillip began. "My parents are amicably separated, so my father, Vader, and I travelled here to visit his sister several times. Tante Suze lives in the Tjikini neighborhood. She's taken in female boarders to help meet expenses. I'm glad your family chose men." His grin showed even, white teeth. "I've never experienced a Batavia tour from a professional guide."

Annika's cheeks grew warm. "I hope I can match your expectations." The admiration in his eyes told her she'd made progress on appearing mature by wearing the dressier short-sleeved aqua linen jacket and pale-yellow blouse ensemble instead of trousers. The striped ribbon on the band of her hat matched perfectly. And now, the perfect time had arrived to begin describing historical landmarks. She leaned a tad forward and pointed across his broad chest. "That Portuguese Church was built around 1690, during the VOC period. Pappie made certain my brothers and I knew the history of Batavia and how the VOC – the Vereenigde Oostindische Compagnie – had public shareholders in the 1600s, unlike how other foreign governments controlled all aspects of colonial life."

An automobile's beep-beeping sent their buggy wheeling to the far edge of the road. Annika clutched the seat and Phillip grasped her forearm to steady her. Two jeeps filled with men in military uniforms whizzed past, an odd sight for a Sunday. She motioned to the vehicles. "I've never seen so many uniformed men in Batavia."

"You'll see more soldiers in the days to come."

"I noticed you met Uncle Bajetto last night," Annika said. "He's an excellent horseman and he always entertains me with old stories about the esteemed Dutch cavalry. Your conversation appeared serious."

The carriage passed under a row of tall trembisi shade trees, their leafy green canopies more than forty feet wide. Beneath them, vendors waved bright-colored fruits and vegetables as they called to the sado driver. He ignored them and kept a steady pace.

"War is imminent, I'm afraid," Phillip said. "But let's shelve the issue for the day, please."

"Of course." Annika swallowed hard. He must constantly deal with the threats, while she only heard whispered fears. "Next, we'll arrive at Sunda Kelapa, the Harbour Canal flowing out to the Java Sea. I wonder how it would feel to travel the ocean in one of the wooden Buginese schooners."

The driver stopped alongside a sidewalk near the dock. "I can wait for your return," he suggested.

"Please do," Annika replied to the driver. She donned her wide-brimmed hat and caught Phillip staring again, this time at her profile. Could such a tall and handsome lieutenant consider her pretty enough to be the wife who advanced his military career? That's what she'd heard officers wanted, to move up in rank. "A walk will be perfect to stretch our legs."

"Yes, mine get a bit cramped in tight places." He led the way to the sidewalk.

Sweet and pungent smells filled the air alongside the canal. Ahead sat a row of Buginese schooners piled full of wooden crates and canvas bags. Broad at the middle, the boats quickly narrowed to a pointed bow. "Their rigging reminds me of pirate ships. I can imagine them cutting through high seas in a chase. Which one do you think would win?" she asked.

"I'd pick the darker one holding the tallest mast.

She's not elegant and sleek, but I'd bet she can outlast the rest."

"Hmm. Same one I chose, for her mismatched pile of sails and weathered hull. She's ridden through some storms and met the challenge."

Phillip tapped the edge of his eye. "Good observation. Rugged often outshines refined." His genuine smile could've melted chocolate for ganache. "May I take you to lunch at the Hôtel des Indes? I've heard the food to be excellent."

"Oh." She smoothed her jacket. Thank goodness she'd not chosen to wear trousers or an informal sundress. "I'd be delighted. Mamma and I sometimes eat there after shopping trips."

Phillip kept his body five or six inches from hers on the leisurely stroll returning to the sado.

Two well-dressed young men in suits approached. From a few feet away, they smiled at her, removed their Panama hats, and bowed.

Annika did a mock curtsy and waved them past. Phillip moved to an inch from her side. She slowed her pace to enjoy every moment of closeness and breathed in the scent of his crisp, clean aftershave. "A lovely Sunday brings out the best in everyone," she said modestly. Even if he wanted, no hand holding was allowed while in uniform.

He'd straightened to even taller. "As does a pretty lady," Phillip asserted. She took the arm he offered to assist her in climbing aboard the tippy sado. "To the

Hôtel des Indes, please, via the Tjikini neighbor-hood," he instructed the driver. The two-wheeled cart made a sharp U-turn and followed old Kali Besar thru Town Hall Square. They continued the peaceful ride along Mills Canal, shaded by trimmed tamarind trees. Vibrant art deco office buildings sat beside elegant 17th and 18th century homes. At the southern end of Sunda Kelapa, the port, stood a skinny three-story white building with a red upper level and trim. "Oddly-shaped structure," Phillip said.

Annika perked up. She'd noted this one. "That's a watchtower from 1831, once the office of the Harbor Master. Next, we'll be passing by the large Chinese Quarter in the Glodok neighborhood. The Chinese first arrived here as early as the 13th century, although not in large numbers until the 1800's. Mamma and I often visit their shops for special spices."

"Now I know the secret to the delicious and exot-ically spiced meals at your home," Phillip said. "Along with your history and language aptitude, can you write in Chinese?" He pointed to the beautiful script advertising restaurants and businesses.

"Not yet." she quipped, "but I could learn." She swiped the air with an imaginary pen.

"I'm certain you could."

The sado driver stopped at the entrance to a narrow drawbridge and waited for oncoming vehicles to pass. On the other side, rows of vendors lined the road. Under makeshift awnings they sold tools, batik cloth, and produce. The smell of ripe bananas hung in the air as a man waved a bunch of them. The Indonesian men were generally Annika's height or shorter, with black hair and dark brown skin. Most of them wore a straw hat and a sarong skirt topped by a boxy, mid-thigh length shirt. Shoeless children in dusty clothes wove in and out of customers. They balanced on their shoulders three-foot long, narrow planks of wood which held suspended woven baskets loaded with kitchen wares, toys, and clothes.

Annika watched a young boy who waved a pair of shoes for sale. She fiddled with the pristine hat sitting on her lap and swallowed. "I wish the children didn't need to work. How their little bodies must ache at night."

"Children are gifts to be treasured." Phillip's voice had softened. "I've wondered what they must think of a monstrosity like that." He motioned toward a sprawling two-story white mansion ahead. The bright red roof and window shutters stood out. He shook his head. "Displays of excessive wealth amongst poverty breeds contempt," he said quietly.

Annika had never considered how the ornate Dutch buildings would seem to the Indonesians. But it did sound as if Phillip liked children, too. She bit her lip. A lady wouldn't discuss either of those subjects on a first outing. As the sado passed the mansion she offered quietly, "That manor belonged to Reynier de Klerck, Governor General of the Dutch East Indies from 1778-1780. I'm not certain who lives there now."

"You really know your history," Phillip said.

The sado horse's hooves clip-clopped an easy beat as they entered the Tjikini neighborhood.

"Truth be told," she confided, "I revisited a history book of Pappie's just before we left."

"Preparation has always served me well," Phillip responded. "My turn. Tante Suze mentioned that Queen Emma Hospital is the official name of the next building. The locals call it Tjikini Hospital."

Annika leaned across him for a full view. A sprawling grassy area held a wide, three story white building. Ten or twelve steps, done in a half circle, stretched across the front and led to the entrance. A slatted balcony wrapped around the second floor, where interior patients' rooms opened onto a wide veranda. A gabled roofline with multiple peaks gave it a look of elegance. "Whatever it's called, I want to walk those stairs one day as a nurse."

"I hope you do." In the next block, Phillip pointed to a small home fronted by a tidy garden of blooming flowers and vines. "That's Tante Suze's home. They moved close to the hospital when my uncle needed daily treatments. After my uncle died, his mother came to live with Tante Suze. We'll stop to visit them someday if you'd like. Tante's mother-in-law is Indo and makes fabulous rice desserts."

"Sounds perfect to me. I'd love to meet them," Annika replied. Family introductions moved her plan forward.

The sado continued onto the main thoroughfare, and at the Hôtel des Indes, Phillip paid the driver. "Selamat jalan!" The men exchanged cheerful Malayan goodbyes.

He helped her out of the buggy as a streetcar rounded a bend in front of a stately, white building on the south side of Harmonie Square. Three tall pillars marked the entry. Annika motioned toward the pillars. "Pappie belongs to the Sociëteit de Harmonie. I could take you his club for a dance." She held her breath. Did he know only the top ten in Batavian society were members?

"I'd love to see the inside of that renowned social club." Phillip stepped back for her to enter the cool interior of the hotel. "As long as their band plays a tango."

"I'll request one." She could've squealed in delight, but instead she raised her chin ever so slightly and did her best to walk in a dignified manner across polished marble floors. Ornate shaded chandeliers hung from tall ceilings. In a corner of the lobby, a man sat at a grand piano, his soft music filling the background as numerous men in beige suits strode past. Their female companions wore slim fitting bias-cut dresses or tailored skirts and jackets. Most carried parasols or wide-brimmed hats and looked prepared for a leisurely stroll in the sunny square.

Annika smiled at a couple who approached. The pair stopped in front of her, and the gentleman spoke. "Juffrouw Annika," Dr. Subroto, a friend of Pappie's, smiled broadly at her and said, "how nice to see you." He bowed slightly and nodded in acknowledgment toward Phillip as well. Dr. Subroto, a native of Java, turned to his companion, touched her gently on the shoulder, and then turned back to Annika and Phillip. "Please allow me to introduce my wife, Geneviève."

Geneviève – Mrs. Subroto – wore a peach linen jacket that set off her reddish-brown hair and pale complexion. Contrasted with his dark skin and black hair, they made a striking couple.

"Bon jour, Madame." Annika watched Geneviève's face brighten. "I'd like you both to meet Lieutenant Phillip van Hoven. Lieutenant, this is Dr. Subroto, the wonderful veterinarian who cares for our horses."

The men shook hands. Dr. Subroto patted his stomach. "Geneviève appreciates the classic French cuisine here. I chose a dish my Indonesian mother fixed on special occasions. Both tasted delicious. Today is our wedding anniversary. We've just enjoyed our yearly lunch here."

"Congratulations, and very nice to meet you

both," Phillip said. "We're also lunching here today. I've been assured we won't be disappointed."

The group said their goodbyes, and then Phillip and Annika walked past a covered veranda where rocking chairs and tables sat on a black and white tile floor. They stopped in front of a kiosk near the entry to the spacious dining room. Behind it stood an Indonesian man with a trimmed black moustache. He wore a white turban, jacket, and pants. "Good afternoon," he said in Dutch.

"A perfect day, indeed. Two for lunch please," Phillip requested.

"My pleasure, Meneer," The maître d's gaze flicked over them, as if measuring the appropriateness of their attire. "I have one space remaining on the terrace." He led them past five-foot-tall, potted palms to a quiet corner where he seated them at a wicker table with matching chairs. A floral appliquéd tablecloth held gold-trimmed Limoges china cups and saucers. Gleaming, etched silverware sat at each place. Their shady seats overlooked Molenvliet Street and bustling Harmonie Square.

Annika settled into her cushioned chair, smoothed her skirt, and placed her starched white napkin on her lap. At the table to her left sat an older, round-faced matron reading a Dutch-titled book. A coffee service sat on the table. Her mauve colored silk day dress and strands of pearls looked comfortably chic in the heat.

A smiling Indonesian waiter brought them ice water, menus, and a fresh sliced baguette in a linen-lined basket. The aroma of wheat and yeast made Annika's mouth water. She scanned the menu and swallowed. The cost of the expensive French dishes hadn't occurred to her with Mamma. Her monthly allowance wouldn't cover even one item on the menu. She sipped her water. Did a lieutenant earn a good salary? Her finger slid to a moderately priced, traditional Indonesian entree. "The udang kukus tempt me. I'm the only one in our family who delights in steamed shrimp tucked inside zucchini."

Phillip nodded. "Glad you didn't choose the extravagant Rijsttafel. I'd bet the rice table served here includes at least forty side dishes."

"Yes," she agreed. "Mamma and I once saw a dozen or more waiters lined up on the lawn to serve it to a table of four."

"That many waiters would make me nervous," Phillip declared. "I'll try the udang curry dua. I haven't eaten a good shrimp in curry sauce for ages. Does their blended guava and papaya juice appeal to you?"

"Perfect for a warm day," she agreed.

Phillip smiled and repeated their order to their waiter.

"I'm glad I finally met Dr. Subroto's wife," Annika said. "He left Java to attend the National Veterinary School of Alfort, near Paris. I believe that's where they were introduced. I think it's very romantic if they met abroad."

"I guess it would be." A frown crossed Phillip's face. "Annika, has your father mentioned any unrest amongst the younger Indonesian people, like Dr. Subroto, who've earned degrees in European universities?" He sat back in his chair and steepled his fingers at the edge of the table.

"Dr. Subroto and Pappie are more like friends who share a love of horses." Annika thought for a moment. "Pappie's mentioned someone named Sukarno and a nationalist movement."

"Yes. There's growing motivation for reform by Indonesians and Indos who belong to that political group. I'm glad you're aware of these things, but let's leave that discussion for another day." He smiled. "The deer grazing on the grounds are charming." They chatted for a few minutes before Phillip's focus shifted to a troupe of uniformed servers. Scents of shrimp, rice, and freshly roasted peanuts filled the air. The staff arranged the entrees and drinks on the table and left.

"A meal fit for royalty. Eet smakelijk," Phillip added the Dutch salutation to eat.

"Bon Appetit," Annika countered in French, and lifted her fork. While they ate, he described in detail how Bandoeng's topography compared to Batavia. Every morsel tasted delicious while listening to her husband-to-be.

Phillip ordered the special Toradja coffee to finish the meal, delivered alongside a doily-topped saucer that held two chocolate truffles. They both reached for the one not adorned by finely sifted cocoa. "I concede to the lady," he teased.

Annika brushed her fingers across his hand, then lifted the dusted piece and tapped its edge on the plate, reducing the odds her suit would acquire a cocoa shadow. "No need. I'd never wrestle you for a mere chocolate, lieutenant."

His cheeks colored to a perfect shade of mulberry.

CHAPTER 4

Annika homed in on the rise and fall of Maggy's canter. It didn't help settle her stomach. She shouldn't have invited Phillip to their stable. She shouldn't have set up so many jumps and she shouldn't be so nervous. Maggy lengthened her stride on the long side of the arena and Annika inhaled in hopes that the warmed-up, horsey scent would calm her.

It didn't.

What a ninny she'd been to extend their perfect outing. The romantic sado trip and lunch should've been enough. But no, she'd encouraged Phillip to join her while she exercised Maggy. While she'd swapped her linen suit for jodhpurs, he'd changed into casual cotton trousers and a short-sleeved shirt. Her stomach felt anything but casual. She shouldn't have eaten every mouthful of the delicious lunch at

The Hôtel des Indes—another bad idea. She glanced to her right. The tandem bike they'd ridden to the barn sat parked against a tree. If she had any brains, they'd still be bike riding. Too late. Phillip stood outside the arena fence, his arms on the top rail. His intense scrutiny followed her through the circuit of jumps, worse than a judge in a show ring. Her fingers tightened on the reins.

Stop it. Use Pappie's coaching and concentrate on your horse and the next obstacle. Maggy's shoulder muscles bunched and released at each stride. Annika's own muscles remained twice as tense as before her ballet performance. Pounding hoofbeats set a demanding tempo on the soft earth of the arena. Why had she set up the entire course? A line of sweat rolled from under her riding helmet and into the corner of her eye. She blinked it away and slowed Maggy to a trot alongside the far wall.

Looming to Annika's left, in the center, sat the double-railed oxer used to exercise Pappie's jumper, Noir. Without a rider, Maggy had flown over it several times. At the corner, she flipped her mane in anticipation.

They'd prepared for this, why not jump? Annika leaned over and whispered, "We're ready." She circled Maggy, relaxed her body, and aimed her at the three-foot, three-inch oxer. She rose to a half seat, and let her hands go soft to allow Maggy to gauge the jump stride on their approach. The mare crouched and leapt. Annika inhaled and kept her weight in her heels but leaned forward until her chest grazed Maggy's neck. Flowing mane brushed her cheeks while she exhaled and they sailed over both top rails, spaced three feet apart. Even staring straight ahead, she could sense Phillip's eyes still glued to them.

Maggy landed into a canter on her front feet, and smoothly pulled her hind end over the bar in a continuous, agile movement. She tossed her head and shook the bridle.

Annika took a gulp of air. "That's right! Good girl on your first try." She patted her horse's sweaty neck and released the chinstrap on her riding helmet. "I need to walk her to cool her down." She beamed at Phillip. "Then she deserves a drink, a refreshing shower, and a longer walk in the woods."

"I've never seen anyone jump in person. You appeared at one with your horse."

"Thank you for the complement. Maggy's a gem."

Phillip stood quietly while they circled the arena at a slow walk. He met her at the gate and held it open for them to pass through. "I held my breath as you glided over the wide gap," he admitted. Foxy trotted to Phillip and bumped his knee. He leaned over and plucked a leaf from the dog's furry back.

"Nicely done, Maggy!" Annika patted her horse's shoulder. "The gap seemed plenty wide from my vantage point, too." She dismounted and hung her helmet on a hook near the barn door. "I've been riding since I received Penny, my pony, as a gift for my fifth birthday. Maggy gets the praise for an impeccable performance today without even a hoof tap." She scratched her horse's neck and got a dusty nose bump of thanks on the sleeve of her white blouse. "I'm so lucky to ride the fleetest-footed mare in Batavia." She removed Maggy's sweat-dampened saddle pad and hung it on the fence. "Oh good— Newt-newt decided to make an appearance."

The monkey approached Phillip and touched the cuff of his trousers.

"Cute little guy." Phillip patted his head. "I assume the carrot pieces we brought belong to Maggy and the banana is for him?"

"Yes. Feel free to pass them out. I already gave one to Penny. Leave a chunk of the banana on top of the fence post." She pointed to where she wanted him to put Newt-newt's reward.

Phillip removed the animals' treats from the basket of the tandem bicycle. For Maggy, he held his hand flat and grinned as her muzzle lifted off several chunks. Newt-newt scampered up, sat at Phillip's feet, and covered his eyes, then his mouth, then his ears, as Annika had taught him.

Phillip's deep, hearty laugh made her chuckle. "See no evil, speak no evil, hear no evil. Clever mistress and monkey." He placed half the banana in Newt-newt's outstretched hand, put a chunk on the post, and gave a piece to Foxy. The dog gulped it and ran to the pasture, his tail wagging.

Annika's furry friends treated most people skeptically, but not her Phillip. Annika felt as if she was still sailing over the oxer the entire time she hosed off Maggy. Newt-newt even claimed Phillip's shoulder for their walk—a much less slippery perch than a wet horse's back. "Newt-newt senses you're an animal lover and trusts you."

The monkey chattered happily, and Phillip grinned like a teenager. "Thick fur," he declared. When he reached out to pet Newt-newt's arm, Annika caught a glimpse of the watch he was wearing. Something about the watch seemed odd.

Annika looked again. The watch face sat on Phillip's wrist at an angle to the band. "Yes, and scratching beneath Newt-newt's ears wins you favor," she said. "Am I imagining things, or does your watch dial sit crooked on the band?"

Phillip extended his arm. "Another astute observation. The design allows an airplane pilot to view the time and operate the chronograph quicker while in the cockpit. My father splurged and bought it for me, knowing my interests and hoping I'd choose to be a military pilot. It's a treasured gift."

"How thoughtful." Annika turned toward the pasture. "Foxy, time for our walk," she called. Maybe she could change Phillip's mind about being a pilot. Flying airplanes for fun was one thing, but pilots died in battles. Worrying about Rudy crashing was bad enough. "Parents are uncanny at knowing our dreams." She clipped a lead line to Maggy's halter. "Pappie encouraged my interest in riding early, on one condition. He won't tolerate students who view horses merely as tools. He also taught me to scrutinize how people treat animals. The ones who are mean to their pets often disrespect people of a different social status. When I'm a nurse, I'll treat everyone the same." She led Maggy to the pasture, where Foxy chased a yellow butterfly.

"You're a wise young woman." Phillip strode beside her through field grass. "Animals have no voice. Same as less fortunate people."

"I've heard Mamma tell stories of how Pappie reprimanded other Dutch folks for disrespecting their servants." They'd reached the shady forest. Red-billed parrots flew overhead and displayed green feathered wings. Foxy dove in and out of the underbrush, and Newt-newt chattered happily from his high seat. Annika felt the need to continue. "I'd bet it came as a surprise to some of the wealthy Dutch. Pappie is regarded as one of the top ten of Batavia."

"Oh, a society ranking," Phillip murmured. He put his hands in his pockets.

"I guess so. The Great Depression shrunk his income, but not his scruples." Annika took a deep breath of the mild scent from a pink shoe flower beside their path. "Mmm. I love the fragrance of flowers," she remarked, and waited in a ladylike manner for Phillip to respond.

Maggy's hooves clopped on the soft ground.

"Our families share a respect for others." Phillip petted Newt-newt's tail. "And also, animals. I had a dog as a child," he said. "I've missed that connection."

"The four of us spend a lot of time in these woods," she scratched Maggy's neck and listened to the rhythm of their footfall on leaves and twigs. Silence between her and Phillip wasn't uncomfortable. When they spoke, conversation flowed easily.

Too soon, they reached the gnarled tree. "Here's where we turn around." Newt-newt chattered and jumped from Phillip's shoulder to a high branch. "We play a game," Annika explained. "The reward's the banana you left." She signaled to Newt-newt. "Beat me back!" she challenged. In a flash, he launched himself into the trees. His brown butt swung between limbs until it disappeared.

Phillip chuckled. "We don't have a chance, do we?"

"Not on foot, and not on horseback these days, either," Annika said. They retraced their steps through the woods, then walked into bright sunshine on the pasture. An unfamiliar, small convertible sat near the hay barn. Next to the car stood a slim, perfectly-coiffed blonde woman dressed in a cobalt blue suit. The woman's pencil skirt, matching jacket with turned back cuffs, and flowing floral scarf constituted a design à la mode, or of the latest fashion, at least by Mamma's standards. She noted the model of the flashy two-seater car for Claude. "Oh, good," Annika said. "A new riding lesson client for Pappie."

"Afraid not." Phillip shook his head. "That's Lisa. Her father's a colonel, and he recently transferred from their home in Bandoeng to the Batavia military base. She and I dated in college. I'm surprised she took time out to visit. She's studying to be a lawyer." His brisk pace slowed.

"Oh." A lawyer. Annika's ribs squeezed tight. An old saying resounded in her brain. Nou breekt mijn klomp! *That breaks my wooden shoe!* Good thing she wasn't armed with one. Judging by the freshly applied red lipstick, seductive smile, and open arms directed at Phillip, Lisa did not consider him a past boyfriend. Annika tucked stray locks back into her barrette, knowing full well she sported smashed, stringy, helmet-head hair. She stopped twenty feet from Lisa and let Maggy graze on tall grass growing outside the arena. Newt-newt scampered toward Annika from out of the barn and Foxy nosed a broken cockroach leg being dragged near her feet by a frenetic squad of yellow ants.

Phillip plodded on ahead toward the fancy car.

"Finally!" Lisa dropped the cigarette she'd been smoking and used the toe of her pointed and very high-heeled shoe to snuff it into the dirt. A second line of ants scurried over to inspect. "Darling," she cooed, and opened her arms for an embrace. "I tracked you from Marta's home to where you've rented the room, then way out here. I got horrible directions to this farm by a lazy servant."

Annika gritted her teeth. How dare she call one of their servants lazy. Her mouth opened to voice a protest. She watched Phillip's posture stiffen as he reached Lisa.

"None of their servants are lazy." He took hold of Lisa's shoulders, pecked her cheek, and backed a few steps. "Quite a quest to find the stable. I'm not a bit surprised you succeeded." He turned to face Annika, his lips tight. "Annika Wolter, please meet Lisa Visser." Phillip scratched his eyebrow.

Interesting. Annika's brother, Claude, rubbed an eyebrow when irritated. If Phillip bore the same mannerism, Annika might still be in the running for his affection, *might* being the key word. She looped the lead line over Maggy's back and approached them. Good thing she'd been taught to take on unpleasant people with dignity. "Pleased to meet you, Juffrouw."

Lisa shook Annika's hand with the grip of wet hay. "Oh, you're the Wolter's daughter. Marta mentioned that you chum around with her girls," she said dismissively.

Heat rose in Annika's chest. The twins had

turned eighteen months ago. "Yes, we're all in our last year of gymnasium, with plans for university, or – in my case – nursing training."

Lisa shrugged. "Nice that your family could accommodate another boarder. Phillip, darling, you should've said something." She tugged his earlobe. "I'll put a bug in father's ear, and you'll be living on base in no time."

Phillip took a step sideways. "Please don't mention my accommodations, Lisa. I wouldn't bother a colonel with something so insignificant."

"Tsk-tsk." Lisa waggled her finger at him, as if scolding a naughty child. "If you're going to prepare for war, your lodging should be convenient." Her gaze skimmed over Annika's dusty black boots, paused at the brown nuzzle splotch Maggy had left on her white sleeve, and ended at her flat hair. Next, Lisa looked at the barn and wrinkled her nose, as if the earthy smell of fresh straw and horses offended her.

Foxy ran forward and bumped Lisa's leg, his way to get new people to scratch his head. Lisa recoiled against the car and brushed off the hem of her skirt. "So many little creatures here." Her gaze flicked to Annika, then back to Phillip. "Be a dear and take me for a drive to see the local sights."

Would he? "Foxy, come here," Annika called, every sense on high alert. The dog bounded to her and stopped before he collided with Newt-newt.

Phillip motioned to the bicycle they'd ridden to the barn. "I wouldn't want to inconvenience my guide from today," he said to Lisa.

Not inconvenienced, annoyed. Annika turned to hide her face. Curses on the war, and curses on her female competition. This one could've stepped off the cover of *De Gracieuse Fashion Magazine*. How could she keep Lisa and Phillip from a romantic candlelight reunion dinner without appearing jealous? Annika retreated to Maggy and grasped her horse's lead line. Phillip was paying her parents for room and board. She took a breath and slowly turned. "Lieutenant Van Hoven, on behalf of my parents I'd like to invite Juffrouw Lisa to join us for dinner. Kokkie prepares enough to feed your entire regiment."

Phillip's tense jaw relaxed. "How hospitable of you after already availing yourself as the well-versed historian." He turned to Lisa. "We toured Batavia earlier today. After visiting points of interest, we stopped the sado on the way home to listen to The Royal Dutch East India Army Infantry Band playing a concert in Waterloo Square. They performed a stellar rendition of work by Franz von Suppé." The faraway look Annika had seen on Phillip's face earlier now returned, as if he were recalling their recent stroll. The band performance had been the perfect impromptu finale to a wonderful outing.

Maybe she'd only imagined his delight. Annika cleared her throat and lowered her voice to sound older. "I also enjoyed the Can-can beat of the Jacques Offenbach piece."

"Never heard of him." Lisa flicked her hand in the air. "Silly Phillip," she trilled, and playfully punched him in the shoulder. "You and your fascination with dusty old composers. Maybe we can find more contemporary entertainment. Ready?"

Phillip rubbed the back of his neck and glanced at the bicycle. "We should transport you and the tandem to Boxlaan, Annika."

No chance they'd all fit, and by Lisa's scowl at the idea, the one wearing jodhpurs would be perched on the rear bumper. "Thank you. I'm capable of riding the bike solo. Enjoy your drive. I need to rub down Maggy."

Phillip threw Annika a mock salute and grinned. "We'll be back by seven." He tapped his watch, then turned to Lisa. "You'll be delighted when you taste one of Kokkie's delicious dinners."

"Can't wait," Lisa muttered. She tucked her silky scarf over her soft curls. She wore her hair in the latest chin-length style, which framed her blue eyes. "Let's find someplace quiet to catch up." Her hips swung as she walked to the driver side. The car's tires threw gravel as it roared toward the highway.

Out of sight, out of mind. Annika's heart hit the heels of her dirty leather boots. She leaned into Maggy's flank and allowed the horse's thick copper coat to absorb the tears. "He'll never choose a hazel-eyed, outdoorsy tomboy," she moaned, "even if Oma Elodie did teach me to crimp my finger properly while drinking tea." Foxy leaned against her leg and Newt-newt climbed onto her shoulder, his little paw gently patting her head.

A warm muzzle rested against her back, and Maggy let out a soft whicker of sympathy.

~

C ycling home took considerable strength without Phillip's prior enthusiastic assistance from the rear seat—that or the assault to her ego had also taken a physical toll. Annika parked the tandem in the shed against Pappie's tall ladder and lifted Foxy out of the basket. She rubbed her hand over the wooden ladder's rungs and recalled how years ago she'd flown her kite onto the roof. Rudy had insisted she drag the ladder to the lowest eave and had showed her how to pick her way across red roof tiles to free her toy. How proud she'd felt to impress her oldest brother. Horse jumping aside, Phillip probably considered strength and agility unbecoming to a lady.

She stepped outside the garage. The distinctive, almost cigar-like smell of a freshly lit coal fire hit her nose. Dinner preparation would be under way. Foxy dashed into the house while Annika removed her boots. She followed him through the annex, past the ballet bar Pappie had installed a decade ago for her daily practice. The Victrola sat silent, but in her head echoed the music she and Phillip had danced to until after midnight. She pretended to be held in his arms and lifted her right palm to the top of his imaginary broad shoulder before she twirled around the room.

A knife striking wood took her out of the delicious daydream. Visible through the door leading to the kitchen, slender Kokkie stood at the wooden, six-foot long butcher block center island. Neat stacks of freshly picked beans, slices of bok choy, mung bean sprouts, potatoes, and water spinach lay in mounded piles. In the sink, rice drained in a colander. Simmering spicy peanut sauce perfumed the room. This afternoon, even the thought of Kokkie's tasty gado-gado dish failed to entice Annika. Had she read Phillip's irritation at Lisa correctly?

Kokkie glanced her way, straightened the lightweight green silk jacket she wore, and continued to chop. "If you and Foxy came hunting for your usual after-riding snack, I made a batch of pineapple preserves to go with fresh bread."

"No, thank you." Annika nibbled the end of a slender yellow wax bean and threw the remainder to Foxy. "I invited Lieutenant Van Hoven's former girlfriend to join us for dinner tonight. Do you need me to pick any more vegetables from the garden?"

"Ah, Nonna Annika, that's why the long face on my lovely girl," Kokkie said. "Luther struggled to remember directions to the stable for the demanding woman." She winked. "We have plenty of your favorite dinner. Don't you worry about anything." She gently patted Annika's arm. "Mevrouw requested you to shower and join her in her bedroom as soon as you returned. I heard she's cleaning out her closet with you in mind."

Annika smiled. Mamma wore beautiful clothing. "Thank you. And tell dear, loyal Luther, that he's a treasure," she whispered. He could make the trek to the stable blindfolded. Even knowing the staff was on her side, her feet felt like bricks as she trudged upstairs and into the bathroom. Would Mamma give her a fashionable outfit for tonight? Cool shower water pelted her skin and revived her will to succeed. She put on clean undies and her pink robe and glanced in the mirror at her tanned skin and shoulder length hair. Trying on Mamma's elegant clothing could be compared to dressing Newt-newt in a swallow-tail coat and breeches.

Foxy sat outside the bathroom door. His tail wagged across the tile.

She petted his head and whispered, "I'm going to be a lady if it kills me." The first step required squeezing herself into elegant pieces from Mamma's walk-in closet.

The door to her parents' bedroom sat ajar. Annika entered and scanned the array of garments laid out on their four-poster bed. Colors ranged from amber and honey gold to pale cream and dark teal.

Mamma stepped out of her walk-in closet. "I heard tell that Luther directed a friend of the lieutenant to the stable. I assume she arrived?"

Inside Annika winced, outside she faked nonchalance. "Yes. And I invited her to join us for dinner. I thought you'd have done the same." She looked to her mother for a nod of approval, although not giving a hint of why she'd made such a calculated decision.

"Lovely idea. I'm impressed." Mamma lifted a turquoise-colored blouse to Annika's forearm. "This shade subdues your tan. Considering the latest style of shorter hemlines and your height, items from my wardrobe should suit you well."

"I'll turn sixteen in six months. It's time I dressed more appropriately." She slumped onto the corner of the bed. "But I don't know. A custom-made dressage saddle doesn't land a plow horse in the winner's circle."

Mamma released a long sigh. "You and your horses, schatje. Pappie won't allow you to spend all your time at the barn after you graduate. You've done well on difficult Latin studies in gymnasium. Why not enroll in stenography and typing classes in preparation for applying to nursing school at eighteen? I'll provide you with a wardrobe of appropriate and ladylike attire. I can have the seamstresses rework a few of my suitably-colored evening gowns, in case you meet any nice university boys."

Boys? Too late. The idea of sitting in mind-numbing classes tied her empty stomach in a knot. She picked at a thread on her robe. However, if playing along got her sophisticated outfits to wear when she was with Phillip, she'd comply. "Nurses need to take accurate notes, so enrolling in those courses is a wonderful idea." She smoothed a dun-colored skirt lying next to her on the bed. "And I know the value you put on your clothing. I appreciate your willingness to share."

"I'm thrilled you're finally concerned about your appearance other than your choice of jodhpurs. A lady is always on display. Coming from a family with high social status, you will find, as Oma Elodie states, Hoge bomen vangen veel wind." *High trees catch a lot of wind.*

"What?" Annika asked.

"Important people attract more attention."

Belonging in the top ten of Batavia meant little to Phillip. "I don't feel important. Maybe your clothes will help. Thank you." She scooped up the pile of skirts and blouses. The clock struck the half hour. Thirty minutes until dinner.

S triking yet feminine? Annika stood in her bedroom and assessed the teal blouse, cream colored skirt, and silver jewelry she'd put on for dinner with Phillip and Lisa. She couldn't ask Mamma's opinion. Thunderation! She stuck another hair pin in the French twist at the nape of her neck. Had the invite been an impulsive mistake? Maybe Lisa thought a family dinner too mundane, or her high-ranking father had requested her presence tonight. If only she possessed Aladdin's magic lamp for a wish or two. She put her hands on the waistband of the skirt and twisted her shoulders. Her reflection in the vanity's mirror wasn't all bad. One of Mamma's stretchy, woven-elastic corsets might nip in her waist a smidgeon.

Voices came from the hallway. She tilted her head and walked to her closed door. Her mother's lilting voice chuckled, and Pappie gave his deep, robust laugh. The sounds faded. Perfect. They'd be headed to the living room for a cocktail. Annika cracked the door open and saw no one, and then snuck into her parents' bedroom. They'd left the slatted doors open to their balcony. She glanced at the middle of the cement, under the railing, and spotted the word "Annika" cut in six-inch letters. Surely Mamma wouldn't mind her borrowing an appropriate foundation garment.

A shiny, peach corset lay folded in the top drawer

of her mother's wide dresser. Annika pulled it out, shucked out of her clothes, and wiggled the tiny, stretchy tube of material over her hips. Tugging it to under her bra took effort. She managed a shallow breath. The tummy panel prevented deep breathing —a minor inconvenience for a waist as defined as Betty Grable's.

The clock struck seven.

Her bare feet stuck to the cool marble floor as she opened the door. Shoes! Mamma's collection of dress shoes sat in a double row of wooden cubbies from the floor to the ceiling of her closet.

A knock sounded from below. "Good evening, Lieutenant Van Hoven, Juffrouw," Luther's dignified tone resonated from the entry.

Verdorie. Lisa hadn't begged off on her dinner invite. Annika pulled out the tallest highest-heeled sandals Mamma owned and squeezed her feet into them. Her long toes hung a tiny bit over the front. She loosened the strap and slid her heel back. Walking in shoes a size and a half too small reminded her of walking on sharp stones while barefoot. She wobbled and clung to a column of her parents' four-poster bed. Perspiration beaded on her upper lip.

She slid her feet across the hall tiles, gaining confidence at each step. The staircase handrail provided support as she descended toward sounds of introductions being made in the living room, a few yards from the entry. She took in the deepest breath possible, held her head high, and teetered down the final steps.

Across the living room, Mamma faced her, seated on the wicker divan against the far wall. She laughed at something Pappie said.

On the last tread, Annika's heel slipped off the shoe and she plunged forward.

Mamma's eyes grew wider than a Javan Scops Owl.

Annika grabbed the final curve of the handrail on the bottom post, clamped with her fingers for dear life, and did a half pirouette. Her free hand landed against the grandfather clock, which stopped the turn. She leaned her head against its solid wood, caught her breath, and wiggled the fingers that had saved her from plunging into the living room.

Had anyone else seen her? Slowly turning, she checked. No one looked her way. Egads! She would've belly-flopped right between the overstuffed chairs holding Phillip and Lisa, seated with their backs to her. "Thank the Lord," she murmured, and raised her eyes to the ceiling. The gilded angels atop the old clock seemed to point their trumpets at her. Annika slipped off the deadly shoes and slunk upstairs to change into flats.

On her return, Pappie frowned at her tardiness, then ushered her to take her place at the dinner table, beside Emily. "Nice of you to join us, Annika. You've met our guest, Lisa?"

"Yes," she said, and placed her napkin on her lap, not meeting Phillip's gaze from across the table. She sat quietly while Ahmad and Luther brought in fragrant dishes.

Lisa pushed around her food and monopolized the conversation, recounting tales of her legal expertise and name dropping the who's who of the wealthy Dutch aristocracy living in Bandoeng. She took a tiny bite of rice, then waved her fork. "Your city is quaint," she declared. "I heard tell Baroness van Heemstra brings her young daughter, Audrey Hepburn, to the local ballet studio for lessons each time she visits Java."

"Yes. Audrey's father and Frederick play tennis together at The English Club." Mamma affirmed. "Annika takes advanced classes and creates the choreography at the same dance studio. She's one of the star pupils. The Hepburn girl is several years younger."

"Have you performed together?" Phillip smiled at Annika from across the table.

He might as well be an ocean away. "No," Annika replied. "But I've seen her. She's pretty, with large, doe-like eyes. And she has long feet." Why had she brought that up?

Mamma pursed her lips, then relaxed them into a

smile. "Do you care for a slice of bread, Lisa?" she trilled, handily changing the subject.

The remainder of the meal was a blur. Annika ate only half of the crystal parfait glass full of Kokkie's double chocolate pudding topped by whipped cream. Nothing tasted good and everything felt strained, especially her corseted waist. She absentmindedly bounced the silver sugar bowl on the table, waiting to squish any rogue ants. None appeared. Even the ants had been bored by Lisa and left.

After taking a few sips of after dinner coffee, Annika politely excused herself and plodded upstairs. Whining came from her parents' room. She pushed their door open and Foxy circled her ankles, his tail wagging. "Oh dear. In my haste, I trapped you." She scratched his head. "Poor thing, need to go outside?"

The dog dashed downstairs. Annika followed, and passed Phillip in the entry, alone. Did she have only hours under the same roof? Not knowing how soon he'd move to the base hung like a guillotine over her head. "When will you leave our home?"

"It depends on the availability of my quarters." His sincere tone relaxed her taut nerves. "I insisted Lisa not bother her father about speeding the process." He patted Foxy and opened the front door to let him out. "I enjoy family living. I won't have that opportunity again until the war ends. Your father and I decided upon study sessions on

Wednesday afternoons and Saturday at one o'clock, starting this week. I hope you agree."

"Oh, yes," she managed. His warm smile could melt her into a puddle of freshly made ganache. The challenge remained for her to appear as demure as a Gibson Girl.

Phillip's twice weekly tutoring took precedence over any other events in Annika's life. As the weeks passed, the twins incessant chatter became more and more irritating. That and the fact that they could call their teacher Phillip, and she needed to use Meneer. Pappie could be so old-fashioned!

Determined to impress Phillip, Annika had given her full attention to the subjects they were studying, and she felt confident she'd do well on the final tests. But her friends might not, due to their constant prattling. Today would be different. Both the twins adored sweets and ate them with gusto, and Annika had planned a strategy with Kokkie.

She turned sideways in the mirror and smiled. Mamma's A-line navy skirt and matching print blouse accented her slightly curvy figure, without a pinching undergarment. She checked her nails and chewed a small mint candy. Clean nails and fresh breath were essential during classes. "Meneer," she repeated quietly while descending the staircase.

Someday, if her luck held, she'd use his name, or an endearment befitting a boyfriend.

The sweet smell of fresh coconut hit her nose as she entered the annex where Phillip held classes. On the sideboard sat a mounded plate of klepon – tiny, green, sticky rice balls covered in freshly shaved coconut. Those would keep the twins occupied. Bless Kokkie!

Phillip had taken his place at the narrow end of the worktable and rose as she entered. His face seemed even more serious. Did he share her despair that it was their last session?

"Good evening," she said. Each week she'd glimpsed snatches of Phillip's humor and intelligence. She shot a look out the window to the space where the twins usually parked their bicycles. Her pulse quickened. "Am I your only student?"

"Yes." He smiled and ushered her to the preferred seat to his right. "It'll be a quiet session. Marta phoned me. Their visitors from Holland are taking the family to dinner at the Hôtel des Indes."

Joy rippled through Annika. She slid onto the chair and scooted it to the table. Socializing with the twins was fine, but not their non-stop banter during tutoring. "Lucky them. Not to demean Kokkie's delicious cooking, but our lunch there was wonderful."

"Agreed. And contrast creates appreciation." A thick folder sat at his place. He opened it.

On top lay the corrected practice tests he'd given

them last week, hopefully showing how much she'd paid attention to his prior sessions of schooling. Did his reserved manner mean she hadn't done well? "The tests were difficult," she said.

"I might dispute that." As he slid the papers to her, his hand brushed along hers. "I'll have to try dinner at the Hôtel des Indes someday. Maybe for a special celebration."

Tingles began in her fingers and radiated through her body. She idly straightened the tests he'd placed in front of her. Fiddlesticks on physics and calculus! His touch had seemed on purpose. Or was she imagining? She had to check. Slowly, she peered up at him.

Hope sparkled in his eyes.

She'd happily join him for sandwiches in a chicken coop, but telling him that would have hinted at a schoolgirl crush. "If you enjoy veal cutlets, I've heard the Escalopes de Ris de Veau are to die for." Her brain whirled as she browsed each paper. Could that be right? She scanned the pages again. Not a red mark in sight.

"I do enjoy a good cutlet," Phillip said. "Kokkie fixed them marvelously last week, never had the French version." He patted his flat stomach. "Regarding school, you excelled at calculus, chemistry, and physics." His deep voice made it difficult to concentrate, much less keep her fingers from shaking. "With your aptitude in these subjects, you could've tutored the twins." He studied her, his arms crossed.

"That would've been a real challenge." She dropped her eyes to the test papers. "I'm confident to take the graduation tests on Friday, thanks to your help. If I think I've done well and you aren't busy, maybe we can take a celebratory walk in the woods on Saturday? June flowers will be blooming."

"I'd enjoy that very much, and I bet you'll pass every subject with flying colors," he added. "By Saturday, I may know if my application to be a pilot has been accepted." His voice held a spark of excitement she hadn't heard before.

Verdorie! Somehow, she'd forgotten about the darn special-edition aviator watch from his father and his intent to become a pilot. "Oh." She rose from her chair and retrieved the plate of sticky sweets. They no longer held any appeal. She set the platter, a stack of dessert plates, and napkins on the table, then used a silver tongs to dish three coconut covered klepon for him.

"Thanks. These look decadent." He popped one in his mouth, chewed, and smiled. "Delicious. You may be ready to take a final exam, but if I'm accepted to the program for pilots, I'll be the one doing classroom work in Batavia. Final flight training is handled at an airfield near Bandoeng where the squadron of planes is located."

No! Bandoeng was three hours away. The smile

froze on her face as a horrible memory surfaced. The night Rudy voiced flying for the RAF, Pappie's composure had broken. He'd maintained that dogfights often resulted in the pilot's death.

Newsreels predicting war couldn't match the bomb Phillip had just dropped.

~

Annika spotted the fresh stack of mail lying on the credenza next to the gramophone in the annex. The piece she'd been expecting for the last week sat on top. She ripped open the envelope from the Educational Records Division of the Dutch Government and studied the scores from her recent exams. "Yes!" she proclaimed. "I'm ranked in the top five percent in every class."

"That's wonderful," Mamma said from the living room, "but, not surprising." She stepped to Annika's side and patted her shoulder. "When the time comes, excellent grades will assure you a place in the nursing program."

"Lieutenant Van Hoven helped me improve in my difficult subjects. Might we invite him to dinner to celebrate?"

"Good idea." Mamma nodded. "He left a number for messages at the base. I'll phone him and see if he's available on short notice."

Annika shrugged, stifling her glee. "Okay," she

responded blandly. She'd endured three long weeks since Phillip's move to the base. Her excuses to see him had run thin. Mamma would catch on how much she missed him if she wasn't careful. "I smell Kokkie's spicey roast lamb." She sniffed the air. "And fresh cheese rolls."

"Emily's bringing home Quinn, the gentleman she's been dating. Marta introduced them and said he's a well-connected businessman, but a tad too serious for her twins. If things work out, it will be a good match for your cousin."

"How wonderful for her," Annika gushed, hoping to cover her own joy. "I'll dress carefully for dinner." She skipped upstairs, Foxy at her heels. An inkling told her Phillip would make himself available. She showered and scrunched her hair while it dried so that waves framed her face. If she lowered her eyelids, she could mimic the poses struck by Hollywood stars featured in Mamma's latest American fashion magazine. "What do you think, Foxy?"

The dog tilted his head and barked.

"Approval. Good. Now for the perfect ensemble." A navy-blue silk blouse and light gray skirt woven with navy threads hung at the back of the closet. She slipped into them and pivoted in front of the mirror. Her gold earrings and matching chain suited the outfit. She rubbed between Foxy's ears. "Good counsel."

From her open bedroom window, the rumbling

engine of a motorcycle grew louder. Phillip turned the big, low-slung, black bike onto their driveway and steered to the detached garage. He parked, then ran his hands through his thick hair.

How soft would it feel? Phillip's hair was finer than the broomstick-coarse texture of her brother Claude's mop. Someday she'd run her fingers through Phillip's hair. Annika put her hand to her heart. Her knight with shiny locks would rescue her from dull dinner conversation. She walked downstairs and greeted everyone.

Soon after meeting Emily's beau, Annika thanked her lucky stars she'd found Phillip. Quinn wore an expertly tailored linen suit on his short, stocky frame, but nothing disguised his outright bragging each time he opened his mouth during cocktails in the living room. He was far from a refined gentleman. As Oma Elodie said, horse droppings were not figs, and this man proved that appearances were deceiving.

"Dinner is ready to be served." Pappie ushered them to the dining room, where name cards written in Mamma's calligraphy sat tipped against water goblets.

Emily and Quinn sat across from Annika and Phillip, with Mamma and Pappie at the narrow ends of the long table. Rudy had moved to Bandoeng, and Claude had gone out for the evening, depriving them of his funny stories.

The actual guest of honor, Quinn, blathered on about contracts and prospects. He'd pause long enough to shovel in forkfuls of tender lamb, fried rice, and spiced yams.

An air of tension kept Annika eating quietly. Polite nods came intermittently from Pappie and Phillip. Mamma signaled Ahmad and Luther to move the three-course meal along at a brisk pace.

Phillip's face neither showed interest nor boredom. The only one who appeared unusually chipper was Emily. In fact, she smiled frequently, had added a touch of rouge to her cheeks, and wore her best dress – custom designed for her by Mamma from a dark green silk. She turned toward Quinn, and candlelight sparkled off her necklace, a large emerald surrounded by diamonds. She raised her glass of wine, and a gold bracelet topped by another emerald graced her wrist.

Annika leaned forward and blinked at the new jewelry. No wonder Emily hung on every word from Quinn. Their relationship must've surpassed the casually dating mark, even though they'd been introduced only a couple months ago at the most. What was shy Emily doing that she wasn't?

Coffee served by Luther on the veranda completed the evening celebrating Emily's beau and Annika's high scores. A breeze lifted her hair gently from her shoulder. She sat on one of the cushioned wicker couches beside Emily. Quinn and

Phillip sat in rattan chairs on either side. Mamma and Pappie occupied the other couch opposite them. A conversation lull allowed the thrum of insects to set the backdrop for an owl hooting in the distance.

"I heard gas rationing could begin on Java now that Hitler's invaded Poland. There's rumors the Germans will ally with Japan and Italy," Quinn stated, and puffed out his portly chest.

Mamma gasped and no one else responded, so Quinn fed off the stunned silence. "If things get tight, I'd imagine that each D.E.I. family would have an imposed weekly limit."

Mamma rubbed her forehead. "Oh dear, I can't bear the thought of Nazis or Japanese soldiers here. I'll speak to our chauffeur about where we might conserve, so we can do our part. Annika, you'll need to pedal your bike to secretarial school, voice, and ballet classes."

"I understand," Annika said. She'd watched Phillip's face show tight lipped irritation while Quinn spoke, then change back to his current state of a relaxed jaw and parted lips after Mamma's request. What good could Phillip think would come from gas rationing? Annika chose to remain silent and wait.

"My motorbike uses little petrol," Phillip asserted. In the evening light, the angles and planes of his face softened to make him even more handsome. "I'm still out of uniform by four fifteen on weekdays. Might I assist by transporting Annika?"

"Oh, that's a kind offer," Mamma began, "but our daughter's more comfortable riding astride her bicycle or a four-legged, whinnying creature."

Annika flinched. Not in this case she wasn't. Her beau-to be couldn't have offered a more appealing solution if he rode on the back of Pegasus. She gripped the edge of the cushion to hide her tense fingers under the fabric of her skirt. She had to appear resigned, to not act a bit excited.

Pappie set down his whiskey glass. "Claude recently took a spill on his motor bike."

Annika bit her lip. Her numbskull brother had broken an ankle and torn tendons in his other knee because he'd been reckless. Thankfully, it happened when she was not riding behind him. Claude had sworn her to secrecy each time she'd climbed aboard. Should she admit he'd taught her how to lean into a curve? Of course not, at least not to her parents.

Phillip cleared his throat. "Yes, I noticed his crutches. I'm so sorry. I'm a slow, steady driver," he said earnestly, and looked from Mamma to Pappie. "My Francis-Barnet Cruiser isn't new, but I keep Fanny B in good repair and have never come close to an accident or injury. There's a seat on the back and foot pegs for a passenger."

Pappie's narrowed eyes flicked from Phillip to

Annika. Being on the hot seat was nothing new. She demurely crossed her ankles, folded her hands in her lap, and tilted her chin in the most ladylike manner. It was now or never if she wanted to plead her case. "The route to the college and the Kunstkring Theater are short, flat stretches. The distance to the ballet studio may be a challenge," she said, and wrung her hands, "but I believe I can manage pedaling there and home afterward."

Mamma rubbed her throat. "They rely on Annika to dance as well as choreograph for the younger students. She needs all her energy."

Her father patted her mother's knee. "Claude can be a dare-devil. I trust Lieutenant Van Hoven," Pappie said. "As long as this isn't an inconvenience. Her ballet classes are each Tuesday and Thursday from five to six. You'd be welcome to dine here afterward on those days if you'd like."

Annika held her breath as she watched Mamma open her mouth, glance at Pappie, and say nothing. Odd, Mamma was a typical Dutch mother, voicing an opinion on everything. Tonight, Hitler's war intervened in her long-term plan for success. She casually smoothed the side of her skirt and waited for what seemed like an hour for someone to respond.

"Excellent," Phillip said. "Ballerina chauffeur will be added to my resume. Helping friends will never constitute an inconvenience." He pinched his side at his waist. "I'll add extra sit ups to my morning routine to offset Kokkie's delicious fresh bread and pastries." He turned to face Annika. Success radiated from his broad smile. "You may want to wear slacks, as my cycle didn't come equipped with a side saddle. I haven't transported a lady before, but I'm certain we'll manage."

Lisa, the girlfriend, never rode his bike! Hope fluttered in her chest. "I'm certain we shall." She met his dark, thoughtful eyes for the briefest moment.

The two of them were meant for each other, and no Nazi would deter her.

CHAPTER 5

DECEMBER 1, 1939

Clinging to Phillip's crisp cotton shirt while riding on Fanny B's passenger seat rated highly on Annika's favorite Tuesday and Thursday non-dates. Thank the Lord her father didn't have a clue as to her real feelings, even after he'd scrutinized her behavior during Phillip's previous two week stay at their home as a boarder and each night that he stayed for dinner after ballet.

Luckily, Pappie had never seen Annika riding behind Phillip on his motorbike. Nothing beat the closeness of her cheek against his shoulder and her legs snugged against his thighs. If she held out a little longer, her parents should allow her to date after her sixteenth birthday next week.

How would Pappie respond if twenty-three-year-old Phillip asked to court her? The question bothered her constantly. Prior to their very first motorcycle trip to ballet class, Pappie had voiced his opinion again on the age difference between her and Phillip. "You will continue to address him as Meneer," he'd begun in his French Inquisition tone. "My daughter isn't going to moon over a man eight years her senior. Lieutenant Van Hoven is being kind to the family, not romantically pursuing you," he'd emphasized. Pappie seldom misread a person, but she hoped this might be one of those exceptions.

What if Phillip never wanted to date her? Another question which bothered her constantly.

The movement of gears downshifting to slow the motorbike brought Annika to the present. Fanny B tilted into the last curve to the ballet studio. Annika's favorite portion of the trip required the tightest grip on Phillip's waist. At times like this she admired the noisy, wheeled beast as much as she appreciated Maggy's rocking canter. They cruised onto the gravel drive which led to the low building and Phillip parked in the usual spot, under the twisted branches of a shady monkey pod tree. The motor went quiet, and he shoved down the kick stand with his boot.

Annika slid one foot to the ground and threw her other leg over the rear fender. She stood and adjusted her backpack, then waited patiently as Phillip extracted from his pocket the chocolate bar he brought for her every time.

He got off the bike, stood for a second, and then sat sideways on the bike's seat to face her. "A snack?" He nearly dropped the bar.

Her comment about loving chocolate from Mamma's birthday party had not gone unnoticed. But why did he seem nervous today? Had she done something wrong? Oh dear, had Pappie said something? "Thank you," she said, and carefully opened the red wrapper. Please, oh please, let him ask the typically polite questions regarding her day spent learning boring-as-dirt stenography. He never strayed a smidgeon from impropriety but remained the soldier Pappie trusted. Today, he seemed more jittery than reserved. Had Pappie put the kibosh on their trips?

He ran his finger around the collar of his white cotton shirt. "Annika, if you ever marry somebody, what kind of a man would you marry?" he asked, and then tilted his head as if he wanted to catch every nuance of her response.

Oh dear, she couldn't tell him the truth. His intense, dark eyes searched her face. "He would be an officer like you." She'd blurted the first thing that came to mind.

"Yes, there are certainly more of them in town," he said. His jaw tightened.

"And he has to be a nice man like you. And everything like you." Too late, she realized how forward and juvenile her words sounded. Her throat went bone dry.

He let out a long breath. "I prayed you thought so. If you approve, I'll ask your father permission for us to date," he said hesitantly.

Finally! How she wished she could do a double pirouette, right here in the grass. Or kiss the remaining worry off his handsome face. But then he might regret his wonderful idea. She smiled warmly and nodded but held back the scream of delight threatening to escape. "I approve."

"Good." His foot tapped on the grass. "Your father's family holds titles and social status. Mine does not." He rubbed his lower lip. "I'm concerned that might come between us."

"It won't, I promise." She crisscrossed her heart. "You've been around Pappie. He takes pride in not being a snob. So do I. Truth be told, my brothers have influenced me as much as strict Oma Elodie."

The studio bell chimed five times, a warning to prepare for the afternoon session.

He grinned. "That's what I hoped." His manner shifted to relaxed. "I shall plead my case to your father. I must confess though, it shocked me when your mother invited me to your sixteenth birthday party. I honestly thought you'd already turned eighteen. You act and look mature, and graduating from gymnasium threw me. I agreed to attend the party, but in my surprise, failed to note the date."

"It's December eighth, next Saturday. Mamma

has you on the guest list." Phillip wanted to date her! Annika swung her backpack in an arc, stopped herself before doing a full spin, and slung the strap over one shoulder. Pappie had to let her date at sixteen. He had to. And she needed to act mature. She corrected her posture to that of a prim lady. "They advanced me in school two years, to my relief. Having older brothers and a father with high expectations, I never felt comfortable with students in my classes. Does the age difference bother you?"

"It would have if I'd known initially." He cleared his throat. "Annika, I assume you haven't dated?"

At least that wasn't painfully obvious. "No."

"I'd be honored to be the first to court you. I'll mark my calendar for Saturday. Perhaps that would be a good time to put in my request with your father." He pulled out a book from the saddle bag and rested his back against the tree. "See you soon." This time, his return smile could melt a chocolate bar three times as thick as the one she clutched in her hand.

She grinned at him, then pivoted and dashed into the building, knowing he'd feel safer about his social standing now, after she'd given her promise that neither she nor her father were snobs. Her lineage may be part of her, but nothing matched her love for him.

~

A light evening breeze blew into Annika's room – perfect weather to celebrate her sixteenth birthday. Goose bumps rose on her forearms. She stepped to the window. Far to the right side of the property, Budi, their chauffeur, bent to check on spinach, eggplant, peppers, beans, carrots, cabbage, and cucumbers planted in the garden. Kokkie would use many of them tonight in gado-gado, Annika's favorite dinner.

On the bed lay her mother's remade, copper hued evening gown. Tomorrow she'd compliment the seamstresses for their efforts to convert the expensive silk into a knee length dress in an updated style with pleats on each side of the inset waist. They must have made the final alterations while she'd taken a head-clearing ride on Maggy this afternoon.

Annika rubbed her temple. At sixteen, Pappie had granted adult privileges to her brothers. But boys always got more concessions. Well, the only item on her wish list concerned Phillip's request to date her. What if Pappie refused? The fluffy towel wrapped around her hair after showering felt double its normal weight. She put on undies and stared at her reflection in her bedroom mirror. Not really ugly. She turned and studied her filled out bra, decent waist, and long legs. One might even say hers was a pleasingly feminine shape. Still, Phillip could've changed his mind about dating her after seeing her bedraggled appearance twice a week after sweltering through ballet classes. Then what? She stood in the breeze at the window and fluffed her hair dry.

A soft knock sounded on her door, and Mamma stepped into the room. "Hello, schatje. Phillip arrived a few minutes ago for an appointment he made to speak to your father. Any idea why?"

Annika swallowed. Right now, in Pappie's study below her bedroom, her life's future hung in the air. "I believe he's going to ask if I'm allowed to date him."

"I figured as much. There's been an attraction between the two of you since my birthday party. Do you like him? Feel special when you're with him? You're very innocent about men."

No more pretending. She sat on her vanity chair. "Yes. I've fallen in love with him."

"You're still a child, you're only sixteen." Mamma picked up the wide-toothed comb and began untangling the back of her hair.

"So what? I can still have feelings. The lieutenant has treated me respectfully, as per Pappie's orders. And I have reciprocated."

"You're so young and so vibrant with life." She leaned over and kissed the top of Annika's head, then positioned a beaded hair comb at each of her temples. "Phillip strikes me as a patient and kind young man. A bit serious, but I've noticed his sense of humor."

"We make each other laugh, one of the things I enjoy about his company."

"That's important." Mamma pulled from her pocket the pouch holding the antique French diamond necklace she'd lent Annika once before, and a smaller pouch holding the matching earrings. "Oma Elodie gifted me these on our twentieth wedding anniversary, during the height of the Malay Depression. She knew Frederick had lost his business and couldn't afford to buy me one of his fabulous presents. They're treasured heirlooms of the de Fisicat family. I want you to have them now, as I have a feeling you will soon be attending formal events. If you had lived a few generations before Oma Elodie, you would be presented at French court while wearing them."

"I'm glad to bypass court and debutante balls." Annika smiled. "The diamonds are beautiful, though. I'll cherish them always." She lifted her chin and Mamma laid the jewel against her neck and secured the clasp.

"I longed for a baby girl and God blessed me with you. That's why we named our home Mansion Annika. Wear them with pride, my beloved daughter. You have become a beautiful young woman." She fingered the large diamond studs before she handed them over.

"I will. Thank you." Annika put them in her ears

and pushed her hair aside. The diamonds sparkled. Could she match their elegance?

Mamma stepped to the door. "Your whole life lies ahead of you. Take time to find the right man. Promise?"

She'd found the right one six months ago. "I hope to."

The door clicked shut. Annika took a deep breath, slipped on her heeled sandals, and proceeded to where she heard male voices in the living room. Today, the smell of tangy peanut sauce had no effect on her. Her future had been decided.

Phillip rose from his seat to greet her. The light in his eyes and radiant smile gave her the answer she needed. He reached into a sack by his feet and extracted a fifteen-inch square box of chocolates tied with a red ribbon. "For your birthday, Annika."

"Why thank you." She read the label. "Milk chocolates and nut chews. My favorite. I'll limit myself to one a day." She shook her head. "No, probably three a day."

Phillip chuckled. "I'll give the box a week," he said for her ears alone, and then pointed to a large bouquet of pink roses. "I recall that you like scented flowers."

Annika leaned over the roses and inhaled. "Mmm. Lovely. Thank you." Their rich, sweet fragrance would be another memory she'd cherish.

"Come sit by me, birthday girl." Pappie patted the

couch cushion beside him. "I've agreed for you to date Phillip. There are conditions."

Of course, nothing worth gaining came without conditions. "Whatever you say," she stated in her most agreeable voice.

"You shall continue to address Lieutenant Van Hoven as such, or as Meneer." Pappie took a sip of his whiskey and Annika bristled. "You'll need an escort on any dates that are more, shall we say, intimate surroundings, such as taxi rides or the movie theater in town."

"Claude likes to get out and sees every new film, I'm certain he'd accompany us," Annika said hopefully.

"Good idea. Anything to take Claude's mind off missing the opportunity to start college due to his broken ankle."

Claude wasn't a spoil sport. Satisfaction smoothed the rough edges of resentment against Pappie's demands. The birthday dinner proceeded festively. Annika responded to questions and ate as if in a dream. Her real-life fairy tale now moved toward the hoped-for happy ending.

After Luther cleared the entrée plates, Pappie slipped a leather ring box onto the table.

Annika gripped the edge of her chair. Might it contain the same ring her father and brothers proudly wore, one engraved with the de Fisicat's family crest? She opened the tiny leather case and ran her fingertip over the emblems carved into a heavy, gold, signet ring. Two lions stood on their hind legs and bore a shield between them. "Oh, Pappie, it's marvelous." She slid the new jewelry onto her right ring finger and held it out for everyone to admire.

"Noblesse oblige, Annika," Pappie stated in his serious voice. "You are old enough to bear the family responsibility of obligations to others." He smiled tenderly. "Opportunities will soon be presented to you, I'm afraid."

He meant in war times. "Of course, Pappie." She pulled her hand back and nodded. Would Phillip think it boastful? As a man of integrity, certainly he understood.

Phillip sat quietly, taking in the scene, his dark eyes studying her family members. He looked straight at her and smiled warmly, as if knowing his approval mattered.

"Nonna Annika!" Kokkie stepped out of the kitchen carrying a triple layer chocolate cake aglow with lit birthday candles. Swirls of ganache decorated the outside. The other staff trailed her. Each one passed by her chair, patted her shoulder, and whispered their congratulations. Their voices resonated with the affection she felt for them all.

Pappie began the first words of "Lang zal ze leven," and everyone sang the Dutch birthday song to her.

Yes, she planned to live long, with Phillip by her side. Kokkie's cake had never tasted richer or more decadent. The frosting must've been an inch thick in places. She cleaned every crumb off her plate, as did the others.

At the end of the evening Phillip cleared his throat. "Thank you for including me in this special birthday dinner. Annika, may I speak to you for a moment?"

"Walk Lieutenant Van Hoven to the door," Mamma suggested.

Annika left the living room and as she passed the towering clock, she raised her eyes to the trumpeting angels and winked. Phillip walked a few feet behind her. She stopped at the door. "Yes, Lieutenant Van Hoven?"

"The cinema has a new film playing," he said in his smooth voice.

"Is it a Janet Gaynor movie?" Annika asked excitedly.

Phillip smiled, "No."

Was he teasing? Two could play the game. "Claude mentioned a new Gary Cooper movie, *Sergeant York*. I admire a man in uniform, even if it's an American boy." She cocked her eyebrow.

"When that movie is playing, I'll have to bring you an extra chocolate bar," Phillip teased. "This movie is about Frédéric Chopin, I recall that you danced to his music."

He recalled so much about her! Annika clapped. "*La chanson de l'adieu* or *Farewell Waltz*. I've wanted to see it."

"I'll take that as a yes, then." He took her hand, sending chills up her arm. His eyes were bright. "I learned today that I'm in the running to land a coveted assignment of flying one of the new Koolhoven trainers in Bandoeng. It'll take me months to complete my current instruction, in addition to the required hours in the cockpit. It's the only non-academic goal I've ever wanted. Wish me luck."

Non-academic and dangerous. "Of course." Annika crossed her fingers and forced herself to appear overjoyed.

"Great." Her handsome beau waved goodbye, trotted out, and climbed onto his motorcycle.

She waved back and shut the door. "Please," she whispered to the trumpeting angels, "let Phillip not be smart enough, or dedicated enough, or too tall. Anything to keep another man I love out of those airplanes." Something told her this request was also in vain, same as wishing for Rudy not to fly into battle.

But not her wish for perfect dates with Phillip. The next months rolled by in a whirl of movies and bicycle trips. On a beautiful Tuesday, Annika left the ballet studio tired, but looking forward to the ride home and another family dinner with her official beau.

His smile looked forced as she approached the motorbike. Even sitting with his back against the tree, he looked stiff or tense. What had changed? Her chest tightened.

Phillip stood and ran his hands through his hair, then placed his book in the saddlebag. He stood and patted the passenger seat for her to sit. He cleared his throat, as he frequently did when something made him nervous. "After your classes, I delight in how your barrette loses the battle and your damp hair curls around your chin." He tucked a loose strand behind her ear.

His tender touch made her body go soft. She looked into his eyes, now a deep, rich shade of brown.

"Annika, you once told me all about the man you would marry." He took her left hand. "I am an officer, and I love you. I know you are still young. Might you consider marrying me some day?"

Sparks shot through her body. "Oh, yes," she trilled. "I share the same love for you." He hadn't officially proposed, but that didn't matter. Phillip wanted to marry her! She stood and wavered, her legs as limp as overcooked noodles.

He threw out his hand to steady her and kissed her cheek. "Excellent. I needed to know," he said, and climbed on the front seat, "As long as you feel that way, we'll keep dating and at the proper time, if you still agree, I will speak to your father. Shall we take the long way back?"

"Yes please." She lifted her foot over the wide rear fender and placed her hands at his waist. Dear, sweet, serious Phillip. He was so handsome that she'd fallen a little in love the first moment she saw him. Now he'd professed the same feeling for her, and she should be delirious. So why did a bit of foreboding linger? Maybe it was the result of growing up and realizing the obstacles in your path. Or the horrible war! Phillip was smart, dedicated, and not too tall to fit in a plane. Newsreels showed movies of the German Messerschmitt fighters in the sky. They were sleek, metal, fast, and deadly planes. Pilots in Holland's Fokker fighter planes had shot down many German aircraft. The Koolhoven biplane their Air Force on Java trained in seemed toy-like in comparison.

Phillip started the engine and the motorcycle glided onto the straightaway. She clung to his starched tan shirt, the material rough against her cheek. Be courageous like Timon Mas, she told herself. Oudje often repeated the old Indonesian folktale of a girl fighting a giant, and now her words replayed in Annika's brain.

In the tale, a widow prayed to be blessed with a baby. A dream told her to search in the jungle for a wrapped bundle. She searched, found the bundle, and inside she found a cucumber seed. Behind the woman appeared a horrible green giant. He instructed her to plant the seed, then warned that when the baby turned seventeen, he'd take her and eat her.

The woman wanted a baby so badly, she planted the seed. A magical golden cucumber grew and held a baby girl inside. She named the girl Timon Mas, or golden cucumber. The girl was beautiful, and the mother sought the help of an old hermit to conquer the giant. The hermit gave her four bags and told her to have her daughter throw them when the giant chased her.

The ugly giant materialized on the girl's seventeenth birthday, as he'd forewarned. Timon Mas did as she'd been told and threw out the contents of the first bag at the giant. The bag contained cucumber seeds, which sprouted huge vines to trip the giant. He persevered, so she spread the contents of the second bag – sewing needles – which transformed to sharp bamboo that pierced the giant. Still, he kept pursuing her. The third bag contained salt, which the girl threw. The salt formed an ocean but it didn't block the giant's path. Nothing stopped the green monster.

Weary and desperate, hearing the giant's thundering steps grow closer, Timon Mas dumped the final bag which held terasi, or shrimp paste, and watched as boiling volcanic mud surrounded the sinking giant. She returned triumphantly to her mother and lived happily ever after.

Annika closed her eyes. The war was her ugly, red, swastika-clad giant, bombing and firing from an ocean away. She may not be beautiful like Timon Mas, but she knew she could run fast and think. If the war came to her island, she'd find the elements to thwart it and protect those she loved—no matter the distance to travel or what price she'd pay.

CHAPTER 6

NOVEMBER 10, 1940

Annika scowled at the monkey pod trees through the side window of their car. She'd been dating Phillip nearly a year and nothing more had been said about getting officially engaged. The war continued to plague everyone's lives. Since receiving the horrific news six months ago of Germany's invasion of Holland, they had not heard a word from Mamma's parents who lived in Amsterdam. Phillip's father and mother thrived in Bandoeng, but his extended family lived in the Netherlands and no news came from them, either. Maybe months of not knowing their plight wore on him.

Tonight, Phillip had brought Annika a huge bowl of beautiful pink roses, but now, en route to yet another movie, he spoke less than usual. Budi, their chauffeur, and Claude joked back and forth from the front seat. They parked on Koningsplein and walked to the entry of the two-story Deca Movie Theatre, lit by white lights and a huge marquee advertising the current film.

Bristling, restless energy surrounded the people ahead of them in line to buy movie tickets. Each week everyone's uneasiness waiting in the theater line felt more ramped up, as if they were race-horses now loaded into the starting gate at the nearby track, ready for the ear-shattering pistol blast. Annika rubbed her brow and fell in behind Phillip. They'd heard a radio broadcast in late September announcing how Germany, Italy, and Japan had signed the Tripartite Pact, as Quinn had predicted. It created a defense alliance to deter America from entering the conflict. That's when the underlying turmoil had begun. More than ever, Annika dreaded the newsreels played before the featured film. They'd likely see a new one tonight. She'd overheard Pappie say they'd be lucky if the Dutch East Indies didn't surrender as the Nether-lands had done in May. The year 1940 was producing good and bad events that she'd never forget.

Claude nudged her arm to step aside and get out of the ticket line while Phillip handed the cashier money in exchange for four tickets. Two he handed to Claude, then pulled out a pack of Camel cigarettes and gave it to Budi. They spoke a few words, and then Phillip waved Claude and Budi to go on ahead.

Phillip smiled mischievously, took her hand, and led her to the back row of seats.

"You never carry a smoker's stench." Annika sniffed his jacket. "Emily told me kissing a smoker would be like licking a dirty ashtray."

He chuckled. "As a gentleman, I won't comment. I believe I'm one of the few non-smokers in the military. I purchase cigarettes on the base where they are cheap, and they make a good bribe to civilians. You're not the only one who's familiar with the bribery tactic."

"I don't understand about you needing a bribe." Annika slid sideways to the middle. Claude and Budi strode further down the aisle and sat in the second row from the front.

"Privacy." Phillip sat beside her, helped her remove her linen jacket, and then settled it carefully across her shoulders.

Hope bubbled in her chest. Might he finally kiss her? She snuggled a bit closer to his side. The opening newsreel featured gruesome airplane and ground battles in Europe. She pulled the lapels of her jacket together to steady her nerves. Rudy might be flying one of those planes. They hadn't gotten a letter from him in ages.

"The Young in Heart," starring Janet Gaynor, opened with a scene on the French Riviera. Phillip leaned close and whispered, "Someday, I'll take you there." He reached for her hand and squeezed it gently throughout the movie.

She made no answer – an appropriate response escaped her. Phillip's courting to date rated strictly prim and proper, which drove her berserk. Even on dinner dates, one of her brothers sat in the front seat of the taxi as an escort. The only kiss she'd received so far had been on her cheek. Tonight, Phillip seemed intent on showing his feelings, and oh, she so longed to really kiss him, to show him hers.

The film slowed in the middle. Phillip draped his arm over her shoulder and drew her to him. With his fingertip, he tilted her chin upward, and placed his warm lips against hers. His gentle kiss stirred feelings she'd never known. He tilted his head back and stroked her cheek. "Did you enjoy that?"

Nothing on earth matched her first kiss. "Oh yes, very much."

"Good, my sweet Annika. Good."

The movie ended happily, and Annika left smiling. The ragamuffin group of con artists from the film found their happy ever afters, so certainly she and Phillip could reach for the stars.

After the movie, they all piled back into the car and discussed the best parts of the show as Budi drove. A quarter mile from the house, near The English Club, Phillip took her hand. "Would you walk with me part of the way?"

He definitely was up to something. "Sure," Annika replied.

Phillip leaned forward and tapped Budi on the shoulder. "Please let us out here for a short walk. Can you pull over and enjoy the smokes, then return in about ten minutes?"

The car eased onto the shoulder. "As you wish. Enjoy your stroll," Budi said. He and Claude chuckled.

Phillip helped her out of the car and held her hand while they walked around the bend in the road onto Boxlaan. He stopped and turned her to face him.

"Annika, I told your parents last week how crazy I am about you. Your mother knew you had a crush on me. You're not even seventeen, however I view you as much older. I'm uncertain how to proceed." He lifted her hands and stroked her palms. His dark eyes held concern.

"Don't worry." She smoothed his furrowed brow. "This isn't a crush. The first moment I saw you, as you strode across our lawn, something deep inside told me you were the one. I not only love you, but I like your gentle manner."

"I'll never push you. I promise. Your parents and I feel you are too young to get married, but they consented to us becoming engaged." He dropped to one knee. "Annika, will you be my wife?"

She gasped and her hands flew to her cheeks.

He'd formally proposed! Oh lord, he'd proposed! "Yes, yes, yes!" She leaned over and pulled him to his feet, then threw herself in his arms. "Being engaged to you makes my dreams come true." She peered at him, and even in faint moonlight, elation shown from the depths of his eyes. They kissed again, a long, slow kiss she'd remember forever.

He lifted her hand and smoothed the skin on her ring finger. "I have something in mind for this very spot."

Goosebumps rose on her arms. "Surprises are wonderful."

Tires crunched on gravel and Phillip stepped back. Headlights swept slowly around the bend and illuminated pavement in front of them. Phillip helped her into the back seat, and they rode home holding hands, their faces cheek to cheek. Life was perfect. Claude and Budi probably guessed, but she'd relish the news privately for a few more heavenly minutes.

Too soon for Annika's taste, Budi turned into the driveway. The bright beams swung across a dark sedan parked in the middle of the circular drive, opposite their front door. "That's Uncle Bajetto's car," Claude announced. "Odd he'd be visiting this late on a Saturday night."

The three passengers left the car and climbed the porch steps. Phillip escorted Annika onto the veranda. Hairs rose on the back of her neck. In the screened sitting area, her mother sat off to the side, her hands folded tight in her lap. Pappie sat rigid in his overstuffed chair. Uncle wore his military uniform, not the casual clothes of a relaxed visit. That was unusual, as Uncle Bajetto had become a cherished member of the family after his son had married Mamma's sister.

A decanter of liquor and two untouched drinks sat on the coffee table next to Phillip's bowl of pink roses. Pappie stood. "Major General Bajetto, you remember Lieutenant Van Hoven." He studied Annika's face for a brief second. "He's asked for Annika's hand in marriage, which we agreed to, after at least a two-year engagement. The war will be done by then and life will return to normal. I believe from Annika's face that she accepted." He lifted one of the glasses and took a long drink.

Annika pressed her lips together. Everything focused on the stupid war. Her engagement deserved a smile, a toast, or a congratulations, but Pappie's manner remained somber. "Yes, Pappie, I did accept." She smiled directly at him, hoping to coax one from him. None came. "May I address my fiancé as Phillip now?"

Pappie nodded, clearly distracted. "Sure. We all will. Phillip, we need Annika for a few minutes. Would you please excuse us?"

"Of course, Meneer Wolter. I was on my way out. I have an early day tomorrow."

Pappie's behavior bordered on rude. Uncle Bajetto and her father needed her? Annika swallowed and walked Phillip to the entry. "Thank you for the lovely evening."

"You are very welcome." He picked up her hand and kissed the top. "Our ride to your ballet class Tuesday can't come soon enough, and if you're available Saturday night, there's a formal military dance at the Sociëteit Concordia. I'd be honored to escort you there."

"Oh my. One of the fanciest clubs in Batavia, I've heard." She preened her hair, then crooked her pinky finger. "Sounds perfectly mahh-velous, Phillip," she crooned. She never could have guessed saying his name out loud for the first time would bring goose bumps to her forearms. She knew a silly grin spread from ear to ear on her excited face. Fiddle-faddle on the war. . . Phillip had officially proposed tonight!

"Plan to dance the night away to a full orchestra on Saturday, a perk of military life. Right now, you'd better return to General Bajetto. He's a highly respected officer in the Defense Department who shouldn't be kept waiting. I'll get demoted if he thinks it's my fault." He leaned in, kissed her lightly on the lips, and dashed down the steps. At his motorcycle, he blew her another kiss.

She blew one back. He started the engine and roared off into the night. Lovestruck Phillip thrilled her scads more than polite Lieutenant Van Hoven.

She touched her lips. Warmth rose to her cheeks at the thought of their heated kiss on the road.

"Annika," Pappie's voice demanded.

She hustled back to the veranda. The men's serious expressions doused her jubilant mood. Perspiration dotted Pappie's brow. Mamma exited the room. What was going on?

"Please sit on the couch," Uncle said. "We need you for a mission of sorts and I'll come right to the point. There are sensitive military documents about the war which need to be delivered by a trusted, and non-political person between my Department of Defense and Dutch government buildings in Batavia. There are Indonesian and Indo military men who'd welcome a change in government and are assumed to be spying at every juncture. I suggested engaging you as our courier to your father, and he concurred."

Neither of her brothers got this feather in their cap. Annika threw back her shoulders. "I'd be proud to do my part."

"That's my daughter," Pappie stated. "Noblesse oblige. This time your country needs you." Ice clinked loudly as he shakily lifted his whiskey glass. "Annika, I wouldn't have agreed to put this pressure on you if it weren't absolutely necessary."

Uncle Bajetto cleared his throat. "Nor should I. You will be paid a small stipend. A car will arrive here for you on Monday and Wednesday afternoons at three sharp, after you're home from college classes. Instructions will be in the packet I'll send via the driver. Dress like a secretary. You will discuss this with no one outside of this room, not even Phillip. Understood?"

Relief shot through her. Motorcycle riding with Phillip wouldn't be interrupted. "I understand."

"Good. You were my first choice, and you'll start Monday. I'm proud you are my niece. Other young women don't have your courage. You began showing spunk as a toddler, running alongside Rudy and Claude." Uncle Bajetto rubbed his chin. "Yes indeed. Courage will serve you well, my dear, with what lies ahead." He patted her hand, told her goodbye, and walked beside Pappie to the door, both men speaking in low tones.

Courage wasn't precisely what she felt. Her world tilted up with Phillip, then dropped, at the thought of war.

For now, she'd concentrate on being engaged and ignore Europe's problems, even seeing stalwart Pappie rattled.

Annika shifted in the car seat, practicing genteel posture for her first ball at the Sociëteit Concordia, the elegant club for military personnel in Batavia. Phillip looked so debonair in his pressed white jacket, with a stand-up Nehru collar and gold buttons. No doubt he'd be the hand-somest man in attendance.

"Penny for your thoughts," Phillip jested.

A siren blared from a passing ambulance. "I wonder if they're transporting an injured person to Tjikini Hospital?" Annika said. "I may have mentioned that if I'm accepted into the nursing program, that's my first choice for training."

"Yes, the one near my aunt's home. I got so busy that I forgot I promised we'd visit her." Phillip leaned forward and tapped Budi on the shoulder. "Could you turn right at the next corner please. He turned to Annika. "I'll show you where my room-mates and I live."

Waterloo Square loomed ahead, flanked by the Court of Justice, the Finance Department, the Mili-tary Hospital, and Sociëteit Concordia. The car entered a street lined by well-kept yards and medium sized bungalows. Someday, she and Phillip might live in one. None as grand as her home with live-in servants, but she wouldn't care one whit, even if she had to learn to cook and clean.

"I believe your Uncle Bajetto lives there now." Phillip pointed to a two-story house at the end of the block. "He probably moved to be closer to the base. My rented home is this next small bungalow. We're near the barracks and not cramped in bunk beds." He took her hand. "Now on to the better part of the evening. I'm excited about the ball tonight. Are you? You're kind of quiet."

"Oh yes." She slunk into the seat and closed her eyes.

"Then what's bothering you? Are you feeling well? You seem tired."

Pappie must've given him mood-deciphering lessons. An image of a flaming airplane plunging toward a blackened field gave her ongoing nightmares. "I haven't been sleeping well."

"That's not good. Do you need to see a doctor?"

His earnest concern deserved an answer. "Phillip, why do you wish to fly?" she tried to sound casual. "The Dutch planes I saw are flimsy two-seater biplanes. In the open cockpit, you need to wear an aviator hat and goggles. Isn't it dangerous?"

"Those are trainers. Regardless of the plane, I might die," he said. "If I die, it's my time. I studied hard in school to qualify for university. I studied harder in the military academy to make lieutenant. Flying will give me a freedom I'll never get on the ground. Does that make sense?"

Annika squeezed his hand. "Unfortunately, yes. Pappie's friend took me in his Piper Cub several times and let me take the stick. I felt the freedom of flight, without a Messerschmidt on my tail."

"Hopefully the only foreign aircraft I'll see will be ahead of me," Phillip assured her. "Banish those war thoughts from your mind. We've reached the ball."

"And I'm allowed to dance the night away until one," she responded.

Their car entered the cobblestone circular drive of the stately Sociëteit Concordia. Budi joined the line of cars crawling to the front of a palace-sized, white brick building. Marble pillars supported its flat roof, outlined by a row of white balustrades, which resembled a fancy picket fence. They were next in line.

"Thank you, Budi." Annika put her nose to the window. Men in formal attire escorted women in an assortment of stylish evening gowns into the building through carved doors at least eight feet tall. She turned to observe a few couples who occupied the round, wrought iron tables and chairs on the lawn beyond the driveway. In the center, a fifteen-foot fountain spilled water into a low marble bowl. Surrounding the fountain, four statues of women in saris held lit orbs overhead, their once coppery forms now the pale turquoise patina of weathered, stately bronze.

"Lovely outside gardens," Annika said. "It's a different setting than the Sociëteit de Harmonie. I'll take you to the upcoming Sint Nikolaas dance there if you'd like."

"I'd be delighted to escort you to any event. My military rank allows me to attend these balls. I never thought I'd be accompanied by a woman who could be mistaken for a princess."

"You're too kind." Her cheeks grew warm.

The car stopped. "I'll return for you at one Nonna Annika," Budi said. "Enjoy your evening."

Phillip sprang out. While she slid off the seat, he kept the translucent, Georgette fabric of her gown from being caught on the car's door.

Royalty walked with grace. She placed her left hand on Phillip's outstretched forearm and with her other fingers gathered the floor-length skirt of pale coral to rest slightly above her heels. "I'll do my best to earn the princess title." As they entered the regal building, Oma Elodie would approve of her carriage —refined, yet approachable. By sweeping her head in a slow circle, she took in four-foot-tall crystal chandeliers lighting every inch of the corridor leading to the ballroom. Marble floors echoed with the clicks and taps of high heels from other guests.

At the far end of the stadium-sized ballroom, a troupe of Dutch military band members assembled music stands and instruments. Floor to ceiling white marble arches ran on either long side of the rectangular dance floor. Between and behind the pillars, tables and chairs held men and women drinking and chatting. Phillip led her to the opening and stopped.

Male servers dressed in white clothing embellished by brass buttons carried trays of champagne flutes, sherry snifters, and wine goblets. Annika's nose caught the scent of hot, spicy hors d'oeuvres. Another waiter passed by from her left, dodging guests while he balanced two trays with dishes hidden under silver plate covers.

The band struck a few chords, the maestro tapped his baton, and the empty dance floor filled with women escorted by a stream of men in military dress uniforms like Phillip's. A few civilian men flaunted the heat in traditional black tuxedos, but most wore the stylish short white jackets and black bow ties. They maneuvered their female partners who wore floor-length, sleeveless gowns of silky, satiny, or flouncy fabric. Many women wore black, the on-trend color of the wealthy.

A tall, slender, blonde lady had accented her pale blue dress with a feathery white capelet. Her gown narrowed at the knees and flared to the floor, in a mermaid's tail effect. She threw back her head and laughed. Dangling from her ear lobes and neck hung teardrop-shaped sapphires. Annika touched her diamond necklace. Oma Elodie's mother had worn the pendant and earrings to events put on by French nobility. She was now proud to be wearing the family jewelry anywhere with Phillip.

He squeezed her hand twice, as if knowing her thoughts. "You're truly radiant, Annika." He brushed a soft kiss onto her cheek, then scanned the crowd. "Ah, there's my friend."

A red-haired young man in a pressed white uniform waved from a table to their right.

"Come on, he's saving us seats." Phillip wove her

between occupied chairs, his warm hand securely gripping hers. Their attempt to make introductions over the sound of the band proved fruitless. They gave up, joined the others on the ballroom floor, and danced every song. A particularly invigorating cha-cha ended the set. Annika took her seat and sipped a cool glass of Riesling during the break. The men's conversation at the table touched on Hitler and Mussolini. The tone changed to anger when they discussed Japan's Emperor, Hirohito, and his growing military strength. The women sat in silence, looking as worried as Annika felt. Phillip got into a discussion pitting a German Messerschmitt 109 against a newly-minted Japanese Zero. Annika frowned. Didn't they care that either airplane could make mincemeat out of a Koolhoven?

She turned her head back to the dance floor. The band played the opening chords of Bing Crosby and Frances Langford's "I'm Falling in Love with Some-one," the same song they had danced to for their first ever dance. Her eyes misted over. She couldn't lose Phillip to the war.

"They're playing our song. Do you remember?" Phillip leaned in and asked.

"I do!" It made her happy to know they both treasured this memory. What a lucky girl she was to have a beau who remembered such details. "Of course. Mamma's birthday party remains the best event of my life."

"Mine too," he whispered, then kissed her cheek. "You're a marvelous dancer. You float in my arms."

She met his eyes. "I can relax, my mind confident of your guidance."

Phillip's cheeks grew pink. He stood and then clasped her hand. "I hope to never fail you."

PHOTO SECTION I
PRE INVASION PHOTOS

My favorite photo of
Mamma and Pappie,
dressed to perform
in the 1919 stage
play "Prince Negoro
Joedho: a Vorsten-
land's Comedy of
Manners in
four acts"

Mamma dressed
me up for a
kindergarten photo

From 1938, an overhead view of our neighborhood.
How wonderful a photographer captured this
from an airplane!

Mamma fashioned my dress for
her 50th birthday party like these dresses
from the Roaring 20s.

Our wonderful tour through Batavia included the trolley. I considered it our first date!

Batavia is busy on a Sunday!

The Buginese schooners hold a lot of goods
to be traded between islands.

Molenvliet Canal

Dances at Sociëteit de Harmonie on
Harmonie Square will be more exciting
with a handsome lieutenant escort!

The Chinese Quarter/Glodok neighborhood
where we buy spices.

Tjikini Hospital, where I hope to work someday.

Lined up sados, awaiting train passengers

Lunch at the Hotel des Indes was fabulous.

Their staff welcomed us in perfect Dutch.

Wouldn't it be fun to stay here like a real lady!

Dancing in the Sociëteit Concordia
ballroom was fabulous!

More officers are in Batavia than ever before.

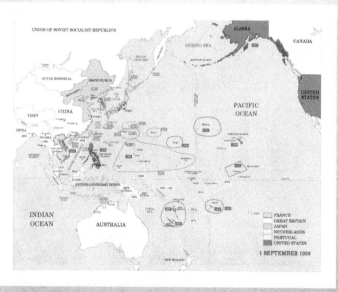

I've learned that Japan is enlarging its holdings
in the Pacific Ocean.*

Our engagement party on December 14, 1940.

CHAPTER 7

DECEMBER 14, 1940

SIX DAYS AFTER ANNIKA'S SEVENTEENTH
BIRTHDAY.

Flutter's filled Annika's stomach. Tonight, she'd
be officially betrothed to Phillip! She swished
downstairs in her white floor-length engagement
gown, created by Mamma. Inside the scoop-necked
bodice she'd tucked a gift for Phillip – a tie tack.
Hopefully, he'd wear it. To get the perfect stone,
she'd wiped out her stash of pin money.

Halfway down the staircase, she was greeted by
sweet fragrances rising from the living room, where
Mamma stood beside a dozen or so elegant arrange-
ments of gladiolas, chrysanthemums, and lilies.

Assorted vases sat on end tables, on the floor, and atop tall pillar stands.

"Annika, I kept the flowers hidden until now. You and Phillip received presents as well." Mamma kissed each of her cheeks. I'm so proud of the young woman you've become. Phillip looks at you adoringly."

"I love him Mamma, and he feels the same way. Thank you for believing I'm ready."

"I'll always believe in you. Come here. Your corsage arrived a few minutes ago." She opened a green florist's box and extracted a long spray that included tiny pink roses and feathery greenery. She pinned it on Annika. The corsage – truly a showpiece – began at her shoulder and curved to the gathered waist of her dress.

"It's lovely, thank you," Annika said, and touched a flower petal. "I do wish Emily wouldn't have married so hurriedly." A mound of gifts sat on their coffee table. "She missed out on all these fun parties. I can't forgive Quinn for insisting they elope before he headed to Australia without her."

Mamma nodded. "It may have been for the best. Australia's officially at war. He might have seen it coming and wanted to protect her. Or maybe he wanted to make sure to get his new business branch established before war broke out there. Perhaps both."

"Then he chose well. She'll be safe with us."

Annika rotated a cut-glass vase holding a dozen pink and cream lilies, willing all of them to be safe. Lord forbid they ever receive white funeral lilies.

A knock sounded. Luther rushed thru the entry to answer the door.

"Good evening, Luther. Please take me directly to Annika." Phillip's deep, excited voice brought goosebumps to Annika's forearms.

Annika walked quickly, smiled at Luther as they passed, and met Phillip in front of the clock. She tugged him into the space between it and the door. "I'm delighted you're here," she said in her lowest, sexiest voice.

"A private spot. Good." Phillip gave her a warm, sensual kiss, sending tingles to Annika's toes. "I love kissing you," he whispered and pulled a velvet ring box from his pocket. He opened it to reveal the darkest blue sapphire she'd ever seen. He took her hand and slipped it on her finger. "I wanted this for your engagement ring, as you embody what the stone symbolizes." He kept hold of her hand and searched her eyes. "We're going to face some challenges in the months to come. Sapphires represent loyalty, trust, and truth. I promise to uphold those principles in our life together, as well as faithful love to you."

"I promise the same to you and I will cherish my beautiful ring." Annika reached under her neckline and removed the tie tack she'd hidden for him. "I heard the significance of a sapphire, that's why I bought one for you to wear." The stone in hers wasn't as dark, but the oval shape matched the ring from Phillip.

His jaw dropped. "You're utterly amazing, my sweet. And we'll be amazing together. I have a wonderful secret to share." His face flushed.

"Tell me, don't tease."

"I've been officially accepted into the Military Aviation Division, or ML, of the Royal Dutch East-India Army. I've a bit more course work here, then I'll transfer to Kalijati Airfield." His eyes narrowed, as if he read the concern in her mind. "Don't despair, it's near Bandoeng, so only a train trip away from you." He squeezed her hand, his excitement palpable. "In the meantime, I'll be pulling double duty to prepare for the ML-KNIL, so I won't be able to transport you to ballet classes. I didn't shirk my chauffeur responsibilities, though. I cleared with your father and Claude that I'd teach Budi to drive Claude's motorcycle. It landed on sand, so hardly was damaged in the accident. I'll give Budi money for chocolate bars, to keep you happy."

Chocolate would never be a substitute for his presence, but this wasn't the time to pout. "That's so thoughtful. Congratulations." Annika kept a joyous smile on her lips.

Pilot training. Icy shards of fear pierced her heart.

At the end of March, Batavia suffered through one of the rainiest monsoon seasons ever. Forced inside, Annika spent her days finishing her stenography and typing courses and her afternoons missing Phillip. Time seemed irrelevant and moved slower than a heavy cart on a muddy road.

On a sultry summer day a few months later, the downstairs clock chimed three o'clock. Annika laid aside the old medical journal she'd been reading, grabbed her purse, and headed outside. In a few minutes, the familiar black car pulled onto their driveway. She stepped off the front porch, ready to complete another courier delivery for her Uncle. The mission posed to her as top secret and mysterious was more akin to a mail carrier being driven in a private car. But it could be the calm before the storm. "Good afternoon, Bram," she said through the open window.

"Sorry I'm a bit late. A buggy with a broken wheel blocked the road as I left General Bajetto."

"No apology necessary. Mamma and I rely on small sados to run errands. I've had many lovely trips in them without a break down." She slid onto the back seat and recalled her trip around Batavia in a sado, seated beside Phillip. She couldn't help smiling. Bram handed her a manila envelope, and she opened and read the folded note taped to the top.

"Today our route begins at the Department of Finance, please. We'll travel next to the Department of Economic Affairs Building and then we're done for the day." Her shoulders relaxed into the leather upholstery. This shorter assignment would allow her time for a long, mind-clearing ride on Maggy on a dry day and a chance to bring Newt-newt home for a visit.

Familiar neighborhoods changed to blocks of commercial buildings as they motored to the uptown center of Batavia and their destination on Waterloo Square. They crossed the bridge over the bendy River Ciliwung and onto busy Salemba Road. Car horns, rumbling motors, and fumes grew louder and stronger. Bram braked as the streetcar bumped and rolled across the tracks in their path. Bicycles, motor cars, and sados all jockeyed for position. Horses whinnied and pedestrians waited for a signal to cross. Their car stopped at the drop-off area of The White House, the location of the Department of Finance, on Waterloo Square.

"Five minutes," Annika promised Bram as she shut the car door. Long strides put her inside the stuffy marble building. Turning left at the first corridor, she entered the office listed on the note. A young, uniformed man looked up from paperwork on his desk.

"From General Bajetto," Annika announced, and

watched with satisfaction as the he came to attention. She handed off her documents.

"I wasn't expecting a lady courier." He unlocked a cabinet and extracted a tan envelope larger than the one she had just delivered, but similar in appearance. "I'm to give you this one."

"Thank you and good day." Annika took the pouch and returned to the waiting car. *Department of Economic Affairs Rm 103* was written on the outside in black ink.

She returned to the car. The police officer who directed traffic from the raised roundabout circle at Citadel-Sluice Square flagged them through. Their route along Noordwijk Boulevard's string of beer houses, a monastery school, and elegant shops, became crowded by horse drawn carts full of loaded baskets, large and small vehicles, and young men on bicycles. Heat poured in through the car windows. As the heavy envelope sunk into her lap, she stared at the address on the front – a location near Mills Canal West. Would Phillip be affected by orders being issued from Finance to the Department of Economic Affairs? She'd never know; the lady courier didn't get to peek.

Bram double-parked in front of the building housing offices for the Dutch East Indies Agriculture, Industry, and Commerce departments. She marched into the correct office, relinquished the sealed envelope, and left.

Another dutiful day complete. If she knew Phillip remained out of battles, she'd welcome news on the war's progression, but thicker packets couldn't be a good sign. While they headed home via Koningsplein, she pressed her fingers to her forehead and stared out the window. They passed a row of sprawling villas. At one corner stood her family parish, Menteng's Nassau Church. The stained-glass windows shone in the sunlight. Someday she'd say her marriage vows there, after spending two years of somedays waiting to meet Pappie's wishes for her to be older. She smoothed the creases between her brows with her fingertips.

Bram reached the open road and covered the route to their house on Boxlaan in record time. The clock struck half past five as she tromped into the entry. She was eager to get to the stables. Exercise invigorated her and was good for Maggy, too. She hustled upstairs, changed to riding clothes, and dragged her black Gazelle ladies' bike out of the shed. "Come on, Foxy. Stable time."

The little dog ran in and sat at her feet. She set him in the woven brown basket strapped to the handlebars beside a couple of carrots from their garden and a banana.

Pedaling down the driveway, a breeze fanned her warm cheeks and helped temper the heat en route to the stable. She parked her bike beside the barn and rolled her shoulders. Maggy and Penny bugled their familiar greetings. Annika relaxed—one part of her world remained as it should be. She lifted Foxy from the basket and he dashed into the barn.

"Annika. Join us, please." Pappie waved her over to their veterinarian's olive-green car, parked behind the barn. The two men stood side by side at the rear bumper. Pappie wore jodhpurs, and Dr. Subroto was dressed in a white shirt and white pants, typical of an Indonesian professional. A girl of about ten years old sat in the passenger seat of the doctor's car. Annika guessed the child must be his. Her reddish-brown hair was very similar in color to Geneviève's.

The veterinarian smiled. "Annika, please meet my daughter, Mina." The young girl made eye contact, offered Annika a limp handshake, then looked down at her lap. "She's a bit shy, but she commented earlier on Maggy's beautiful copper coat," he said.

Annika wanted to put Mina at ease. "Wise people save words for the right moments, Mina. Maggy loves having admirers." Annika smiled at the men. "What are you two conspiring about today? Vaccinations aren't due yet, so it must be something else."

Pappie's face turned solemn. "Today I learned that I passed the government's physical test, which means I'm required to serve in the Dutch Militia for men over forty." He clenched his raised fist and bunched his bicep. "I'll need to learn marksmanship, though." His stiff laugh wasn't normal.

"I can't picture you with a gun, Pappie," Annika murmured.

Dr. Subroto shuffled his feet. "Your father and I came to an agreement. If he's sent to war and I'm not, your animals will be cared for at my veterinary clinic."

Annika's stomached tightened. No Phillip, no Pappie, no Maggy? She sucked in a breath and let it out slowly. Wise people planned. "How kind of you to make that offer."

"That's not all of his kindness," Pappie added. "Mamma's been worried about the family crystal and silver, should things become tense. If we pack them in our sea trunks, Dr. Subroto offered to hide them in his hay barn."

The doctor smiled broadly. "I'm honored to help your family."

"And we feel honored to know you." Pappie glanced at the road. "I see Budi just turned onto the lane. I've got an errand to run downtown. Enjoy your riding session," he said, and jogged toward the car.

"Pappie speaks often of your friendship and knowledge," Annika said to the veterinarian. "May I introduce Mina to Maggy? Maybe she'd enjoy riding lessons from me until this all blows over?"

A sad look crossed his face, then he smiled. "That's a nice idea. Thank you." He opened the passenger door for his daughter. Her pale blue blouse and matching shorts accented her dark olive skin and complemented her auburn hair.

A warm nose pressed into Annika's ankle. She bent to pet Foxy. "This is Foxy. He loves people. When I'm at the barn, he'll be here."

Mina crouched and scratched Foxy's chin. "He's sweet."

"We've had him since I was seven or eight. He runs alongside me when I ride in the woods on Maggy, who trotted into our family on my tenth birthday. She's a wonderful mare and a good listener." Annika looked at Mina's feet. "I think I have boots and a helmet in the tack room in your size, if you'd like to ride."

She flashed a bright smile like her father's. "Yes! Thank you. Papa said I could have lessons someday."

Annika brought Maggy from her stall and showed Mina how to groom and tack a horse. Mina grinned the entire time, like a true pony-girl in the making. "I have another friend for you to meet. He's a wonderful horseback passenger and enjoys racing us home." She poked her head in the first stall and noticed the empty wooden box. "Newt-newt," she called.

The monkey scampered into the barn. He clenched a banana in his fist and chattered at Annika. As if he sensed their future friendship, he held out the fruit to Mina. The girl's cocoa brown eyes widened. "I adore monkeys. Especially generous ones." She took the banana, stripped off the peel, and popped a piece in her mouth. The remainder she returned to Newt-newt. "Good boy."

He gulped the treat, flashed the smile that showed his canine teeth, then stroked the girl's bare leg.

"Touching your leg is his way of asking if he can sit on your shoulder. Hold out your hand and he'll swing up."

Mina did, and Newt-newt climbed aboard and tugged one of her long, reddish-brown pig tails. She giggled and the monkey cackled in joy.

"He likes you. I'm not able to spend as much time at the barn as Maggy deserves. She's very well trained and doesn't have naughty habits. I can give you lessons for a couple weeks. You are welcome to ride as your father sees fit. The trails are cool, and your furry friends know the way home."

"Nonna Annika, I promise I'll be the second-best friend Maggy and Newt-newt have," Mina promised. "I go to Kartini School in Batavia and have afternoons free."

Annika smiled. "Kartini School, I've heard of it." She recalled Pappie speaking of its merits. Dr. Subroto's practice must be successful, as few Indo or Indonesian families could afford the school's tuition for their daughters. Educating sons was a different story. "A school named after the Indonesian women's rights advocate, Lady Kartini, as I recall?"

"Yes. I'm excited to tell the girls in class of my good fortune. Papa has so many injured animals in his care that we don't have any of our own . . . yet." Mina grinned mischievously, then later proved her dedication to the well-being of animals during their first short lesson. She listened to instructions, gave deserved compliments to Maggy, and hopped off when Annika said the mare had worked enough in the sun. "How can I tell if she becomes overheated?" Mina asked.

Annika looked at the veterinarian. "Good question for your father. Right now, you can cool Maggy by hand-walking her around the arena."

Dr. Subroto stood at the fence and smiled at Annika. He'd stayed to watch his daughter's lesson. "I use a formula of temperature plus humidity to know when a horse can safely exert itself. I'll teach it to you. You may ride during cooler times, Mina."

"Good plan." Annika's stomach rumbled and she checked her watch. Six-forty. She'd need ten minutes to pedal home. "Time to give Maggy a shower."

"Annika, you've made Mina's dream to ride a horse come true," he said. "It's getting close to your dinner hour. We'll hose off and dry Maggy and then stall her. Your father has taught you well. He is known among the locals for his generosity. Please know your animals will always be in good hands, no matter what the future holds."

Annika swallowed away the dryness in her throat.

Everyone expected that the future held war. "Thank you for your kind words and for your offer, Dr. Subroto. My pets mean the world to me."

Pedaling home took longer than usual in the heat. She entered their garage to park her bike. Two kids prowled the back in the semi-dark. "Hello," she called. Kokkie and Henri's girls twirled around and stood at attention.

"Good day, Nonna Annika," they said politely in unison. Ratih, the oldest, must be fourteen and Legi, her sister, a year or two younger.

"Hello," Annika said. Odd, she rarely saw them, even though they lived in quarters only a few yards from the main house. How little she knew about the lives of any of their servants besides Oudje.

The tousled, dark head of their younger brother emerged from behind a spare tire. Annika smiled. "My brothers and I played hide and seek in here, too." She coaxed the little boy to come over to her and whispered in his ear. "The best hiding places are behind Pappie's tennis equipment cabinet or laying out flat in Penny's old hay manger."

The boy's eyes flicked to the opening leading into the little stall where her pony had slept years ago. "Thank you," he whispered back. "I'm Ardi." His dark eyes shone in delight.

"Happy hiding, Ardi," Annika called, and stowed her bike. She entered the mansion through the veranda, removed her boots in the annex, and set them on the mat. Ahmad would have them polished by morning. How many hours a day did their servants work? She took the boots outside and knocked them together to remove the worst of the dirt.

"I believe this will be a pleasant surprise for you." Mamma waved an envelope from the back steps.

The return address showed it originated from The Office of Nursing Programs. "But how? I haven't applied, as I'm not eighteen."

"Pappie and I felt you deserved a leg up, as you'd say in horse terms. We purposely maintained our social status, even after losing our money in the Great Depression." She handed Annika the envelope. "Pappie knows men at the Sociëteit de Harmonie who are on several hospital boards. Your high scores and our family reputation may have garnered enough approval to enroll you in the program that starts in a couple weeks."

"I'll be shocked if they were willing to work around the age requirement." Annika ripped open the seal, scanned the opening paragraph, and hugged Mamma. "I'm in!" She kissed her cheek. "You rate the purple and gold ribbon of a grand champion. Thank you!"

"You picked an admirable career. Let's get changed for a celebratory dinner." Mamma indicated the stairway. "After you, my favorite nursing student." She stopped, her face serious. "Anna, long ago your father and I realized you're not meant to sit at a desk or be married off to someone who'd judge you on your embroidery skills. The world needs nurses who may have to face the human toll from horrible battles, and you needed to learn a variety of skills to be a great nurse, which I know you are capable of."

"Thank you, Mamma. I hope so." She took her mother's hand, and they climbed the stairs together.

Her mother shook her head. "Don't ever doubt yourself. Pappie noticed even when you were a toddler that you never feared attempting something difficult or dangerous."

They'd reached Annika's open bedroom door. "I have you and Pappie to thank for my confidence." On her armoire hung an array of freshly laundered, dressy skirts. A breeze caught the material of two long, flowy ones which she'd borrowed from Mamma. "I need to return the ones I wore to fancy dinners. Phillip and I prefer to spend time together here or at the barn. I hardly see him now that he's putting in so many hours at the base."

"Of course." Mamma placed them over her arm. "He's a determined young man and that's good."

"Yes. I have another request." Annika opened her drawer and pulled out her most serviceable A-line skirt, sewn to include several pockets. "Could you please have your seamstresses make me several white ones in sturdy cotton to wear to the hospital?

And I'll need a black leather belt and white, short-sleeved blouses." She redid the band on her ponytail. "During nursing classes I'll keep my hair braided. I'm glad you showed me how."

Mamma beamed. "That's the daughter I admire. The one who knows what's needed to get things done. And trust me, you have the beauty to model if you mind your appearance."

Only Phillip made her feel beautiful. "Your dresses allow me to fit in with the elegantly dressed women at Sociëteit Concordia. Though, I'm realizing that's not my true self. Phillip and I walked the grounds before the last dance. I saw a flock of Merak Birds, fanning their long, iridescent tail feathers as they strutted for peahens. I contemplated their fate. Today the peacock, tomorrow the feather duster. You and Pappie encouraged education. I know what a lasting gift you gave us."

Mamma added the plain skirt to the pile of others. "I'll have the skirts sewn. Let's hope all your patients will be expectant mothers or adults needing routine exams." Her strained smile didn't hide her fear.

~

FALL NURSING SCHOOL OF 1941, TJIKINI HOSPITAL

Annika volunteered to assist doctors performing surgeries within a few weeks of beginning classes at Tjikini Hospital. All the students completed medically-oriented coursework, but by two months in, her supervising nurses delegated her to suture small wounds and give shots. The challenging work kept her from constantly worrying about Phillip graduating to a fighter plane after he finished training.

Hers weren't the only taut nerves. Anxiety seeped into the cracks and crevices of the hospital walls, where confident doctors snapped more often at a drop of blood or a delay in receiving an instrument. Warnings traveled through the corridors from business travelers. The Japanese hunger for dominance had increased after their occupation of French Indochina in 1940. Word spread that their military could easily move south, sighting in on Java to meet their thirst for oil.

Nothing matched the horrific news of lives lost at Pearl Harbor on December 7th, 1941, when the Japanese attacked American ships and other targets. The bombing occurred the day before Annika's eighteenth birthday. Claude had gone to visit friends, and Phillip didn't leave the base during the week, so only Annika and her parents went through the motions of dinner, cake, and presents. The evening dragged on as they listened to snippets of radio news detailing the previous day's tragedy in Hawaii and the other countries the Japanese had simultaneously bombed. Annika took deep breaths and focused on unwrapping hand printed paper from her last gift. She opened the box and lifted a gauzy white jacket. A Mamma original. "Thank you." She smiled. "I'll wear it if Phillip gets leave for the New Year's Eve dance at the Sociëteit de Harmonie. He promised he'd escort me . . ."

"He'll be there," Pappie stated flatly. "I'd bet, come hell or high water, he will arrive."

"Not if they send him to train in those rickety planes early." Annika's lower lip trembled. "I'm so nervous about losing him."

Pappie patted her hand. "You don't have to be nervous. He has a lot of common sense."

"I know. I hate thinking about him being in the air soon, dependent upon balsa wood and canvas."

A loud knock sounded from the front door. Annika jumped. She put her hand to her mouth, worried someone came with bad news.

Luther rushed to open the door. "Good evening, lieutenant."

Thank the Lord. Only one lieutenant brightened her world. Annika jumped out of her seat and ran into Phillip's open arms. She squeezed him tighter than ever before. "I'm so glad to see you."

"I wouldn't have missed your birthday for anything, my sweet." He slid his palm to her waist, directed her to stand in the private corner beside the clock, and pressed a warm, stirring kiss onto her lips. "We'd better join your family," he whispered. "But first, tell me truthfully. Are you in favor of getting married sooner?"

Annika gasped. "I'd love to. But—"

"I'd prefer to explain in front of your father." He cradled her elbow and escorted her slowly through the hallway, his voice quiet. "The night Frederick gave us permission to become engaged, I agreed to postpone marriage until you were older. Yesterday's attack changed everything." They entered the dining room, and the loud, synchronized, machine-like beeping of cicadas came through the open door of the veranda. Repeated chirps and clicks of other night bugs joined them. Her parents normally would be chatting, tonight they remained solemn.

The silver coffee service sat beside Pappie's monogrammed whiskey decanter and matching crystal glasses. Mamma stared into the night and dropped a lump of sugar and – unknowingly – its ant passenger into her cup of coffee. Lingering scents of chocolate cake and liquor filled the air.

Pappie rose and shook Phillip's hand. "Good job, son. Didn't know if you'd make it tonight. How about joining us for coffee, or something stronger while Luther gets the plate of food we set aside for you?" He motioned to his golden colored liquor.

"Thank you. In a moment." Phillip gave Annika a loving smile. He stood to his full height. "Tonight, I am afraid I am on a more serious mission than just a birthday celebration." He faced Pappie. "I love your daughter. And I want her cared for, now and in the future. I may be relocating soon. Annika agreed to a shorter engagement. Conflict is imminent. If we are married before it starts, and God forbid, I'm killed, she'd receive my military pension for life."

No! Annika's racing pulse stilled. Not why she'd agreed. The vicious Japanese couldn't come to Java. No, no, no. Her fingers pressed into Phillip's arm.

The porcelain cup Mamma held tinged as she returned it to the saucer. She shrunk into her chair, her face pale. "I knew war would find us. I pray to God every night for all of your safety."

Annika put her hand to her throat. Life with Phillip had barely started.

No one spoke. In the center of the long table, tall white candles cast flickering light around the room from their perches atop a pair of French baroque candelabras. Shadows darkened the ornate filigree on the polished sterling bases. The light breeze in the room grazed Annika's face, cooling the warm tears trailing down her cheeks. She hastily raised a hankie to her eyes. The soft cloth felt stiff, unyielding.

Pappie clasped Mamma's shaking hand. Annika

watched as she squeezed back. "We agree to your request. Johanna dreamed for years of an elegant wedding reception for Annika's nuptials." Pappie brushed moisture from Mamma's cheek with his fingertip. "We'll begin planning tomorrow, won't we love?"

Mamma nodded. "Would mid-January be too late?"

"I pray not," Phillip said. "If I get wind of anything, I'll phone immediately."

Get wind of anything, like Foxy picking up a scent? The docked American ships hadn't stood a chance. Annika's body felt numb. "I'll help Mamma. We can keep things simple," she said.

"Fair enough," Pappie said. "Now join me in a whiskey, Phillip." He poured a large measure and handed it to him. "Johanna and I will be proud to have you as our son-in-law." He raised his glass, and the two men clinked their crystal tumblers.

Glass on glass, too strong a knock and they'd crack. Annika wasn't fragile, never had been. But how much could she really handle? The noise echoed through her, a sound sealing her future.

CHAPTER 8

JANUARY 14, 1942

Church bells pealed from above the bridal dressing room in Batavia's Nassau Church. Annika jumped. The band of her veil dropped to her eyebrow. She pushed it back up to the crown of her head with her finger. "Sorry Mamma. I don't know what's gotten into me. I'm not nervous. I've dreamed of marrying Phillip for two and a half years!"

"Every bride has jitters. I'll add bobby pins to secure your veil." Annika watched in the full-length mirror while Mamma's nimble touch skillfully centered the petals of her faux silk apple blossom bridal crown and then pushed hair pins onto either side of her temple. They skimmed Annika's scalp but didn't hurt. Mamma stepped back and appraised her work. "Perfect."

"Thank you," Annika said, and tilted her head from side to side, then swished in a half circle. "A spring monsoon couldn't dislodge it now." The attached veil trailed below the gathered waist of her white silk gown, a dress Phillip hadn't even glimpsed. She squeezed her mother's shoulder. "Mamma. Tell me truthfully. Are married men less likely to go into battle?"

"I'm afraid not. Why do you ask?"

"At the rehearsal dinner, I overheard Uncle Bajetto and Pappie discussing the news about our General Archibald Wavell manning a post in Singapore and the Americans' General MacArthur landing in the Philippines." She met her mother's concerned eyes. "War against Japan means it's likely Pappie and Phillip will join Rudy in battles."

Mamma touched Annika's cheek. "Not if the generals arrive at a defense plan first. General Wavell and Hein ter Poorten, the commander of the Royal Netherlands East Indian Army, are meeting here in Batavia on the twenty-second of this month. In case they don't finalize a strategy to deter Japan, Pappie warned me that the Defense Department has arranged to begin drills using air-raid sirens. He's not certain when, but we all must take cover if we hear them. I knew I'd forgotten to tell you something." She patted Annika's arm. "Enough of such talk on your wedding day. Our world will change as your life will change today. If you ever have questions about the, ahh, more private side of marriage, I hope you'll ask me."

"Of course, Mamma. So far, Phillip's been very patient. I've read romance books, so I have an idea of what to expect." Heat rose to her cheeks. She bowed her head and slipped into her high heeled shoes.

Mamma touched her heart. "No book can describe how fulfilling your life will be. Yours is a love match, same as mine. Frederick and I met as actors in a play. Sparks began immediately. We are both lucky girls."

"I feel especially lucky today." She swished the six-foot train of her dress. "You and the seamstresses created an amazing wedding gown quickly."

"The women worked non-stop for us. Fortunately, I purchased the entire bolt of the white Georgette fabric years ago and stashed it away for this very purpose," Mamma said. She reached to the neckline and straightened a tiny leaf below the delicate silk apple blossoms that adorned the gown, then checked her watch. "Five minutes before ten o'clock. Your wedding shall begin on time, my beautiful daughter."

Her fairy tale day. Joy rippled through Annika. "I love you." She hugged her mother.

"I love you, too. More than you'll ever know, unless you are blessed with a baby girl someday." Mamma kissed her cheek, then bent over and lifted the folds of crêpe fabric that formed the train. "Time to make your grand entrance."

They descended the staircase slowly. When she reached the bottom step, she blew out the breath she'd been holding. "I managed the stairs without tripping. That's a good sign."

Emily stood smiling at them from a corner of the narthex. "You've always been graceful," she whispered, and moved to a side table. She withdrew from a florist's box a nearly three-foot long spray of white flowers, ferns, and greens. "Your bouquet is gorgeous, Annika," she said quietly. "You are gorgeous. I'm proud to be your Matron of Honor." She smoothed the skirt of her lavender silk sheath. "I only wish Quinn were here too, instead of in Sydney."

"I know," Annika agreed and squeezed her hand. "In the meantime, I'm glad you're living with us. No girl has had a more patient and helpful cousin. You're more like a sister."

Emily beamed and they kissed each other's cheeks.

Bach's "Jesus, Joy of Man's Desiring" rang out from the pipe organ, loud enough to echo off the high ceiling of the nave. Annika grasped the wrapped handle of the lengthy flower spray and pulled it to her waist. She fiddled with the soft ribbon and inhaled sweet aromas from orchids and lilies and the earthy scent of chrysanthemums.

From behind her, Mamma spread out her bridal train. "I'm off to the front row." She blew her a kiss and left. Annika peeked around the door. Her mother's crouched form moved up the side aisle toward the front row of padded benches.

A baby cried and a woman cooed to the child in a soft voice. Annika sighed. Phillip had mentioned the gift of having children. So many possibilities would bring them even closer together after today.

The final chords of music faded in the large church, where fifty or sixty people who sat in the pews cleared their throats and tapped their shoes on the wooden floor. A processional song began.

Emily walked to the aisle and turned, "Everything will go smoothly," she mouthed, and then began her measured steps to the altar.

Annika bowed her head. Please God, bless us with a long and happy marriage, she prayed silently, before she stepped to behind the last row of pews. Forty feet away, at the front of the church, Phillip's warm smile radiated an unwavering belief in their wonderful future together. Tingles of excitement ran up and down her spine. Her faithful defender waited for her alone. Out of all the women he could have chosen, he'd picked her. Restless energy coursed through her. How she'd love to kick off her shoes and do a series of grand jeté leaps down the aisle, ending in his strong arms. Instead, she smiled joyfully back at her almost-husband, standing proudly in his dark blue ceremonial uniform. Golden-yellow braid crossed his chest and was anchored by two tassels at his shoulder. In his left hand he held his kepi cap, its white feather plume resplendent against the blue. His gleaming sword hung at his side.

War wouldn't ruin her happiness. Not today, not ever. Annika stepped onto the edge of the white runner and glanced over her shoulder to find Pappie. Her grip tightened on the flowers. He should be here by now to escort her down the aisle.

The organ went silent, then the opening notes to Mendelssohn's "Wedding March" rang out.

Seemingly out of nowhere, Pappie rushed to Annika's side. "Had a slight disagreement with my bow tie," Pappie said in a low tone and smiled. He held out his forearm to her. "I'm bursting with pride today, Annika. You never, ever disappoint me," he lovingly confided.

Pappie's approval brought warmth to Annika's cheeks and a sense of calm to her fluttering nerves. She smiled back, unable to speak, and pressed her fingers into the stiff fabric of his tuxedo, truly prepared to start a new and wonderful chapter in her life. She glanced at the front again. Phillip's handsome face shone with the loving devotion she'd dreamt of finding in a husband.

As she and Pappie walked the aisle, smiles lit up the faces of women in an array of colored gowns, men in smoking outfits, and soldiers in their dress uniforms. Sabers hung at their hips.

Oma Elodie sat on the aisle of the front row next to Mamma, both their smiles wide with loving pride. Annika's heart thumped double time as Pappie kissed her cheek, blessed her, and placed her hand into Phillip's outstretched one. His warm, steady grip quelled her jitters. Their eyes met, and she'd never seen him look happier. Hand-in-hand they stepped to the altar.

The robed dominee blessed them before he welcomed the guests and asked them to join him in singing "We Gather Together" a traditional Dutch song honoring the Netherlands military victory over a Spanish king. Mamma insisted on the choice to please Phillip. His wink to Annika let her know it was an excellent decision.

The ceremony proceeded as planned and ended with them exchanging rings by placing them on each other's fingers. Flutters of joy, or relief, or utter happiness filled her chest. They were married! Annika took a deep breath and listened to the consecration. They bowed their heads in the last prayer and the reassuring tone of the dominee washed over the silent chapel.

Steel crashed onto wood.

Annika twisted her head and scanned their wild-eyed guests. A scarlet-faced young officer grimaced and pointed to the saber he held in his hand, the sword's fastener dangling. He shrugged sheepishly and hooked it to his belt. Murmurs and chuckles swept through the room. She let out her breath and tilted her head toward Phillip. He gently squeezed her hand and grinned.

As long as Phillip stood by her side, she'd handle a life of quiet moments, punctuated by crashing interludes. As long as Phillip stood by her side.

Annika rubbed her gold band. The wedding ceremony seemed more of a dream sequence from long ago, even though only an hour had passed. But she remembered the sweet refrain of the final hymn, "Whatever the Future Might Hold for Me." The words, "show me to carry the present only, with a calm and peaceful mind," would be her mantra from this day forth. As a start, she'd savor each moment seated beside Phillip at their celebration brunch in the Sociëteit de Harmonie's banquet room. She adjusted her unfolded linen napkin to cover her lap and the edge of the side bustle created from the gathered and buttoned train of her dress.

Glasses clinked from a far corner. Many of the soldiers had only stayed for the ceremony, but at least forty guests sat at tables set with gold-rimmed china and sparkling cut glass. Her eyes roved around the spacious room. Due to the impending war, the club had cancelled the New Year's Eve celebration, but the staff had managed to create a dazzling backdrop for their wedding reception from the unused decorations. Thin crystal rods of assorted lengths hung from the ceiling and gave the room a magical appearance as they caught flickers of candlelight. A waiter approached from the front side of their bridal party table. He held a silver tray piled high with golden fried meat ragout balls. "Bitterballen?" he asked.

"Oh yes." Annika inhaled spicy, savory scents and forked three bitterballen onto her appetizer plate. "Please tell Chef that he and his staff outdid themselves and I appreciate their effort. Whomever handled the lovely décor did a fabulous job."

"I will pass on your praise, Nonna Annika, I mean Mevrouw Van Hoven," the waiter said. "Might you and your new husband honor us in a few minutes by starting the buffet line? I'll send the carver and servers out."

"Of course. By then the bitterballen will be a memory." She caught his grin before he turned and left.

"More reasons I adore you, Annika," Phillip whispered." You enjoy eating nearly as much as I do, and you're not afraid to give compliments. The waiter has a spring in his step heading back to the kitchen." He stood and held out his hand. "Join me for a private moment?"

Privacy meant another wonderful kiss. "Of course," Annika declared. "I'd follow you to the ends of the earth and back." He kissed her cheek in response but remained quiet. Nerves made her babble. "Mamma planned the menu to include our favorites." She motioned to a buffet table they passed. "Braised Baron of Beef and a seashell ice sculpture holding crab and prawns. The silver chafing dishes contain spring rolls, bami-fried noodles, and skewers of chicken satay. I smell two of my favorites, fried rice and gado-gado, both waiting to be doused in spicy peanut sauce."

"Quite the selection," Phillip stated, and led her to an empty hallway off the entry. He stopped and turned her so that her back rested against a tapestry on the wall. He tipped her chin. "I sense you are nervous. Please don't be. Everything will be done at your pace."

He read her too well, this time for the wrong reason. "Don't worry about me. I'm not a meisje, a little girl."

"I've never thought of you that way," he confessed, and then stroked her cheek. "Annika, I never imagined I'd find a woman I'd fall so deeply in love with. And I want you to know that the love we share will brighten my darkest nights and keep me fighting until the bitter end. And if I don't return, I'll find solace knowing I did my best to take care of you through my pension."

Oh Lord no! If he didn't return? Her body went numb. Money meant nothing if he died. Still, how did one answer a man baring his soul? No words came to mind. She balanced on tiptoes and placed her hands on each side of his face and drew his lips to hers. His kiss tenderly matched hers before he led her into a heated rush of need. She ran her hands through his hair, never wanting the moment to end. He pulled her to his chest. The saber hilt poked her rib cage.

Phillip moved it to the side. "Sorry, the next time we kiss in private I'll be unarmed." Sparks in his eyes told her he meant every word.

"A statement I'll hold you to, Lieutenant Van Hoven." She used the formal salutation from habit. Her throat went dry.

"I certainly hope so." He led her back to their table and pulled out her chair.

She smiled, knowing that even though his future entailed deadly war, he loved her. After he sat beside her, she took a mental picture of his handsome, movie-star profile. Heat penetrated the thin silk of her gown where their arms touched. Her happily-ever-after life with Phillip had finally begun! Joy filled her while she scanned the intimate setting of her smaller wedding reception.

The room glowed from tabletop candles. Couples murmured and laughed. She and Phillip faced their wedding guests from behind an oblong table, with her parents seated on one side of them, and his parents on the other. Scents of all the delicious food enticed her as the servers removed lids from the covered dishes. "Should we start the buffet line, dear husband?"

"After you, dear wife." He stood and supported her elbow with his hand while she rose. Guests clinked their glasses and teasingly puckered their lips. Phillip leaned in and gave her a quick kiss. "It's the least I can do for folks who came on short notice on a Wednesday. I'll never need encouragement to kiss you," he whispered. "Your family organized a perfect wedding day in record time."

"Befitting my perfect husband," she added.

An hour later, coffee aromas wafted over the room as the waiters poured the steaming, dark brew from filigreed sterling silver pots. Annika relaxed in her chair with a full tummy. A petite woman in a classic brocade dress approached their table.

Phillip stood to greet her. "Tante Suze, I'd like to introduce my wife, Annika. Annika, please meet Tante Suze. She and my father are siblings. Her home is the one I showed you near Tjikini Hospital."

"Lovely to meet you," Annika said.

"The delight is all mine. Please call me Tante." She smoothed her brown hair, done in a classic French twist. "We hoped Phillip would find the ideal bride. From all he's told me of your beauty, your athletic skills, and your desire to be a nurse, you are much more. He deserves the best," she declared with pride.

"I hope I can live up to your compliments. Phillip does deserve the best," Annika confirmed.

"Dear nephew, bring your lovely wife for tea soon." She grasped Annika's hand. "If you ever work a long shift at Tjikini Hospital, you are welcome to stay overnight. Any time. God bless your marriage." She smiled warmly and moved on to visit Phillip's parents.

Well-wishers stopped by to chat while they sipped coffee and enjoyed slices of the ornately decorated, three-layer wedding cake. The smallest layer, at the top, remained untouched, adorned with a topper of blown glass swans. Their arched necks and touching beaks formed a heart.

Pappie tapped his wine glass and stood. "Thank you for celebrating Annika and Phillip's wedding with us today. After coffee and cake, please join us at our home to watch the newlyweds open their presents. I know it's not customary, but it will give us a little more time together. I've secured a case of French champagne for—"

Air raid sirens shrieked their attack warning—the ominous low wailing rose to a nervous crescendo, one blast overlapping another.

Annika's coffee cup clattered onto its saucer. "No!" she cried. Her body went cold.

"I'll get you safe, then help others. Don't worry!"

Phillip grabbed her hand and pulled her toward the door.

"Call out if you need assistance!" Pappie shouted to the fleeing throng of guests. "The hillock on the far side of the parking lot holds the nearest bomb shelter. It has plenty of room!"

CHAPTER 9

The long, flat, all-clear tone of the air raid siren blasted into the Harmonie parking lot before Annika and Phillip passed Pappie's car. "Thank the Lord it was a drill." She loosened her death grip on his hand. "We married in an anxious time, is that an omen?"

"No, not for us." Phillip wrapped her in a tight hug, his strong arms precisely what she needed. "The world around us may change, but my love for you will never waver. Don't ever forget our sapphire promise." He led her to their car. His eyes pledged the same devotion she felt.

"Congratulations." Budi ran from across the parking lot, opened the car's rear door, then walked to the driver's side.

"Thank you," Annika and Phillip said in unison.

She stopped and whispered to Phillip, "I won't

ever forget our sapphire promise," then gave him her best smile of reassurance. "Cross my heart." She traced an X on her bodice before she gathered her dress and slid onto the seat.

Phillip jumped in, kissed her, and snuggled her to his side. "I love the quaint little things you do, meisje." He kissed her again and brushed the tip of her chin.

Meisje. Coming from Phillip's lips, the little girl nickname was sweet. "If I'm to be your meisje, you're going to be my liefje. Because you are my darling, my sweetheart." She put her hand to his cheek.

"I'll answer to anything you call me. Liefje. Never thought I'd earn that endearment." Horns honked from behind them, and he grinned in the boyish way she'd grown to adore. "Sounds like we'll have a parade following us to your home. French champagne provided a wonderful enticement and a great distraction from the sirens."

"I hope so. Pappie ordered a special vintage the day you first mentioned your wish to marry me. He heartily approves of our union. Mamma as well."

"Then I will do my best to retain their confidence." They cuddled together during the short trip to arrive at Mansion Annika's front door. Phillip hopped out and held the car's door for her.

"In my mind, you've accomplished the feat. My parents adore you." Annika lifted her side bustle of fabric, stepped out and planted a quick kiss on Phillip's lips. Behind him, garlands of flowers wove around the veranda's posts. She took his arm, climbed the steps, and paused to smell the sweet, clean scent of gardenia blossoms. In the entry, tiny gardenia buds peeked out from the horns of the golden trumpeters atop the clock.

Their smiling servants stood together to meet them in the entry "Congratulations!" they cheered. The men wore their best white linen jackets, and the women wore colorful batik saris. Oudje's smile beamed from her wrinkled face.

Annika smiled back. Until now, the thought hadn't crossed her mind about them not attending the service or reception. "Thank you," she said. "Please, join us in a toast." Pappie had walked in the door. She caught his eye and he nodded approval.

Most of their staff requested fruit punch, but Luther, who wasn't Muslim, took a flute of champagne from Pappie. Henri held up his punch glass. "Kesihatan yang baik, hehidupan yang baik!" he spoke in Malayan.

Good health, good life. Annika would drink to that. She raised her champagne flute. The crystal clear, pale yellow liquid sent a flurry of bubbles to the rim. She swirled the glass and inhaled the fruity scent. As she breathed in, she also caught just a tiny hint of freshly baked bread. She sipped the soft, crisp beverage and let the tightly knit bubbles burst on her tongue. "Pappie chose well," Annika said to Phillip and touched his glass, "as did I, my liefje."

"I couldn't agree more." Phillip kissed her cheek.

They all sipped their drinks, and in a few moments, the servants took their stations to serve the refreshments they'd prepared. Soon after, twenty or so guests had arrived. Pappie greeted each one and poured them champagne.

Mamma put one arm around Phillip's waist, and the other around Annika. "Time to open gifts." She led them to where a tall stack of elegantly wrapped packages covered the round table in the living room. None of the golden and russet hued wood of the polished top showed. Several packages were decorated with floral bouquets and colored satin ribbons instead of bows. "Phillip, please hand the large gift on the left to Annika. The sender needs to depart soon."

Annika sat next to the coffee table and Phillip placed the heavy parcel on her lap. She untied the lace ribbon, lifted the cover from the oblong box, and folded back tissue paper. A gift card was tied to a sterling silver sugar bowl decorated by a pattern of inset vertical lines. Under it sat a matching twenty-inch oval tray, a teapot, and a milk pitcher, all outfitted with shiny ebony handles. She flipped the card and searched the onlookers. "Uncle Bajetto, and Tante thank you for the beautiful silver tea service," Annika began. The craftsmanship was marvelous and surely expensive. Another package wrapped in tissue held a matching sugar scoop, delicate teaspoons, and their caddy. "We'll have you over for tea soon."

"You are very welcome, dear Annika," her uncle replied. "I appreciated your assistance." He kissed her cheek, shook Phillip's hand, and the older couple said their goodbyes to her parents.

Annika watched as Bajetto strode out. He was another proud, honest man determined to prevent war. Somehow, they'd make time for tea. Annika pulled a small package to her lap and then admired the cut-glass bud vase from Tante Suze. For a half an hour they unwrapped china, crystal, and more lovely gifts to outfit a home. In between they drank champagne and nibbled fondant-covered petit fours and green klepon balls covered in fresh coconut, all created by Kokkie. Relatives, close friends, and Phillip's three roommates lingered until dark, as if they knew that with the impending war, they'd better enjoy every moment of this celebration. Mamma and Pappie attempted to keep conversation cheerful, but Annika heard snatches of discussion about battle threats.

After the last group departed, Phillip ushered Annika into the empty annex. "My beautiful bride, I booked the honeymoon suite at the Hôtel des Indes for tonight. There wasn't a home for us to move into, and I'll only be here for two weeks until I leave for Kalijati Airfield."

Two weeks before he left! Annika's breath hitched. Even the champagne couldn't dull her distress. She opened her mouth to protest, then stopped. Nothing would ruin her wedding night. She batted her eyelashes, mimicking the coquettes in the movies. "I packed an overnight bag, just in case." Warmth rose in her cheeks at the thought of the negligee gifted to her privately from Emily. "Mamma and Pappie suggested we could stay in my room if you didn't have temporary housing for us. It's at the quiet end of the house."

"Perfect for after tonight. I'll need to work long hours on base during the week, but I'll be able to join you the next two weekends. I alerted your father of my plans for tonight, and he insisted Budi should transport us. That idea seemed preferable to balancing you on my motorbike—although those were the most wonderful days of getting to know you." He kissed her tenderly and wound a strand of her hair around his finger. "I began to fall in love while I watched your ballet performance the night we met and became the happiest man alive when we started dating. Today, I am even happier. Rest assured, though, tonight we will go at your pace, Annika."

"I love you and trust you." She squeezed his warm hand. "Give me a few minutes to change out of my wedding dress." After blowing him a kiss, she lifted the skirt of her bridal gown and bounced upstairs. Oudje met her at the top, a mischievous look on her face.

"Mevrouw Van Hoven," Oudje teased, "the staff heard your romantic plans." Her sweet nanny ushered Annika into her bedroom and unhooked the tiny pearl buttons at the back of her dress. "I expect you will give us full details about your suite at the best hotel in Batavia. Didn't I tell you the first night not to worry? That the lieutenant would value your gifts?"

Annika grinned. "You did. And now I'm ready for the other gifts he brings to our union."

Phillip clasped Annika's hand the next morning as they strode out of the elegant Hôtel des Indes lobby—both of them sorry to leave their sumptuous room behind. She held up her sapphire ring to catch a ray of sunshine. Memories of their night together matched the brilliance of the sparkling stone.

A row of cars waited in line to pass under the covered porte-cochère outside the glass entry doors of the stately building. Columns of stone supported the second floor of the white, hundred-year-old structure, designed so each guest suite offered a sitting room and bedroom that opened onto the veranda. Their room had overlooked Harmonie

Square and Mills Canal. They hadn't spent much time at the window.

"I see Budi three cars back," Phillip said. "Ready to return home, sweet meisje?"

His loving smile sent shivers up her spine. "If we must." A whistle blew, taking her away from recalling how often she'd felt those same shivers over the last twenty-four hours when Phillip had shared with her his brilliant smile and more. Warmth crept into her cheeks. Would she always blush at thoughts of their romantic moments? Who cared! She grinned and looked toward the road.

The Hôtel des Indes sentry, dressed in a pressed white uniform, blew the whistle again from his covered station. He waved vehicles in and out of the hotel drive, then signaled Budi to approach the entry. Annika climbed into the back seat while Phillip pointed out their luggage to the bellman.

Phillip slid in and draped his arm across her back. "I have four more days off. We'll make the most of every minute."

She tucked against his side. "While dating we've gone to movies or dances on Saturday nights. My family typically assembles in our living room on Saturday evenings to play instruments and sing," she began. "Mamma invited us to join them this week, unless we have other plans."

"My plans centered on marrying you. I'll clap from the sideline if you'll sing."

"I'm a bit above caterwauling," Annika joked. "Uncle brings his cello, Oma Elodie plays piano, and Pappie excels in violin solos. Claude may grace us with an appearance. My brothers think they can carry a tune. You can be the judge of their vocals."

"I'd never critique a talented family. I'll need to mesmerize you all by my clapping prowess." He clapped using only the tips of his finger.

Annika giggled. "You've mesmerized me." She tickled the top of his ear and ran her fingers through his thick, perfectly textured hair. "My voice lessons came long after ballet classes, so don't expect a prima donna."

"You've already exceeded my expectations, meisje." He kissed her cheek. "Everything else constitutes ganache frosting on the proverbial chocolate cake."

Annika laughed. "You do know me well."

"More surprises greet me each day." Phillip's eyes shone. "I've been thinking. Should we visit Maggy and Newt-newt later today? I'd delight in your company and the exercise."

"A splendid idea. I'm so grateful you share my love of animals."

"I can't list all the blessings I see in you. Your determination to succeed and your positive outlook are at the top. Someday we'll go on a real honeymoon to an exotic location, like the French Riviera. For now, I'll cherish each day we spend together."

"As will I." Annika glanced out the window. Their car passed her father's preferred place to exercise, The English Sports Club, and then they turned onto Boxlaan, a tidy street where Mansion Annika stood out as its grandest home. Her own choice to marry a military man meant she'd move as his orders directed, probably never to a mansion. But wherever she lived with Phillip, she'd call the place home, even if they lived in a tent near the battlefield.

~

O n a sultry evening in mid-February, Annika studied a medical journal on the veranda. A month ago, her parents would've been seated side by side, listening to music or discussing books, and she'd be anticipating a visit from Phillip. Would those times ever return? Shortly after Phillip's departure to Kalijati Airfield, Pappie and the other able-bodied men had also been instructed to travel by train to Bandoeng to learn further battle skills in the militia.

Mamma sat in the living room, her head bent over a length of purple silk, part of it secured in an embroidery hoop. Her slouched shoulders gave a hint of how much she missed Pappie.

Annika glanced toward the cricket fields across the street. An airplane crossed the sky, then its path curved down to land at the Batavia airport. Phillip's leaving had thrown her into a tailspin. She brushed her lips, remembering their final moments together. They'd stepped into the shadows at the side of the train station and had shared a long, luscious, and passionate kiss, until they were interrupted by the conductor's whistle issuing its warning blast.

Phillip had walked out of her life and onto the train to Bandoeng. That day seemed years ago instead of only weeks. She picked up her pencil to continue note-taking. The medical journals answered many simple questions, and with the doctors' tempers growing shorter every day, finding information this way allowed her to bother them less. Signs of war put everyone on edge, like the thick air before a monsoon storm. Even riding Maggy and taking deep inhalations of clean forest breezes no longer refreshed her.

She sighed. Nothing could revive her like the two overnight visits from Phillip. On the second one, they'd spent a weekend at a hotel in Batavia. Thank the Lord, his letters kept her updated on his progress in the Royal Dutch Army Air Force division. She kept the growing pile of his precious notes stashed under her pillow, all tied together with a sapphire blue ribbon. She'd been so relieved to learn that his lack of flight hours in the flimsy Koolhoven's kept him from joining the squadron. For now. She would never voice her relief to him, though.

The telephone rang.

Annika dropped her pencil. Earlier in the week, Oma Elodie had been feeling tired. Emily had gone to stay with her. She'd been giving Annika a full report each evening, but they'd already spoken tonight. Had their grandmother gotten worse?

Mamma quit embroidering the robe she was finishing for a client, her needle poised in the air. The phone rang again. "I'll get it." She dropped her work on top of her sewing basket and dashed to the annex.

After a few moments, Mamma called to her, "It's Phillip. Please hurry." Strain sharpened her voice.

Annika's stomach knotted as she rushed inside and picked up the phone. "Are you okay?" she said into the black receiver.

"Yes, my love. I have to be brief. Many need to make this call. We may be sent to guard the coast of Bali as infantrymen. I relayed to your mother my concern of an invasion."

The knot in her belly turned to lead. "When will I see you again?"

"If I get any leave, I'll climb a mountain to see you, okay?"

Tears wet her lashes. "I'll be waiting. Rub my tie tac for good luck. I love you."

"I will. I love you, sweet meisje. We'll get through this. Bye for now."

Annika held the phone to her chest. Phillip meant every word. That thought would carry her through the days ahead. "Mamma, I know we need to put the valuables in our steamer trunks and get them to Dr. Subroto. What else do we need to do to prepare for an invasion?"

~

"Hurry, Budi. Hurry," Mamma pleaded from the back seat of their car, already speeding on the empty road at dusk a few days after Phillip's phone call from Bandoeng.

Annika understood her mother's rush, neither of them wanted to miss a moment in their husbands' company during the short reunion. Somehow, thank the Lord, Phillip had arranged to get himself and Pappi on a flight to Batavia's airport to help load military supplies brought in by ship.

As their car pulled into the parking lot of the new Kemajoran Airport, a huge, dark-colored airplane touched down on the tarmac, outlined by the setting sun. Budi parked the car near the fence and the two women threw open the doors and ran through a gate and onto to the edge of the airfield. The plane taxied toward them. It resembled the long, wide passenger models she'd seen in photos. A large truck and four jeeps pulling trailers rumbled onto the airstrip. About a hundred feet from them, the airplane stopped, and the propellers quit spinning.

Unlike her stomach. Mamma squeezed Annika's

hand, both of them trembling from nervous energy at a chance to see their men before they left Java for Bali, the next island to the east.

A large hatch-style door opened near the rear of the plane and Phillip stuck out his head. He flicked them a quick wave.

Annika's heart flip flopped. "Egads I miss him. It's like part of me belongs to him."

Mamma nodded, her focus on the plane. "I've known that feeling for nearly thirty years. There's Pappie!" Her father's head had appeared beside Phillip's.

One of the jeeps parked alongside the plane. Pappie and Phillip jumped from the hatch exit onto the trailer, and then to the ground. Other soldiers began to load wooden crates and oblong metal cases from the trailer into the belly of the plane.

Guns and ammunition? Annika ignored the thought and concentrated on the breathtakingly handsome man who jogged to meet her. Her lieutenant, her husband, her liefje! The uniform suited his muscular physique so, so well. The closer he got, the stronger her heart pounded.

Phillip lifted her off her feet, spun her in a quick circle, and set her down. He kissed her in an urgent, needy, and sexy way. Too soon, he changed to soft, light kisses, and then brushed his fingertip against her lips. "I needed to see you one last time, in case I'm shipped out." He exposed his empty wrist, showing a tan line. "I traded the watch from my father for this trip."

She touched his wrist and pressed her other hand on his chest. "You did? Thank you. I know how much that watch meant to you." She cradled his cheek. "Where will you be stationed?"

"I'm still a dozen hours of flight time short. If I can log those in somewhere, I'll be piloting a plane to hold off the Japs. Otherwise, they'll move us to the coast of Bali to join the infantry."

Annika's knees went weak. The coast, please let him go to the coast and remain on foot. "I'll continue to pray for your safety in the air or on land." She couldn't display her fear to Phillip, and she couldn't meet his eyes right now, so she motioned over his shoulder. "That plane appears sturdy, what's it called?"

"It's a Douglas, from an American maker. Smaller planes are more maneuverable, but she flies steady as they come."

"And she brought you to me like an arrow to its mark." Annika kissed him and then clasped his hand. "Thank you for including Pappie." She glanced at her parents, who'd remained hugged tightly together. "They haven't been separated since they were married."

"Just because we haven't been married long doesn't make it easy for me, either." Phillip's deep voice changed to comforting. "I'll do what I can to keep an eye on your father. Don't worry, meisje." His steady gaze reassured her. "I outrank him and won't be afraid to use my power for protection."

"Rank won't matter to Pappie," Annika disclosed. "He's more concerned about the less fortunate." She bit her lip. "Fighting isn't in his temperament."

Wrinkles creased Phillip's brow. "Nor is fighting in mine, as I hope you realize. I chose serving in the military as an honorable career option, and a way to provide a good living for a family on Java. Someday it shall." His lop-sided smile broke Annika's heart. He couldn't put on false gaiety any more than she could.

"I know you are a family man at heart. Whenever this war ends, wherever you are, I'll find you," Annika promised. "I won't quit searching until I do. Not even the Indian Ocean could stop me." She tugged his arms back around her waist and grabbed the sides of his stiff, brown jacket. "Hold me until you leave, liefje." They stood in silence, her cheek to his chin. She committed to memory how Phillip's spicy cologne melded with his unique essence. Words weren't necessary, they knew what lay in each other's hearts.

Jeeps roared past them and the truck honked its horn. Phillip released one hand and pulled a chocolate bar from his pocket. "We'll be together again, Annika. And until then, your sweetness will linger in my thoughts." He slipped the bar between his shirt and her hand. "I need to leave now. I don't own another watch to buy us more time. I'd never trade away the sapphire you gave me, sealing our promise of loyalty, trust, truth, and my infinite love for you."

"I love you with all my heart." She mustered a cheerful smile. Lord only knew when she'd see him again.

Moisture made his eyes glossy. He kissed Annika and let his lips linger against hers for a wonderful moment, and then stepped away and tapped Pappie's shoulder. Both men trotted to the airplane, now a huge, dark shape in the low light of evening. The big plane's propellers spun faster as the engine grew louder. Mamma grabbed Annika's belt and wrapped her arm around her waist. Tears streamed down both their cheeks. She and Mamma watched their husbands climb aboard and the door panel shut. They both waved at the plane when it lifted off and watched as it disappeared, swallowed by a dull gray sky. Mamma sobbed into her hands.

"They'll return to us," Annika said. Agony ripped through her. Phillip wouldn't have traded away his treasured watch unless he'd estimated a lengthy separation. She put her arm around her mother's slight shoulders. "They'll stick together. Phillip knows the military, and Pappie is worldly wise."

Mamma snuffled and wiped her eyes. "Uh-huh." She pulled a handkerchief from her pocket and dabbed her face. "You're right, Annika. Those two men complement one another."

"As do we. Mansion Annika won't look any different when our men return. Noblesse oblige."

"Funny, your father mentioned that tonight. We have a responsibility to keep things running smoothly in his absence. The servants depend on us. I know Ahmad, Luther, and Henri will help with Frederick's duties." Mamma's hand shook as she twisted her hanky, embroidered with tulips.

Annika patted her arm. "I can help manage the stables. When we get home, we'll make lists of things to be completed—to occupy our time and keep our wandering minds off the hazards our men face."

They walked off the empty airfield tarmac, the faint odor of jet fuel lingering on the evening breeze, offering the last reminder of the visit. Neither women uttered a word on the drive home. Annika pictured the airplane carrying Phillip and Pappie, her final view of it had been a tiny spec gobbled by thick clouds. Beside her, Mamma's slumped form on the car seat mirrored her own despair. One of them needed to snap out of the doldrums. She straightened her shoulders and leaned forward. "Sorry to take you away from your dinner, Budi."

"No need to apologize. We pray each day for your family's safety," he said. The car turned onto their circular drive.

No lights shone from Mansion Annika. Dark and empty, same as she felt inside.

Foxy met them in the entry. He sniffed Mamma and whined, then scratched to go out. "He smells Pappie," her mother lamented. She patted his back with a trembling hand. "They'll be back soon, pup, don't worry."

Annika rested her head on her mother's shoulder. "Maybe this whole thing will blow over."

"Good thought." Mamma brushed aside a strand of hair falling over Annika's smooth brow. "We'll get through this together. Safeguarding our heirlooms tomorrow starts the process." They hugged good-night and plodded upstairs to their bedrooms.

Annika's damp pillow pressed into her cheek throughout the night. Would Phillip and Pappie be put in the front line of a battle? Or fly in a plane to fight the Japanese? Where were Claude and Rudy? What if she'd seen them all for the last time?

CHAPTER 10

FINAL WEEK OF FEBRUARY 1942

Phillip was gone from Annika's life as of last night, but the war wouldn't shatter their love. Not if she could help it. At first light, she dressed and walked to the bathroom to put a cold compress onto her red eyes. She returned to her bedroom and ran her fingertip across the de Fisicat crest of two lions holding a shield, carved into the front panel of the French heirloom antique trunk which Oma Elodie had given her the night of her engagement party. That celebration seemed a lifetime ago. She lifted the trunk's lid and removed her bridal trousseau, most of it never worn.

A tap sounded on her door. "Yes?" she called quietly.

Oudje cracked the door open and stuck her head

inside. "I heard you bustling about earlier than normal. Need a cup of tea?" Her cherished nanny-turned-confidante walked to her side and kissed her cheek. "Our prayers will be answered for the men to return safely. We're all ready to help."

"Thank you." Oudje's voice always soothed Annika. "And tell everyone Mamma and I appreciate each of you." The stacks of clothes on her bed, once planned for an extended honeymoon, teetered as precariously as the current course of Annika's life. She split two piles into three. "Tea sounds lovely. I can fetch my own." She fought to keep her voice from breaking.

Oudje held up her hand. "No dear. I'm headed downstairs. You finish your packing." Her soft foot-steps padded to the door. "I'll be right back."

"Could you please ask Luther and Ahmad to move this wooden chest, along with Mamma's from the foot of her bed, and the two trunks in the storage room into the living room? We'll be stowing our valuables in them today."

A frown flashed across Oudje's wrinkled face. "Yes. May I assist you?"

"Please. Let's plan for an hour after Mamma rises to begin sorting things to be stored in the trunks."

"She's up," Oudje leaned against the door. "I heard both of you from the kitchen."

"Oh dear. I hoped she would sleep later." After Oudje left, Annika dressed, took Foxy outside for a break, and returned by way of the annex. The four trunks sat in the living room. Two steamer trunks, typically used for voyages between Indonesia and Europe, looked nearly as long as she was tall. Inlaid tulips decorated Mamma's dowry chest.

Throughout the morning, Mamma and Oudje packed crystal goblets, blue Delft porcelain, hand embroidered linens, silver candelabras, and antiques into the cedar-lined chests while Kokkie and her daughters brought them items from cabinets and drawers. Annika wrapped her own wedding gifts and stowed them into her trunk. Would all the beautiful silver and crystal gifts ever be used? She placed her cleaned and pressed bridal gown into a cotton bag, laid it on top, and closed the lid.

By lunchtime, they'd filled the trunks. Annika flipped through Pappie's leather address book and located Dr. Subroto's name. The phone receiver felt heavy in her hand. Sending away all their cherished pieces gave the coming war the same emotional drain she'd feel if she were trying to vaccinate against a dreaded disease with an aspirin. She dialed the vet's number. Each click of the finger wheel sent a warning for her to disconnect, to slam the receiver onto the cradle and pretend all was well.

"Hello?" Dr. Subroto's familiar voice answered on the second ring.

"Good day. It's Annika. I'm calling with a favor. We've put our valuables into four trunks. They're at least five feet long and three feet high. Are you still willing to store them?"

"Of course," the veterinarian said. "I'll bring my stock trailer to your home this afternoon. By the way, I've taken Mina to your stable twice in the evening recently and you'll be surprised to see her post a trot on Maggy. Also, I've readied extra stalls in my barn for your horses, should you need them."

"Thank you. I'm praying we can all stay put. That's wonderful news about Mina. I'd bet Maggy loves the attention and exercise. I appreciate your offer about boarding our horses. See you soon." She replaced the phone's receiver. A lump formed in her throat. If the Japanese invaded, she'd herd the horses from Pappie's stable to Dr. Subroto's barn herself before she'd let them fall into the hands of barbarians.

MARCH 2, 1942

Classes continued at Tjikini Hospital, the tension thick in the air. Every spare moment was spent rolling bandages to prepare for an onslaught of wounded soldiers and civilians. The idea of her beloved men being injured kept Annika on edge. On the Monday after Phillip's airfield visit, Bram picked her up from in front of the hospital to begin her courier run. The packets of papers he handed her must have weighed two pounds. "I overheard General Bajetto on the phone while waiting for your orders." He brushed his eye with his sleeve. "Early yesterday morning, the Japanese executed an unexpected landing and took over Kalijati Airport. Our casualties were high. In the air attack we launched, none of our pilots survived." His knuckles turned white on the black steering wheel. "We sent out three squadrons of twelve. Damn Japs shot them all down."

Annika gasped. "The Koolhoven trainers!" she exclaimed. Had Phillip gained his last training hours? Where was Rudy?

"Probably. Not certain if they have Fokkers there." Bram glanced in the rearview mirror. "You okay, Mevrouw? You've turned pale as rice."

"My husband is stationed at Kalijati. He wanted to fly but hadn't quite met the criteria." A strange feeling deep, deep inside gave her hope that by some miracle Phillip had survived. "God bless the souls of the brave men we lost in those downed planes. Maybe the Allied navy will do better." She bowed her head and pulled the envelopes to her chest. "Please God," she whispered. "Let Phillip and Rudy be alive."

"You haven't heard about the Battle in the Java Sea?"

Her pulse quickened. "No. What battle?"

"It was awful." He shook his head. "From midday to midnight on Friday, the Allies tried to reach the Japs' invasion fleet of troop transport ships as they were headed for Java. In the battle, many Allied ships went down. Australia and the Philippines are wide open for attack, now too."

Annika's limp body slunk into the car seat. Could Phillip have been on a ship headed to Bali? "Oh no. That's devastating news." She closed her eyes to recall their wedding hymn. "Dear Lord," she prayed silently, "show me to carry the present only, with a calm and peaceful mind." A tough undertaking, not knowing of Pappie, Rudy, and Phillip's fate.

CHAPTER 11

TUESDAY, MARCH 3, 1942

The radio broadcasts that they heard on breaks at the hospital didn't give much hope that Phillip, Rudy, and Pappie had all missed being part of the Allied air and naval defeats. For the last twenty-four hours, Annika had prayed during every spare moment and debated whether to share yesterday's horrible news from Bram with her depressed mother. She'd purposely not turned on their home radio the last few days. Carrying this heavy secret drained her strength worse than the hard work she did at the hospital. Tonight, though, she must disclose the facts to her mother. Her feet struggled to pump the bicycle's pedals past The English Sports Club and onto Boxlaan.

Annika rounded the corner and turned at their

driveway. Sunset cast orange, yellow, and purple stripes onto the clouds above Mansion Annika. How could the sky above Batavia look so peacefully beautiful when the world reeled from war? Could her mother handle the horrible news?

Mamma ran from the house and met her at the garage. "You received a letter from Phillip." She waved an envelope. "I hope he has news of Frederick."

The postmark, February 28th, was the day before the Dutch pilots had all died. She dropped her bike to the ground. Her pulse hammered as she ripped it open. Please be alive, she prayed again as she unfolded the single sheet of thin paper. She read the first paragraph and let out a long, low breath. "Thank the Lord! Phillip's still ten hours short on flight hours and he and Pappie's militia group made it to Bali as ground support!" She scanned the page. "For now, he and Pappie are near one another. He said that we should be prepared to move to a safer place. Mamma, I need to get everyone together. This is great news for us, but the war isn't going well for the Allies."

Following dinner, she repeated the horrors of the Battle of the Java Sea defeat and the airfield strike to Mamma and the servants. Emily had remained in town with Oma Elodie, so Annika phoned her, and suggested the two of them pack bags in case they needed to relocate. Afterward, Annika climbed the stairs to her bedroom and sorted through her belongings. She piled necessities on her vanity chair and closed her dresser drawer. In bed that night she reread the last line of Phillip's letter, written in his neat script. *"My love will bring me home to you. Stay strong, Annika, stay strong. Forever your loving Phillip."* She prayed for his safety and for all the men still fighting, then drifted in and out of restless sleep.

The next afternoon, Annika waited in front of the hospital for Bram. In a few minutes, the car drove in and stopped. He spoke through the open window. "It's our last delivery. General Bajetto said to thank you. We need to hurry."

"Okay." She hopped in the back seat and shut the door. Her unease increased the faster he drove on an empty section of road. She unfolded her uncle's note. "Ministry of Finance, as usual." The thin envelope contained maybe a dozen sheets of paper. The final missives to prepare Batavia for battle?

Their car made progress in fits and spurts. Sados, trucks, pedestrians, and cars vied for positions at busy intersections. Stops and starts jerked her back and forth in her seat. Horns honked and an exaggerated need to rush buzzed in the hot afternoon air like an angry swarm of hornets. Bram passed vehicles driven by wrinkled, frail old men. None were the stout, middle-aged Dutch businessmen who now served in the army or the militia. Poor Pappie, he'd never owned a gun, and soon he might be wielding one to save his life and the lives of his family. Annika pressed her fingers into her throbbing temple.

Bram double-parked their car near the front doors of the Finance Building, alongside a delivery truck with its ramp extended out the open back door. "Best I can do today," he muttered.

"Thank you. Be right back." She ducked into the lobby and dodged men wheeling hand trucks piled with banker boxes. In the familiar office, the young soldier who'd become her contact kept his back to her while he yanked files from a cabinet and stuffed them into boxes. "Wednesday delivery," she announced.

He jumped. "Oh, my favorite courier." Stress lines drew his lips into a thin smile. "Sorry, we're in high gear at the moment." He took the envelope she offered.

"What's going on?"

"Orders came to secure or destroy anything of potential benefit to the Japanese. I understand you are not a government worker. Thank you for your service." He gave her a short salute and shook her hand. "Glad I got to say goodbye. It's likely that Jap soldiers will take over Batavia soon."

Soon! Enemy soldiers controlling her city? "Ahh. You're welcome." She smiled weakly. "I'm glad I helped in such a small way. When do you think they'll invade?"

"This week." He leaned over his desk and whispered. "The Dutch government has prepared several blocks of houses for older folks, women, and children to move into in case they feel unsafe in their homes. Thought I should tell you." His eyes held compassion. "It's an area called Tjideng Ghetto."

The name wasn't familiar to Annika. "Thank you. I appreciate your letting me know." She exited the building on shaky legs and found Bram parked several cars back. They left and negotiated thick traffic. Drivers and pedestrians moved in hectic patterns. "Bram, have you heard the Japanese may take over Batavia this week?"

He met her eyes in the rear-view mirror. "That's the rumor."

"I was told there may be a secure area for women and children in Tjideng Ghetto. Where's that located?"

"Not in a great part of town. It's next to a railroad and packed by small houses. Northwest of here and near a canal, I think." He turned onto their driveway. "Goodbye, Mevrouw Van Hoven. It's been an honor driving you. Be careful."

"You be careful, too. Thank you." Annika got out of the car and waved farewell to Bram. She walked to the house and pushed open the front door. Fear about the impending invasion overshadowed her relief at successfully finishing the Monday and Wednesday commitment.

Ahmad stepped off the last stair, carrying a large

suitcase. "It's Claude's," he said sadly, then stowed it beside the clock and walked away.

From the living room, her brother hobbled toward her on his crutches. One foot remained in a cast from the motorbike crash, and his pants strained over his other ACE-bandaged leg.

"What's going on?" she asked.

"I phoned Uncle Bajetto. I'm going to take a battery of tests to see what I can do in the war effort. He assured me there's a barracks I can bunk in, as it may take several days, and I don't want to use the car."

Annika's heart lurched. Everyone was leaving. But Uncle would watch over Claude. "Do you need anything else?"

"No, sis. Ahmad came to my rescue." He balanced against the wall. "If I need any medical assistance, I'll request you."

"I spoke to your orthopedic doctor. After your cast comes off tomorrow, you're not to strain either injury. Keep them wrapped in those new elastic bandages. Do you understand?" She stood to her full height, still a head shorter than Claude.

"You've mastered the authority of a nurse." He saluted her. "I vow to show more respect to my body. The ligament near my knee must be healing. No shooting pain from walking. You're going to see me running a marathon."

Typical Claude. Being sidelined must kill him. "In

the meantime, put your brain to use." Annika tapped her head. He laughed and hobbled off the porch and out to Budi, who waited beside their car to take him to town. As the vehicle moved away, something spurred her to run after them. "Claude! Wait!" She caught their car at the end of the circular drive, before it turned onto Boxlaan.

Claude stuck out his head. "Yes?"

She leaned in to kiss his forehead. "Forgot to say goodbye. And Pappie would be proud you aren't using your injury as an excuse to slack off."

"Never!" Claude gave her his brightest grin. "See you in a couple days wearing a shoe on each foot and a fine title," he joked. "Onward, Budi." In a moment, the car disappeared at the curve by The English Club.

She rubbed her neck to lessen the ominous feeling that she'd not see him again for a long, long time.

CHAPTER 12

THURSDAY, MARCH 5, 1942

The next morning, screaming and shouting blared into Tjikini Hospital from the street. Annika dropped a partially rolled cotton bandage and looked out the open window of the break room. She gasped.

Japanese soldiers in jeeps and on tractors camouflaged by branches drove past the hospital. Their flag with the red circle on a white field flew on every vehicle. Horns honked and pedestrians and sado drivers scrambled to get out of their path. Rows of helmeted men on bicycles led a fleet of tanks flying the same flag.

Batavia had been invaded! What now? Annika's fingers gripped the windowsill.

"The Japanese soldiers are everywhere!" The

sweet, old, Indonesian hospital custodian had charged into the room. "They're busting into buildings and houses. Mevrouw Van Hoven, should we fight? You stay behind me."

Bless him for his courage. Annika turned from the window to speak to him face-to-face. White showed around his wide-open, dark eyes. He clutched an upended push broom like a sword. Verdorie! They had nothing to fight with except a few scalpels. Her pulse raced. Teaching ballet had taught her to speak quietly to an anxious student and encourage deep breaths. Anxious was an understatement as to how unnerved she felt. Annika gently patted his shoulder. "Put down the broom, and we'll both take slow, calming breaths. I'd suggest we follow the lead of our doctors." From the corridor, the sounds of boots stomping, shouting, and clatter grew louder. There was no use in hiding. A tremor went through her body as she walked to the open doorway. The janitor followed behind her. Retired Dutch doctors, judged too old or otherwise unsuitable to serve in the military, stood in the hallway beside Indo and Indonesian medical staff.

A contingent of black-haired soldiers marched toward their end of the corridor where Annika and the custodian had joined their colleagues. The soldiers shouldered people aside and yelled in short, rigid Japanese that no one understood. Some of their army wore loose fitting, tan trousers. Others wore knee-length shorts and short-sleeved shirts. All had stern faces. A gray-haired man, apparently an officer, strode forward. The soldiers swung sideways and saluted as he passed. Displayed on the chest of his brown uniform, a row of colored ribbons holding round metal discs bounced as he prowled the hallway. His jodhpur style breeches were tucked into shiny, black leather boots. He bellowed a word, and the melee silenced. His intense glare searched the group of patients and medical staff, and then he walked directly to the kindly, stoop-shouldered doctor who'd recently completed rounds on their floor. The older Japanese man puffed out his chest and patted the medals. "Colonel," he announced in English.

The doctor stepped back and shook his head. "Sorry. I don't understand," he uttered in Dutch.

The balding hospital director slipped through the crowd. "May I help you?" he asked in Dutch, which caused a deep scowl from the Japanese commander. The director changed his polite request to Malay, then Latin.

The colonel shoved his hand in front of the director's face. "English! Now!"

The hospital director shook his head. His eyes swept the corridor and stopped on Annika.

Her throat went dry. She pushed her back against the door frame. She couldn't move or speak.

The Japanese officer's dark, angry eyes skimmed

the onlookers. Patients in hospital gowns shrunk away from the doorways and slipped into rooms.

Annika took a deep breath. The air in the corridor hung heavy with the smells of stinging antiseptic and fear-soaked bodies. What would Pappie or Phillip do? Noblesse oblige. Her stomach tightened. She raised her hand.

"No, Mevrouw. No, no, no," the custodian whispered to her.

Not knowing what he demanded would be worse for them all. "I speak English." Her voice sounded shrill.

The Japanese colonel strode down the center of the hospital hallway toward Annika. Dutch and Indonesians cowered against the walls. A taller, muscular soldier followed directly behind his leader. The man wearing medals pointed at her. "You now interpreter," he commanded in English. He flipped his hand at the hospital director. "Tell him hospital under my rule." He pointed to a group of Japanese men, all wearing a different uniform from the others, who stood in a group. "My doctors make decisions."

Annika ran her clammy hands down the sides of her skirt. English had not been her favorite language. The room stayed silent while she raised her voice and relayed his commands into Dutch and then Malay. Gasps rippled through her co-workers. Feet shuffled. Many stepped backward into the recovery rooms and offices.

The colonel pointed to her again. "You come here every day to translate!" he ordered. "Now show me building and I give you orders."

'Or else' was implied. Annika nodded. She grabbed a notepad and pencil. "Offices and room for recovery from surgery," she began, and motioned to the rooms on either side of the corridor. She stepped forward. The larger Japanese soldier stuck out his hand to block her path. The colonel marched past her, and after he'd gone six feet, the sentinel lifted his arm. Over the next hours she followed the leader throughout the building. She explained in simple English the various facilities in the hospital. Whether he understood or not, it didn't matter. He seemed intent on one goal: to get rid of any non-Indonesians, except in her case.

He ignored darker-skinned Indonesian and Indo doctors and nurses but flicked his hand to dismiss all lighter-skinned staff, whether or not they wore nursing or physician's garb. The same for patients. His soldiers escorted both groups from the building, many of the patients crying.

In the maternity ward, he yelled at a young Dutch woman nursing an infant. Annika bit her lip. A few minutes ago, an Indo doctor had objected to him kicking out a man recovering from gall bladder surgery and the soldiers had hauled them both out.

She had to help the new mother. How to be discreet and not get caught and detained, or worse?

Mamma would go crazy if she didn't return home. When the colonel moved to the next room, she tore a corner of one page from her notepad, scribbled her phone number on the torn piece, and slipped it to the crying woman, who held her newborn tight to her chest. She left the room knowing it was the best she could do for now.

During a bathroom break, she heard two women in the other stalls speaking in Malay. They called the invaders "Japs" and the commander "Medals." Annika flushed the toilet and washed her hands. Appropriate nicknames, given how the colonel and his army showed no empathy for the sick. At the moment, Medals waited impatiently outside for her. She dried her hands and continued the nerve-wracking day.

They'd ended the hospital tour in the storeroom. Medals marched out at four in the afternoon and left the harried skeleton crew to tend the remaining patients. At five, two Indonesian men in army uniforms carried in a teen-aged boy on a stretcher. Below his tattered shorts, a bone in his left leg jutted at an odd angle. Annika pulled off his wet shirt and towel-dried his skinny chest while a young Indo doctor assessed the damage. "Appears you broke your tibia. What happened?" he asked in Malay.

"All the men in the city got captured at gunpoint by the Japs. They pulled soldiers out of the barracks and marched workers out of buildings. They grabbed me and my brother. We'd gone to the port. Saw them load prisoners onto transport boats. A huge ship is anchored far out. During a commotion we escaped." He stuck out his thin chest.

The doctor tilted his head. "I guess you were lucky."

The boy smirked. "Yeah. I ran in front of one of their jeeps. I'd rather suffer a broken leg after I heard the others might be shipped to Japan and put to work as slaves. When the Allies arrive, they'll torpedo the Japs' boats, no matter who's on board."

Annika gasped. Claude would've been with Uncle in a government building. What time was his doctor's appointment today? "Excuse me, please." She ran into an office and phoned Uncle Bajetto's number. Too late. No one answered. She headed to the back door. Her hand cramped as she signed out after the ten-hour shift of nerves and note taking. Clogged streets held Japanese soldiers in vehicles and on bicycles. Indonesian people on foot darted through the soldiers. Street vendors scrambled to steady their baskets. "Make way!" yelled sado and wagon drivers. They urged their struggling horses forward, trying to make progress with their over-flowing vehicles.

The locals were leaving Batavia. Annika panicked. Would Mamma be home waiting for her? Had the Japanese soldiers barged into houses in her neighborhood? Pedaling on the normal route took her twice as long as usual.

Traffic thinned the closer she got to Boxlaan. Dusk became dark. She parked her bike in the garage and ran through the front door. The crystal chandelier illuminated dirty footsteps on the pristine marble. "Mamma!" she screamed.

Her mother jumped from her chair at the dining room table. A pad of paper dropped to the floor. "I'm so glad to see you!" Scissors and implements from her wicker sewing basket were strewn across the table.

Annika ran to her. "The Japanese invaded. They took over the hospital," she blurted.

"They've been here," Mamma said. "Stormed through the door and shouted 'Out!' at me. Marta and the family left a few days ago, but their maid ran over to warn me, bless her heart. They'd hauled away all the male servants. Budi barely got our staff in the car. He planned to drive them to Ahmad's brother in the country. I couldn't leave without you."

Annika kissed her mother's cheek. "Mamma, I would've gone crazy if you weren't home." She pulled out a chair and let her body rest for the first time since the invasion. "I'm glad Oudje and the others got away. Why did the Japanese let you stay? The soldiers at the hospital kicked out the Europeans, sick or not."

"Between pantomime and a little English, I told

them I wouldn't leave my child." She pretended to cradle a baby. "I gave the leader the last loaf of fresh-baked bread and he gave us until morning. Tomorrow, a Japanese truck will transport us to some type of housing in town. We're allowed to bring linens, a small suitcase, and a shoulder bag. At least I think that's what he said in broken English." She handed Annika the pad. "I'm listing what we need to do tonight and essentials to take. Did I miss anything?"

Annika set her mother's list on her lap. Packing felt so trivial. "Have you heard from Claude?"

"No. You sound worried."

"They captured men in town and put them on transport boats. Rumors say they'll be used for slave labor in Japan."

Mamma's eyes flew open. "Dear Lord, Annika. Claude can barely walk." She rubbed her chin. "But he's clever and protected by Uncle Bajetto."

Their close association might mean immediate imprisonment for both of them. Those details Annika would not share. Nor would she mention the horrible part about the Allies sinking Japanese ships. Pappie and Phillip could've been put on a transport boat. Mamma didn't need more stress. "No one answered Uncle Bajetto's office phone earlier. I'll try tomorrow." She glanced at the list. "Let's start by packing small valuables."

"Yes, in apothecary jars." Mamma finished rolling needles, thread, and scissors into a small bundle. "If we stuff money and jewelry into jars, then melt wax on top, they should be fine."

"Why the wax?" The end of the dining room table held four clear glass jars and a partially filled amber colored one.

"Bugs and moisture. They'll be safest buried in the shrubbery around the house. I didn't think to put our important papers in the trunks, so I'll wrap them in oilcloth, and we'll have to think of a dryer spot." She pointed to a tray of cake and a teapot. "I'll find something fresh for us to eat in a few minutes. I hope the servants are all safe."

"Me too." Annika nibbled a piece of chocolate pound cake and thought about possible hiding places. "I heard a mouse in the ceiling over my bed once. Claude took me into the storage room adjacent to my bedroom to set a trap." Her brothers annoyed her at times, but they'd also taught her things. Had she ever thanked them? She pushed the cake aside. "The mouse had made a hole to get into a space between the wallboard and the roof. I can loosen a panel and stick the papers inside," she said, and lifted a folded piece of stiff sailcloth and a tall stack of envelopes and photo album pages from the table. "I'll put these away first. There's a space under a floorboard, too."

"Wait. I started packing our most precious things." She motioned to the amber colored jar.

"Remove your wedding rings and your signet ring. Hide this jar upstairs. Someone may plant flowers."

Annika studied her hands. She'd never taken the rings off. Her fingers shook as she pulled off the signet ring, kissed it, and dropped it into the jar. Warm tears rolled onto her cheeks. Slipping off her wedding band and the sapphire wasn't really severing her tie to Phillip—it just felt like it. She clutched them to her heart. Her precious rings would stand a better chance of survival here. She carefully placed them in the jar and screwed on the lid. Climbing the stairs never seemed so taxing. A bare bulb lit the dusty, narrow, storage room. Think. Where had Claude pried up the loose floorboard to show her his hidey hole? She found it near the back wall in two tries, pulled out a battered toy truck, squeezed in the jar, and tapped the board in place with her shoe. She turned her focus to the walls. A protruding nail stuck out from the thin, ribbed wood paneling behind an old nightstand. She pried a section of the wood free and fit the paperwork behind the bead-board, then again pounded the nail in place with the heel of her shoe. Confident they'd be safe, she hustled downstairs and into the living room.

Mamma's sobbing made her skin crawl. "What happened?" Annika slid onto the couch beside her and put her arm around her shoulders.

She leaned her head against Annika. "Elodie's

heart gave out as the men stormed into her house. She's with our Lord now. Emily phoned while you were upstairs, it only happened a few minutes ago." Mamma dabbed her eyes with a white hankie.

"No!" Annika cried. The elegant woman who'd taught her manners and so much more had died? She sank into the sofa cushions beside Mamma. "I can't believe she's gone."

"Nor can I," her mom cried. "While Emily was teaching at school today, I spoke to Elodie and warned her about the invasion. I told her to be courteous and not to worry. I knew she'd panic about the thought of being a captive, or worse."

Annika glanced at their piano, covered by a white cloth, the piano Oma Elodie had played for them so many times. "I'm glad Emily was beside her."

"Yes. No one should die alone." Her mother took her hand. "None of us knows what to expect tomorrow. A refined woman such as your grandmother . . ." She swept the hankie across her face and handed a blue one to Annika. "I know Elodie would want . . . no, expect, you and I to stay the course for Frederick and Phillip's return."

Annika nodded. "Yes, she'd sit straight, her hands folded properly in her lap, and insist we carry on as ladies. To calm us, she'd glide over to the piano and play Bach."

"Precisely. Let's get started on the remainder of

the family jewelry, a priority to Oma Elodie."
Mamma gave her a sad smile.

It took over an hour to sort Mamma's modern
jewelry from the valuable heirlooms. They stowed
them alongside money into four more apothecary
jars, melted wax, and dripped it on to form a seal.
"The soil should be easy to dig," Annika said, and
grabbed a flashlight before she headed outside. An
owl hooted from behind the tennis courts to her
right. Night bugs thrummed and clicked while she
pushed the shovel into soft dirt. She buried the jars
two feet deep, below the living room windows, and
then stowed the shovel in the garage and walked
inside.

Mamma patted the supply of cash she'd retained.
"This afternoon when we talked, Elodie extolled the
virtue of bribes. Her grandparents successfully used
that approach when escaping from France to Java.
May God rest her soul."

Annika took her mother's hand and bowed her
head. "Oma Elodie guided us so often, please guide
her now, God. Amen." She released Mamma's hand.
"Poor Emily. I hope she's okay being alone in her
house tonight. What about a funeral?"

"Elodie often repeated that life was for the living,
and her Indonesian butler offered to handle the
burial. We don't have a choice. The Japanese soldiers
will return tomorrow for Emily, too. I assume to
transport her to the same housing as us." Mamma

used a steel crochet hook to lift the suede insole of her sturdy leather shoe. "Money can be walked into camp, so to speak." She gave Annika a weak smile. "Where can we hide these items for bartering?" Her finger hovered over the remaining pile of newer pieces of jewelry. "These contain real diamonds and gemstones and should fetch a good price."

"My brain is kapot." Annika, worn out from her long day, yawned and poured herself a cup of cold, strong Dutch tea. Dawn would arrive before they knew it and another duty needed her attention before she could rest. She tapped her toe on the floor. "I have a solution. My ballet shoes."

"How can those help?"

"You'll see." She jogged upstairs to her bedroom, grabbed her ballet shoes, and returned to the living room. Mamma's stitch ripper made short work of the seams on the boxy toes. "If I remove half the padding, you can layer the jewelry inside and replace the stitches by hand." She tossed the shoes to Mamma and glanced out the window into darkness. "I need to change into black clothes and phone Dr. Subroto about moving the horses to his clinic. Pappie planned for their safety. I'll ask him for a sedative to make Foxy groggy. I won't leave him behind."

"Annika," Mamma cried. "You can't move seven horses by yourself at night."

She ignored the comment and retrieved her small

rucksack from the annex cupboard. "I have to move the horses by myself. Dr. Subroto only has a small stock trailer, and he could be in trouble if he got stopped. The horses can't fend for themselves. Pappie taught me that our animals deserve our protection, too. Foxy will help." A tremor went up her backbone.

"Egad. Too close," Annika whispered to Foxy. Another jeep filled with armed Japanese cruised down the main road, the lights becoming dim. Sweat rolled off her brow. They'd gotten close enough for her to see the Dutch jeep they'd stolen. Phillip had taught her to drive in one just like it when he'd been stationed in Batavia. She buried the thought. This was not the time to dwell on the past. Her heart still thumped from the exertion of pumping the bike's pedals to escape. She'd barely had time to veer off the paved road to hide behind a tree. "We're almost at our stable. Dr. Subroto said the Japanese want horses to patrol the rice paddies. They're not going to confiscate ours for that awful job."

Foxy sat in the bicycle basket, his head turned to face her.

She smoothed his floppy ear and unzipped her black jacket. After leaving Mansion Annika, twice

she'd avoided enemy soldiers combing the countryside. A waning moon, a few days past full, cast a pale
glow on the empty pastures. She turned around for a
final look to the left and then right. No one else travelled the road at the end of the lane. For now. Annika
cycled the last fifty feet and parked her bike against
the barn, then lifted Foxy out and pulled her flashlight from her rucksack.

Maggy's nicker sounded from the rear stall,
followed by Penny's call. Thank the Lord the soldiers
hadn't found their horses. The Japanese commander
had kicked sick patients out of the hospital. Annika
clenched her jaw. No way she'd let his army mistreat
their animals, or worse.

The unfamiliar stench of manure hit her nose.
Henri kept the stalls spotless, but Budi must've
collected Henri this morning, on their way out of
town to escape the Japanese soldiers. Their staff's
safety was another blessing. "Hello, ponies." She
entered the stable. "I bet you're all hungry for
dinner," she whispered, then put a couple scoops of
grain into each bucket hanging inside their stalls.
She aimed the flashlight beam on the ground.

Newt-newt climbed from his box and stretched.
He ambled toward her, tilted his head from side to
side and chattered. "I know, we don't typically ride at
night. I'll need to tack the horses. If the Japanese
question Dr. Subroto, I want it to appear that he's
their owner. Being the best veterinarian in town, and

proud of his Indonesian heritage, they ought to treat him well."

Foxy circled her legs, anxious to go on a night walk. "No barking tonight, okay?" She bent to stroke his longer chin hair and held his face. "Stay quiet. Don't let me regret bringing you along." It seemed crazy to talk to a monkey and a dog, but in this world of gun-toting soldiers around every corner it comforted her somehow. She stood up and frowned. How could she move so many horses safely?

Lunge lines and lead ropes hung on the wall. She'd once seen an American cowboy movie showing a pack train of mules. If she strung the horses together, they could make the four-mile trip to Dr. Subroto's in less than an hour. The night was clear, the horses were all strong, and there weren't any hills or rivers. Once they fell in line, they'd all follow the herd's leader. Confident her plan would work, she pulled out the map, unfolded the paper, and ran her finger along the route. They'd cut through her woods, continue straight, and cross a main road. Once they zigzagged through an open marshy field, they'd land on the veterinarian's doorstep. Her gaze shifted to outside the barn and to the dark forest beyond. The moon hung low in the horizon. "Please guide me," she prayed.

Newt-newt watched her put saddles on each horse, bring the stirrup irons onto the seat of the saddle, and then tie the irons together with twine.

She fit a bridle onto Noir and patted the horse's wide, ebony neck. "You have the strongest opinion, so you get to lead the herd. Penny and Maggy can bring up the rear. The girls are my trusty anchors." She walked to her beloved mare and combed through her long, flaxen mane. A tear welled in her eye. "Next time, I'll ride you. Keep those geldings in line, okay? Knot tying isn't a strength of mine." A low nicker affirmed she'd received the message.

Her fingers trembled as she secured each horse's lead line to the stirrups ahead, checked the saddle girths, and brought Penny to stand beside Maggy. The compact, sweet, pinto pony had taken good care of her when she'd started riding at five, now she'd take care of her old companion. She scratched Penny's favorite spot between her ears, then felt her hind leg. "Still free from heat or inflammation. You're a sturdy little girl. You help Maggy, okay, Penny?" The pony's gentle nudge to her thigh brought tears to her eyes. Loving the horses gave her joy. Tonight, she'd prove her loyalty.

After loading the bridles into Newt-newt's box, and securing it to Maggy's saddle, she mounted Noir and let her foot hang beside the metal stirrup. "Time to go, Newt-newt. It's higher, but you can leap," she encouraged. He stepped back, his monkey canines showing. He shook his head and chattered. "Come on, little buddy. Noir will behave."

Newt-newt grabbed her booted foot, bounced

onto the saddle, and swung to his perch. He reached back and tugged her braid, then laced his fingers into Noir's thick black mane.

If her monkey felt confident, so should she. Annika took a deep breath and released it. She nudged the big gelding's flanks and he walked briskly away from the barn, his long stride taking them quickly to the obscurity of the woods. The night bugs went silent. Halters jangled and hooves clopped. The string of horses followed dutifully. Foxy made a circuit from Noir's flanks to Maggy and back.

Annika smiled. Her little terrier liked herding. The Japanese must allow him in the camp, or she'd refuse to interpret at the hospital. She bit the inside of her cheek. From now on, duty to her mother and the need to see Phillip and her family again had to determine every action she made. But she couldn't give up Foxy, she just couldn't. If things got tough, she'd find a home for him.

The heavy night air pushed at her from all sides. "Must be how a mouse feels with an owl overhead," she whispered. Noir's ears moved back, then forward. He'd alert her to any far-off sounds which weren't horse hooves falling on leaves. She took a deep breath but picked up no heavily perfumed scents of tropical flowers. The nighttime forest issued only the damp, earthy smell of decay. Bugs renewed their repetitious clicks as the parade of horses passed the gnarled tree. Foxy yipped and darted into the brush. Her fingers tightened on the reins. On a normal ride she'd call him back, or whistle, then they'd return to the stable. This ride was anything but normal.

Maggy whickered, probably to tell her they'd missed the turnaround. The bushes shook and Noir side-stepped. Annika's stomach clenched.

Foxy dashed out of the underbrush a few feet ahead of prancing Noir. A leaf clung to the dog's ear. "Easy, boy." Annika patted Noir's neck.

"Longer walk tonight," she whispered to Foxy. In response, he cocked his head and looked back toward the barn. Annika shook her finger at him. "Stay by Maggy. No more barking."

Measured cicada chirps and the occasional squeak of some unknown night bug echoed around her, then grew quiet as the woods thinned to reveal an open area ahead. A paved road crossed the expanse. Annika sat back in the saddle and Noir stopped at the edge of the woods, fifteen feet from the pavement they needed to cross.

Foxy bounded up.

"Sit," Annika hissed, and he planted his butt on the ground behind a shrub.

Newt-newt grabbed a strap of her rucksack and jumped to her shoulder. A few of the trailing horses blew out breath nervously. To the right lay empty railroad tracks. To the left, the gray pavement headed into town.

No! In the distance, dim lights from an oncoming vehicle flashed against the tree line. Her pulse thrummed. The distinctive dull rumble of a jeep engine slashed the silence and grew louder by the second.

Noir pawed the ground. He bunched his shoulder muscles, prepared to run.

The Jeep's headlights lit up an area well past the road edge. Annika squeezed the reins with sweaty hands. "Easy," she whispered to Noir and pushed out her breath, willing tension to leave her body. She pressed her legs into his sides and gently tugged against the bit. "Back, back, back," she crooned. The lunge line that strung them together slackened as he obeyed. Noir's rump bumped into the shoulder of the gray gelding behind them. That horse side-stepped and swung his rear to where his dappled butt stood out like a beacon.

Her pulse pounded. In a few seconds, they'd be caught. "Maggy. Back up, girl." She clicked the signal and held her breath. Nothing. "Maggy, Penny, back up."

Newt-newt shifted on her shoulder and faced the string of horses. He chattered and then let out a high-pitched monkey screech. Noir did a half rear. Annika flinched, tugged the reins, and then let out her breath slowly. "Back up, Noir. It's okay."

Nervous whinnies sounded through the quiet night. The line tightened as the horses receded into the shadows. Noir's nose finally reached the shelter of the tree line. "Good job, Newt-newt," she cooed.

The jeep passed without hesitation and sped toward their stables. Her breath came in gasps. She scratched Newt-newt's head. "Monkey smarts, thank the Lord." Seconds ticked by, echoing in her head. An owl hooted in the woods, the only sound above the noisy bugs.

"Okay ponies. Time to move. You too, Foxy." Noir stepped forward. His hooves clattered on the road, followed by clanks of banging stirrup irons, and nickers of the other horses. Dr. Subroto's instructions had been to crisscross the soft ground to avoid sink holes in the middle of his ten-acre pasture. She moved her pack train out in a diagonal across the field, then reversed and continued forward. In a few minutes, buildings came into view —a low barn-like structure and a square two-story home. A light danced on the ground between the two. "Hallo," came Dr. Subroto's low voice. His light beam grazed her and the horses for an instant.

Annika let out her breath. "Made it," she whispered to Newt-newt.

The veterinarian's flashlight then outlined the shuttered barn and clicked off. The pure tone of a few mole crickets rose from the pasture.

The barn door's hinges squeaked as it swung open. An engine approached. The unmistakable rumble of another jeep.

He signaled her to ride the horses inside. "Quickly, please."

Annika loosened the reins and Noir readily moved into the barn. "You smell fresh hay, and I hear trouble," she murmured. "Foxy, come on inside."

"Glad you made it without incident," the vet whispered.

What would've happened to the horses if Pappie hadn't been so gracious to their veterinarian? "We were lucky. The area is crawling with Japanese soldiers in Dutch jeeps." Annika walked Noir to the far end of the barn aisle. She twisted her head. Penny had cleared the door and Foxy stood next to her. "Good boys." She patted Noir and stroked her monkey's tail. "We survived one close call as we left the woods. Smart little Newt-newt monkey screeched the command for the horses to get their rears in reverse to stay hidden."

Dr. Subroto's low chuckle calmed her. He shut the barn door. "You're all safe. Good monkey."

"I'm hoping he's welcome to stay." She dismounted with Newt-newt clinging to her neck. "He'll be great company for Mina on trail rides. He can forage food from the nearby woods. I don't know what he'd eat in the camp."

"Any of your animals are welcome. Your father treated me with respect." Dr. Subroto stepped to the door, cracked it open, and turned his flashlight on and off twice. "I asked Mina to stay put until I signaled." He kept his light pointed to the floor. Clean straw covered packed dirt.

"Pappie valued your skills and appreciated your love of animals," Annika said. "He learned the best way to care for his horses from you." She set Newt-newt on a bale of hay. Six stalls on each side faced the aisle where her horses stood in a bunched line. A donkey lifted its brown furry head over the half-wall of a nearby stall. "You're going to have some company." She rubbed the warm muzzle.

"The furry little mare stepped on something sharp yesterday while pulling a cart. Her owner worried he couldn't keep an infection out and brought her here. While I keep her hoof clean, she'll enjoy your herd."

The door squeaked open. Foxy yipped and ran to it.

Mina slipped in. "Shh, cute little Foxy." She bent and petted the dog, then held Maggy's lead while Dr. Subroto and Annika pushed Noir, the gray horse, and three other geldings into open stalls.

"Maggy and her friends thought a sleepover sounded fun. What do you think, Mina?" Annika walked back to Maggy.

The little girl giggled and handed Maggy's lead line back to Annika. "Papa already told me I couldn't sleep in the barn." She rested her head against Maggy's belly. Newt-newt tugged Mina's pant-leg and she patted his head, then lowered her hand, and the monkey hopped to her shoulder. "We'll take special care of your friends, Mevrouw Annika. I'll start with your pony." Mina untied Penny's rope and led her into the smallest stall. "Here you go, little lady."

Annika's fingers relaxed on Maggy's lead line. Mina handled the animals showing the same kindness and devotion as her father. They'd be treated well here.

Dr. Subroto handed Annika a tiny paper envelope and a light parcel wrapped in newspaper. "The envelope contains three mild canine sedation pills. One of them will quickly make Foxy drowsy for about two hours. The dried fish is good protein for his diet."

"Foxy loves fish. I don't know what I'd do without my furry buddy." She petted the dog's wiggling butt. "It was scary riding over here, and no one knows what tomorrow will bring."

"Mina's bicycle is ready for your ride home. I'm sorry we can't take you in the car."

"I understand Dr. Subroto. You've done so much already."

"You need to stay on your guard at all times." He glanced at the door, then back to Annika. "There are many Indonesians throughout the islands who consider the Japanese their liberators from the Dutch, especially those who've been educated in Europe. They returned home proudly holding degrees but cannot obtain well-paying jobs utilizing their new skills, like I did."

Annika tucked the dog's pills and dried fish into her pack. She'd need to fear the Indonesian people too? "I know some Dutch treat native islanders differently than our family does. I wasn't aware of the job situation. I hope things can be worked out after the war."

"As do I. Unfortunately, the history goes much deeper than what we see on the surface. I've walked in both worlds and use caution these days so as not to put my family at risk. Ties with the Dutch are frowned upon."

Annika glanced at sweet Mina. The rucksack on her shoulders suddenly felt like it held bricks. She hung her head. Trying to keep the Wolters' horses safe was putting Dr. Subroto's family in danger. "Oh dear. Pappie and Phillip both mentioned unrest. Are you certain having our horses here is okay?" she asked.

"I have good standing in the community, so do not worry. Speaking of that, I've heard you will be able to purchase things from vendors during your internment."

A different fear sunk into her limbs. "Internment, like prisoners? We understood housing." She leaned against Maggy's shoulder.

"A friend saw the Japanese constructing a fence around an entire neighborhood crowded with houses. If I'm correct, I'll send you supplies through a man wearing a red belt. His name is Slamet, and he is trustworthy."

"You are so kind. I wish I could tell Pappie." Her voice cracked.

Mina stepped to her father's side and he smoothed her hair braid. He met Annika's gaze. "Your animals will get loving care from our family and I will do what I can to aid you and your mother. Your father was one of my first Dutch clients. Following his endorsement, I received a substantial increase in business. I'll never forget that."

Annika swallowed the lump in her throat. When he and Pappie worked out this plan, they couldn't have imagined the danger. Tears welled in her eyes. "I know you are putting your family at risk to protect our animals and help us." She moved Maggy into the last stall and rested her face against her soft, warm cheek. The touch of her silky hair and horsey scent brought Annika some peace. "I can't thank you enough for being our guardian angels," she managed.

Why couldn't the world be filled by honorable people such as Dr. Subroto, Phillip, and her family? She clung to Maggy's neck. Would she ever see her mare or Newt-newt again?

CHAPTER 13

MARCH 6, 1942

Brakes grunted to a halt on Boxlaan at the driveway to Mansion Annika.

"You're right, Annika. The Japanese soldiers are here to pick us up!" Mamma cried in a high-pitched tone. "Two got out of the big military truck. We'd better hurry." She dropped the curtain. "How did you know when they'd arrive?"

Through their home's open door, the cargo truck's motor grumbled impatiently and broke the stillness of the morning.

Annika rose from the couch and patted Foxy. His eyes were nearly shut as he lay asleep inside her leather satchel on top of a towel and washcloth. "From my bedroom a few minutes ago, I saw their flag on the truck when it rounded the bend by the

English Club. I immediately gave Foxy the sedation pill. Glad it took them awhile to turn the big truck around." She buckled shut her roomy leather satchel's flap, once used to carry her load of schoolbooks, now decorated by a round patch bearing a red cross. "Thanks for stitching the patch onto my bag. The hospital requires all doctors and nurses to wear them on the sleeve of their shirts. I'm praying it fools the Japanese into thinking I'm carrying a medical bag instead of a dog."

"What if they stop you?" Mamma settled the strap of her largest leather purse onto her narrow shoulder. She'd tied an old water canteen to the strap.

"I slipped the stethoscope Pappie gave me inside. I'll pull it out and act like a nurse. Let's go."

Annika and Mamma lifted their suitcases and walked past the grandfather clock. From atop the tall antique, the trumpeting angels watched them. Annika touched one's foot. "Bless us with a speedy return," she whispered, and stepped onto the veranda. Where were Phillip, Pappie, Emily, and her brothers? When would they all be united to sing and joke again?

Neither of them looked back before Mamma shut the front door behind them. Annika's heart and soul felt empty and lifeless, same as Mansion Annika. So many wonderful memories of life in their beautiful home. What would they find at the internment camp? Had they brought enough money to survive? The thick stash of bills in her shoe sole made her gait wobbly. At the boxy, six-wheeled truck, they shoved their suitcases and bundled bedding onto the chest-high floorboard. Diesel fumes surrounded the tailpipe. She maneuvered the bag holding Foxy from her hip to her back. He didn't let out a peep as Annika grasped a bar on the side, placed her right foot on the rear bumper, and heaved herself aboard.

Mamma looked up, her face taut. Tears wet her eyes. "I'm too short."

A soldier yelled in Japanese and swung his gun.

"One minute, please," Annika said in English. She smiled at him and knelt at the edge of the truck's bed. "Mamma, give me your hand and put your foot on the bumper." She hoisted her mother, and they both sat on the plank floor. Recessed in the shadows under the canvas canopy, mothers clutched children, while old men and women cowered in the corners. None spoke. Their eyes showed the anxiety now coursing through Annika's own veins.

She scanned their faces. No Emily and no familiar faces. "Please let Emily be safe," she prayed quietly while the truck lumbered down the road. Its giant tires scattered stones onto pavement heated by a blistering hot day. The hulking vehicle bounced them like rocks in a wheelbarrow every time the gears shifted.

At the edge of downtown Batavia, the brakes

groaned to a stop. Two soldiers approached the tailgate, motioned for the group to exit, and issued orders in Japanese. Annika helped Mamma down, then jumped out and scanned the surrounding warehouses to get her bearing. "Our housing?" she asked in English.

"Tjideng," he declared, and pointed west. "Walk."

"At least we'll stay in Batavia," Annika said to Mamma. "Phillip and Pappie can find us after the war if we don't locate them first." Sweat beaded on Annika's brow. She searched the area. A building with red shutters caught her eye. "We'll walk along Rijswijkstraat, Mamma. The road's lined in Banyan trees."

Her mother barely nodded, her knuckles white on the handle of the suitcase.

"Come on, it's not so far." Annika unbuckled the flap on her satchel and flipped it back to give Foxy air.

Dutch jeeps occupied by Japanese soldiers sped past the slow-moving throng. Women carried babies and bundles. Children sucked their thumbs and dragged teddy bears. White- haired old people lugged suitcases and stumbled along silently toward an unknown future. They all kept their heads down and ignored horse-drawn sados and vendors which transported Indonesian people and goods along the busy street. Annika pulled Mamma off to the side. "Drink some water, you're red."

Her mother tipped the battered canteen to her lips, drank, and then handed it to Annika. "You, too."

Annika took a swig, replaced the cap, and led Mamma onto Laan Trivelli street, followed by the rest of the people. Eventually they crossed the bridge over Tjideng Canal. She gasped.

A wooden fence surrounded Tjideng Ghetto, topped by barbed wire. If the guards closed the gates, they'd be shut in a prison. Her feet felt stuck in cement. What choice did they have? "We've made it," she said to Mamma. They walked alongside their bedraggled companions from the truck and continued through the open gates. They passed a house on one side marked CAMP COMMANDER in Malay and another house marked CAMP OFFICE on the other.

"Wait!" shouted a guard in Dutch.

Annika stumbled to a stop. Her feet hurt. Sweat poured down Mamma's face. They both drank warm water from the canteen. She studied the area. None of the identical beat-up homes near them had been constructed from durable stucco like Mansion Annika. Instead, they'd been built cheaply of ampasiet, a sugarcane matting plastered over in cement. Baked-clay tiles covered the roofs. Many were missing shutters. None had grass lawns, only dirt.

A Japanese policeman wrote their names on his

clip board. When he finished, he pointed at the oldest people from their group and directed about fifteen of them into a nearby house, intended to hold two or three. If the soldiers crammed so many people into the row upon row of houses, the area could hold several thousand.

A different Japanese man, this one in a military uniform, frowned and signaled the rest of them to follow him. They trudged another half mile through the neighborhood. The place had an eerie, vacant feel. In one yard lay a broken basket like the ones carried by the Indonesian vendors. Is this where the little boy she'd once seen selling shoes had lived? Where were these families now? Who had removed them from their homes – the Dutch or the Japanese? Her mother nudged her to move forward.

Concentrate on the present, Annika chided herself. She glanced at the folks she'd come with. All had the light skin of Europeans. Judging by their fashionable clothing, before the invasion they wouldn't have known Tjideng Ghetto existed either.

Pegged laundry hung from lines in back yards, separated by low cinder block walls. The dirty smell of burning coal hung in the air. Kids shouting in Dutch darted across the street, thumping sticks, and chasing balls. At the end of the block the soldier called out names, directed them into houses, and left. Across the street from their designated house lay a small field and a Djamboe tree in full blossom.

The tiny, fuchsia pink flowers resembled miniature chrysanthemums. Behind the cheerful tree lay the newly erected fence and past it the railroad track. Annika tried to swallow down the dust which had settled in her throat.

"Better get inside." Red-faced Mamma wheezed each breath as she lumbered toward the door of their new dwelling.

"Goede middag," said a round-faced woman standing in the doorway. "I'm the Kapala, in charge of the duties and schedules in this house. We arrived yesterday." Offering a strained smile, she ushered eighteen of them into the modest home built for four. "Second room to the left," she told them. "The Japanese require tenko, or roll call, every day—morning and afternoon. Hustle to the front gate when they call you for it."

Annika and Mamma put their suitcases on two of the dozen or so thin, bare sleeping mats in the bedroom. They chose one which lay next to a wall and under a window and a mat that butted up to it, tucked in the corner. "If we put our pillows where the ends meet, we can whisper to each other at night." Annika tried for a perky tone.

Her mother's bedding bundle and suitcase dropped from her hands. She hugged herself, head down, shoulders slumped. The woman who'd always stood straight as a fencepost to show every fragment of her five-foot frame now stood slouched in depression.

Annika bit her lip. Somehow, she'd resurrect the spunky mother she adored. "Lucky Foxy, he must be in doggy dream land." She placed the satchel holding him onto her bed and gently pulled his head out and petted him. His breathing felt normal to her touch and he wasn't too warm. He opened his eyes for a moment before dozing again. "Maybe the red cross is our lucky token." She clipped on his leash and tied it to her heavy suitcase. "You nap a bit more, pup. We'll be close by." She took her mother's hand. "Come on Mamma, let's explore." They walked the narrow hallway, passed a tiny bathroom, crossed through a postage stamp-sized kitchen, and stepped through the back door to a ten by fifteen-foot courtyard. She'd give anything to see her mom's cheerful smile. But how?

"I thought I smelled coal burning," Annika said. To their left, a table held a couple of flat bricks sitting under a small, metal, coal-fired cook stove. The six-inch cylindrical base widened to a foot at the open top, where a grate sat. Kokkie had used one three times that size to cook their meals. A pang of longing made her throat even dryer. Had the Japanese caught Oudje and the rest of the staff escaping? "One of us needs to learn culinary skills," Annika attempted to bring Mamma out of her melancholy. She lifted the lid of a ceramic jar and shook the grains of white rice. "I think I can boil water."

Mamma kept her head down. "I didn't pack a pot," she stuttered.

"You planned for what you knew." Annika pulled her into a hug. "We'll borrow what we need until we can buy one."

"If people are willing," Mamma mumbled in English. "Having been in society's top-ten percent may put us in jeopardy. They'll hate us if they find out." Her tears wet Annika's blouse.

"I don't think anyone's concerned about social status." Annika held her mother's shaking body tight in the hug, feeling her shoulders gradually relax. "We'll get through this, Mamma. All of it. Our family needs us to be strong." In that moment, responsibility shifted. The doting, confident, encouraging woman of last month now needed the very things she'd always doled out lovingly to her three children. Presently, the role of nurturer fell squarely on Annika. She glanced over her mother's back in the direction of the ocean. Had Claude been a captive on a ship headed to Japan, or placed in a POW camp? Was Rudy one of the fliers who'd been killed? Had Phillip and Pappie stayed safe in Bali? Tomorrow she'd take a break from the hospital and bicycle to the Ministry of Defense. They must know something.

Bicycle on what? Her hands dropped from

Mamma's waist. The Japanese commander insisted on her working daily at the hospital. Walking from Tjideng Ghetto to Tjikini Hospital would take at least an hour each way. "I'm ready for a nap."

"Me too," Mamma said, and trudged into their bedroom.

That afternoon, an official Japanese commander assembled the interned group for roll call, or tenko. Annika stood quietly and listened to snippets of conversation in Dutch, and English - spoken by Brits and Australians.

The big soldier who'd kept her six feet behind his colonel, Medals, during the hospital tour stepped forward and pointed at Annika. He uttered a few sentences in Japanese.

Verdorie. Why'd he come here? Without a choice, she became the camp interpreter. Through her translation from the Tjideng commander's fractured English to Dutch, she explained the rules to the new group of internees. Twice a day they'd be called to stand in rows of ten and bow East toward Japan, their fingers brushing the side seams of their pants or skirts in a precise manner. Or else.

Annika woke at five the following morning. Mamma slept with her face to the wall on the thin mat, curled on her side in fetal position. A doctor might interpret it as her desire to protect herself. Prisoners rated minimal protection, like the two-inch sleeping mat on the cement floor. She rubbed her back, then pulled Mamma's nightgown over her bare calves and slipped out of the bedroom.

Foxy darted to the patio and Annika slipped into the bathroom for a sponge bath. Even turning the spigots to fully open, water only dripped from the bathroom faucet. At least it was wet. She soaped up and dried off. Their Kapala had assigned her and Mamma half of the third shelf in the tiny wall closet. Last night she'd tucked her satchel, a clean blouse, and skirt there. Thankfully, they looked undisturbed. After dressing, she walked into the kitchen. At their designated cupboard, she found the perforated metal tea ball, loaded it full of specially blended black tea they'd brought, and set it in a blue and white Delft teacup—key essentials packed by Mamma. Even dry, the citrusy scent of bergamot oil perfumed the air. Her lips trembled. Kokkie always kept a kettle of hot water at Mansion Annika and a silver tea service ready at the family's beck and call. Days gone by. Foxy returned inside and bumped her shin with his warm nose. "Good boy," Annika whispered. From another room, a clock struck six. "Time to start our day."

A mild breeze blew in the open window and brought the stench of stagnant water and coal fires. On the patio outside, a tea kettle hissed. An elderly woman sat in a chair, dozing in the cooler temps of dawn. Across her tanned face fell wisps of gray hair, the rest braided and pinned to the crown of her head. She wore a yellow blouse and skirt, topped by a white apron. "Come on, Foxy, let's meet one of our roommates and get my tea steeping." The dog trotted behind her.

"Goede morgen," she whispered from a few feet away. "I'm Annika."

The older woman straightened in the chair. "Everyone calls me Trinka, and you resemble one of my nieces." Smile wrinkles nearly hid her faded brown eyes. "I put water on to boil." She gestured to the cook stove. "Help yourself. Next, I'll get rice started. They gave us a big bag yesterday, so we figured on more arrivals. We cook in shifts and this morning is my turn." She patted Foxy on the head. "I miss my dog. They're lovely company."

Annika filled her cup and sat on the thigh-high brick wall opposite Trinka. She glanced over her shoulder. On the other side of the brick barrier sat an unoccupied courtyard with the same type of coal cookstove. The neighbors must be asleep. The comforting, flowery tang of her brewing tea filled the air. "How impolite I am! I'm sorry. Would you like a cup of tea?"

"Not yet, dear. Thank you, though."

"Mamma worried we'd be like fish out of water, but everyone's been kind. I'm training to be a nurse at Tjikini Hospital, so if you need any simple medical assistance, let me know."

"It's always good to have a nurse nearby." Trinka smiled, showing gold fillings in several teeth.

"I need a favor. Will you help keep Foxy out of trouble while I'm working at Tjikini Hospital?"

Trinka nodded. "Such a sweet dog won't be any trouble. I'll gladly watch him. And don't you worry. We'll share our talents and muddle through this." She pushed off the chair to rise and kept one hand on the wooden back. "I'll fix you and your mother rice today."

"That would be appreciated. Mamma tossed and turned last night, and I work all day."

"You'll see, it's not so bad," she assured Annika. "Yesterday morning, a Japanese Policeman posted a notice in Dutch. Tjideng Camp will be managed by an economic administration run partly by local Indonesian authorities. We can cook and leave camp to shop or attend church services."

Annika's eyes flicked to the end of the block. Strands of rusty barbed wire topped the bamboo fence. An eerie sense of foreboding passed through her body. She set her tea on the table and held out her arm. "Your words are encouraging. May I help you inside? My Oma Elodie fought stiffness in the morning."

"Me too. Walk me to the bathroom, please." Trinka placed her tanned, gnarled, bird-like, hand on top of Annika's forearm. "You've got muscles. You'll make a competent and compassionate nurse."

"I hope so." Annika led Trinka to the bathroom, returned to the patio, and drank her steeped tea. She found a slice of thick bread for breakfast in the supplies other people shared. She ate most of it and gave Foxy the crust and a bit of the dried fish she'd left to soak overnight.

Trinka, her feet shuffling on the tile, entered the seven-foot by seven-foot kitchen and pointed to a kettle on the counter. "Fill it halfway with water, please. The outside tap runs the fastest."

Annika finished the chore, walked to the cook stove, and swapped out the tea kettle for the pot of water.

Trinka scooped rice into the pot and popped on a lid. "Foxy," she called, and returned to her chair. "We'll take a nap together as the rice cooks." He hopped on her lap and she gently rubbed his ears. "Don't worry about us." Her cocoa-colored eyes held warmth and assurance. Foxy stretched out on top of Trinka's belly and rolled onto his back. She scratched between his front legs.

"You've won him over. He's a lap dog at heart." Annika said. "I'm writing a note to Mamma. My cousin, Emily, should be in this camp. Maybe she can locate her today." She handed Trinka the slip of paper. "Will you hand this to my mother when she awakes? I'll see you all tonight," Annika said, and kissed the woman on each cheek. "So glad we were assigned to your house."

"We're glad you're here." The woman squeezed her hand.

Annika shouldered her leather satchel containing her stethoscope and stepped into sunshine. She passed sleepy-eyed children of assorted sizes perched on the low block walls or standing in open doorways. Shouldn't they be walking to school? Hopefully, they'd get those details sorted out soon. Her pace hurried as she recalled Medals, the impatient Japanese colonel. Would he excuse her absence yesterday when they'd moved?

Women's voices singing a religious hymn floated from a nearby low brick building. A rusty bike rested against the side wall. Its firm tires held plenty of air. She stepped through the open doorway, hoping for a bit of luck.

A nun in a black and white habit walked toward her and smiled. "May I help you?"

"I'm in training to be a nurse at Tjikini Hospital. Might I borrow the bike outside to ride there?"

"Of course, my child. We're not certain who left it here, so consider it a gift from God."

"I will. Thank you. I'm in the house across from the large Djamboe tree, if you need any simple nursing care, ask for Annika."

"I know the area, Ogan Field. We call the tree a Rose Apple." The nun crossed herself. "Bless you for offering help," she said, and waved from the doorway as Annika cycled onto the dirt road. In a few minutes she'd reached the gray pavement leading through the gates. She pointed to her satchel with the red cross patch and the guard waved her through.

Past the camp, crowded Batavia streets reverberated with the high anxiety of sados dodging jeeps, the pounding feet of Japanese soldiers marching in straight columns, and honking car horns. She turned into Tjikini Hospital's driveway and wheeled the old bike to the service entrance. They'd allowed her to stow her Gazelle bicycle in a corner where they kept outdoor supplies, so she parked the old bike in the same spot.

The normally friendly Indonesian guard she saw each day stood frowning at the back door. "It's a nightmare inside."

"Oh dear. May I please use your phone for a quick call?" Annika asked.

"Of course." He ushered her to his desk, tucked against the back wall of the building.

"I'll make it short." Knowing of Claude and Rudy's safety should help Mamma cope. Her fingers shook while she dialed Uncle Bajetto's office number. A woman answered in Malay and Annika replied in that language. "Good morning, I'm related to General Bajetto. I'm inquiring about my brothers' whereabouts. One's a pilot, Rudy Wolter. The other brother, Claude Wolter, may be with General Bajetto. He recently had an ankle cast removed, so would limp. Twenty, light brown hair, always smiling?"

The woman cleared her throat and whispered her reply. "You never spoke to me." Her tone was urgent, frightened. "We have no reports on missing pilots. As for Dutch men in town, the Japanese removed them from the building on Thursday. I saw one fitting your brother's description hobble to a Japanese truck packed with other men and boys."

"Oh no." Annika pressed her palm into her chest. "Thank you. If you do see the limping one again, please tell him to contact me at Tjikini Hospital."

"Unlikely," she replied, and the connection ended.

Claude would be okay in a camp. Besides his motorcycle accident, he'd enjoyed robust health. They all had. Her hand shook as she replaced the receiver into its cradle. "Thank you," she said to the guard, and walked past a stack of boxes holding jugs of bleach. She pushed open the door into the main hospital and gasped.

In the corridor a throng of Japanese carried stretchers holding black-haired men wearing once white uniforms, now ripped and charred. Exposed skin showed patches of scarlet or burned areas. Painful groans were interspersed with jagged shouts in Japanese. An oily smell permeated the air.

"Annika. I'm thankful you're here." Dr. Modjo, an

older Indonesian surgeon, grabbed her arm. "I'm officially in charge." Stress lines marred his face. "The Allies torpedoed a ship carrying prisoners to Japan. There's twenty or so Japanese casualties so far. One of their doctors speaks English."

Her heart lurched. Claude? She scanned the room for paler skinned people or any victim without black hair. None to be found. "Where are the Dutch survivors?"

"I haven't seen any," Dr. Modjo whispered. "You need to go immediately to the make-shift surgery center in the emergency room. Best I can tell, their angry commander asked for you twice."

She would not give up on Claude. All the Wolters were expert swimmers. Annika scurried down the hallway, scrubbed her hands at the wash station, and entered the surgery area. Medals stood nearby, his feet apart and arms crossed. He met her eyes. "How many die?" he demanded.

"I'll check." The sweet smell of carbolic acid and ether couldn't overpower the metallic odor of blood as she passed rows of make-shift operating tables. The internal injuries being sutured by doctors and nurses should've been done in their well-outfitted surgery room, but the space would only hold two patients. She was seeing dozens of patients here.

Doctors in bloody gowns shouted requests for clamps and scalpels. Nurses scrambled to find things in metal carts and murmured sympathetically to calm the moaning soldiers. On the far side of the room, a doctor pulled a sheet over a man's face, his black hair a sharp contrast against the white bedding. Annika circled back to Medals. "Seventeen are in triage, seven are in surgery, two deceased."

His eyes narrowed. "You keep track of Japanese dead. I want full report later!" he commanded in English and left.

The Indonesian doctors ignored him. Several of their doctors flicked a glance to Annika, then refocused their attempts to save dying men. "What was their commander's last order?" Dr. Modjo asked from behind her. His dark skin had paled when she'd translated and repeated the order. If more men died, would Medals shoot the messenger?

PHOTO SECTION II
POST INVASION PHOTOS

Tjideng front gates. Tjideng Ghetto had been converted to Tjideng POW Camp.

Tenko-Tjideng POWs bowed toward Japan twice a day at a minimum

Early living conditions in Tjideng:
cooking in courtyards.

Laundry day when the camp held about 2,000.

The camp jumped to 5,000 POW's and
then 10,000 by the end of the war.

Tijdeng - overcrowding at its worst!

Living conditions were inhumane by the time
Mamma and I were allowed to leave Tjideng.

CHAPTER 14

Dark, empty streets led to the closed gates of Tjideng Camp. A clock somewhere behind her struck seven. Annika rolled her neck to remove kinks from the eleven-hour shift she'd just finished. She felt as if she'd worked twenty hours straight. And the stress hadn't ended when she'd signed out. Dr. Modjo had stopped her at the back door. His dark eyes had constantly darted from the door to the corridor guarded by Japanese soldiers—the same soldiers who had thrown life at the hospital into hell in the past thirty-six hours since their invasion. The doctor had slipped her what looked like a playing card with a red cross on the front and Japanese characters written on the back. The pass indicated her stature as a mobile nurse. But would it keep her safe from the Japanese soldiers roaming the streets? Some Tjideng guards even made the internees bow at their trucks as they passed the camp. Hairs rose on Annika's arm thinking about how nervous Dr. Modjo had been tonight. During his instructions to her to quickly flash the card if any Japanese soldiers stopped her, he had paced nervously as he talked. And he'd repeated twice to her how she should bow as low as possible. Had he given her a street pass meant only for the Indonesian nurses? She stopped her bike a few feet from the center of Tjideng's closed bamboo gate, at the gap where the sides swung to meet each other in the middle. "Hello?" she called in Malay and tilted her head to look through.

An Indonesian guard stood several yards inside the enclosure. Farther back, a Japanese soldier scowled. The two men, who wore different uniforms, approached.

Verdorie. She'd forgotten the doctor's warning already. She removed the card from her satchel, bowed low, and held it toward them for inspection.

"Enter." The closer guard said in Malay. He swung the bamboo gate enough for her to pedal through. "Gates close at dusk. You work late all the time?"

"Yes, I think," she answered, and mounted her bike. "New doctors. Not certain." She rode through and didn't look back. Light flickered from a few dwellings, but she heard no noise from playing children and no music to compete with the repetitive clicks of night bugs. She pedaled faster, needing the warm welcome from her mother, Trinka, and Foxy to offset their barracks-style living. Her bike rounded the corner.

Mamma stood in the doorway frowning. She spotted Annika, put her hands together in prayer, and raised her eyes to the night sky. "Amen. You are safe." She rushed forward and touched Annika's cheek. "I located Emily. They moved her to a different camp today. We pleaded to allow her to stay here, but the commander produced a list. He made it clear that the Japanese follow orders. I couldn't sway him."

Annika gasped. "How heartless. Poor Emily." She tilted the bike against the house. "First her parents dying, then Quinn leaving for Australia, and Oma Elodie . . ." She choked on the last words and bent to pet Foxy, who'd nosed her ankle. "I hope when she and Quinn reunite, they have a fairytale life together." Imagining Quinn in a princely way took more effort than she could muster. Her mother's sagging posture suggested she felt likewise.

"Maybe it will be a nicer camp," Mamma said.

Not likely, from what Annika had heard at the hospital. They'd put most camps in the jungle. "I'm hungry," she said to change the subject. "Any luck bartering for dinner?"

"Of sorts. I've been told it's wisest to cook a

three-day supply of rice at a time. I managed that chore thanks to Trinka.

"I knew you'd appreciate her."

"A few of the street vendors are allowed through the gates. I scavenged bok choy and chicken wings for tonight. Probably paid too much. I steamed it for you. Not gado-gado, but the time I spent planning meals with Kokkie paid off. Foxy enjoyed bits of Dr. Subroto's dried fish mixed into rice."

"See, all's well. And at some point, we'll see Dr. Subroto's contact, Slamet, who wears a red belt." Annika forced her brightest smile. "I found out Medals, the Japanese commander, will be absent on Thursday afternoons. If you can wait until then, I'll help you negotiate prices with the street vendors."

"Yes. I realized something today." Her mother's voice faded to a whisper. "All I can do is wait."

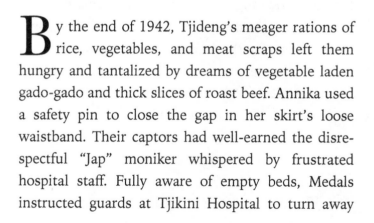

By the end of 1942, Tjideng's meager rations of rice, vegetables, and meat scraps left them hungry and tantalized by dreams of vegetable laden gado-gado and thick slices of roast beef. Annika used a safety pin to close the gap in her skirt's loose waistband. Their captors had well-earned the disrespectful "Jap" moniker whispered by frustrated hospital staff. Fully aware of empty beds, Medals instructed guards at Tjikini Hospital to turn away

Europeans, even if they needed lifesaving surgery. Annika overheard that heartless dictate from an Indo nurse. Still in training, her own assistance to Japanese surgeons grew along with her daily nursing care responsibilities as the enemy soldiers filled the hospital. Each night she returned to Tjideng by bike, barely able to pedal the last few blocks. Translating taxed her brain, and standing for hours on end during surgeries strained her body.

But she'd take the pressure of saving lives over being ordered by the camp's guards to hoe weeds, knit, or worse. Rumors spread of Dutch and Indo boys of only ten being put into slave conditions and young women being forced into prostitution. If Mamma knew, she kept it to herself, but she'd bet they both prayed nightly for sweet Emily's safety. Sitting across from Mamma on the sleeping mat one evening, Annika asked, "Are grade school classes being held later in the day? Each morning I see groups of children milling around."

"You don't educate people you want to rule," her mother replied. "Retired teachers are meeting with students in secret. Elderly sentries whistle an alert if a soldier appears. The children use little pieces of lead from the leaking roofs for pencils."

"Poor little souls." Annika gazed out the window, in the direction of the ocean. "Innocent children aren't responsible and shouldn't pay the price of war."

Mamma barely nodded, her eyes half closed, her body slumped against the wall. A whiff of smoke drifted in the bedroom window. Their roommates were on the patio, sharing a home-made cigarette and voicing complaints.

Annika pulled Foxy onto her lap and scratched his belly. "I can count so many blessings thanks to you and Pappie." She held up her free hand. "A gymnasium education, learning five languages, my wonderful pets, ballet, singing, getting into nursing school, and flying a Piper Cub."

Her mother's eyes flew open. "Frederick let you fly an airplane?"

"His friend let me control it when we were in the air. Very safe." She looked out the window. Endless dark sky rose above the barbed wire fence across the street. "It's an amazing sense of freedom and power. I know why Rudy and Phillip wanted to be pilots."

"I pray each night they survive, wherever they are," Mamma murmured.

"Me too. Using our brains, we will all survive," she whispered in English, a language her mother spoke. "You know, in my absence you'd be helping everyone by translating the Japanese guards' English commands into Dutch."

"No." Mamma shook her head, her coarse hair now grayer than brown since their arrival at Tjideng. "Too much pressure. Each day I do my duties in the garden, I knit, and I pray for your safe return."

This was not the Mamma who'd once taught fashion design at a college, organized a troupe of seamstresses, and rented out rooms to help pay the bills after Pappie's business went kapot. Annika kissed the top of Foxy's head. "Okay. Rumors throughout the hospital suggest that the Japanese are losing their hold to the Allies. Be very careful, Mamma. We're the easiest targets to satisfy their anger."

On a wretchedly humid Thursday afternoon in late November, Annika walked Foxy toward the gate on a mission to purchase a tea kettle without rust holes from Slamet. A handful of Dutch dubbeltjes, the ten-cent coin, jingled in her leather satchel. In the side yard of the last house before the gates, a woman hung threadbare children's clothes on a line. A piece of bloodied cloth covered her head. Annika grimaced and touched the scarf at her throat. Mothers desperate to educate their children would risk a head shaving to barter with a teacher for lessons. If they got caught, the Japanese soldiers didn't care how much they gouged scalps while carrying out their brutal punishment.

Up ahead, the vendors who'd been allowed through the gate were surrounded by customers. A soldier threw a cigarette butt to the ground and a bird swooped low toward it.

Foxy jerked the leash from her hand and barked at the bird, now flying over the head of the inside guard. The man raised his gun, taking aim at her dog.

"Foxy! Stop!" Annika shrieked. The dog spun, and she dove onto him to cover his wiggly body. She stayed crouched and looked over her shoulder. The rifle pointed at Annika.

The distinct racking sound came from a bullet being loaded into the chamber. The soldier closed one eye, his angry face pressed to the gun's butt.

Her body went numb. This was it. Annika bent her head. "Help me, Lord," she prayed.

Shouts in Japanese silenced children, vendors on the street, and shoppers. A different soldier approached her from the side. "You! Interpreter," the same voice said in broken English. "Get rid of dog."

Annika raised her chin. "Thank you." She rose and then immediately struggled to bow while she clutched Foxy to her chest.

"You lucky." The soldier clapped his hands and walked toward the camp's office building. "Go!" he yelled in English. The onlookers scattered. The soldier at the gate had lowered his gun.

Not lucky. Being here was a curse. Annika's legs felt like jelly as she stood upright. A warm hand pressed into her back. "I saw how close you came to being shot," Mamma's voice cracked. "Thank God he recognized you." She put her arm around Annika's shoulders. "I remembered we needed tea and came to find you. What did he say?"

"Foxy's got to leave. I was selfish to bring him." Hot tears streamed onto Annika's face. She set Foxy on the ground and slumped against Mamma. "We have to send him to Dr. Subroto with Slamet."

Mamma took her hand. "I'm so sorry. The soldier with the gun is watching us. We'd better go." She squeezed Annika's fingers and they walked Foxy outside the gate.

"I remember the Christmas I found him as a puppy in a big box under the tree." Annika wiped her eyes and searched the crowd of vendors. "I think I'd just turned eight."

"You'd done so well grooming Penny that Pappie thought you'd handle the responsibility of a dog." They'd reached the street vendors. "And you still do."

"I don't know what to do if Slamet doesn't appear today." Annika stood on tip toe. Indonesian men and boys vied for the best position to sell their wares. Flat, skinny boards lay across their backs, holding ropes attached to deep woven baskets slung at hip level. Each week, the once overflowing mounds of shoes, batik fabric, toys, and housewares shrunk. Now the men carried half-filled baskets. The bigger ones pushed through crowds of ragged-clothed, barefooted children carrying smaller baskets, all of them hoping to earn money to survive.

"There he is," Annika said, and pointed to the smiling man who wore his familiar red belt. He crossed the street bearing his pair of cumbersome baskets.

"Good day," he said, and lifted out the tea kettle they'd requested the previous week. "Found one."

Annika handed him the coins, leaned over, and whispered to him. "Please take my dog to Dr. Subroto. The camp's no longer safe. I'm going to give him a pill, and by the time you leave, he'll be sleepy." She found the slit in the lining of her bag and fished out the envelope which held the last two pills. She petted Foxy and tossed one into his mouth, then rubbed his throat until he swallowed.

The man tilted his head, sadness in his eyes. "You won't be needing the dried fish, then." He tucked a wrapped package under a pile of woven belts. "All will be well. Mina asks about your dog. She's proud to take care of your horses and loves the monkey."

Annika wiped moisture from her eye. "Yes, Mina is wonderful with animals. Please tell Dr. Subroto I'll give you a little money each week to feed him."

"I don't think you need to. He's busy treating the horses the Japs stole. They use them patrolling the rice paddies."

God willing, not their horses. "We all do what we

have to." She looked into Slamet's kind eyes, then removed her scarf and knelt to tie it on Foxy's neck.

Mamma bent to kiss the dog's head and scratch his ears. "Good little Foxy. We love you."

"You'll get to explore the woods again, Foxy." Annika dropped to her knees and buried her fingers into his fur, choking on her words. She rose and faced Slamet. "Please tell Mina that he likes to sleep by my feet. If she puts my scarf on her bed, he should stay put for her, too."

"I will." Slamet handed Mamma the slightly dented-yet-serviceable tea kettle.

Annika lifted the groggy dog and put him in Slamet's basket. Tears wet her face.

Slamet patted Foxy and draped a square of black and white batik over his back. "He will have good care with Dr. Subroto and Mina. I'll head straight to them so as not to keep him in the heat. Look for me next week."

"Thank you." Mamma patted Annika's shoulder and then pulled a scrap of clean cloth from her pocket and dabbed at Annika's cheeks. "Foxy will be fine at Dr. Subroto's."

Annika nodded. She couldn't talk, couldn't bear the thought of losing the little friend who'd accompanied her on so many adventures and listened patiently to her problems.

"I'm sorry for you." Slamet did a quick bow and turned on his heel.

She and Mamma watched him pass by a few vendor's carts on the street. They stood silently until he'd disappeared.

Annika dropped her chin to her chest. "What more can they take from us?"

～

Losing Foxy dimmed any remnants of cheer in their internee household. December of 1943 dawned with no hopes for celebrations or release. Annika tip-toed out of their darkened dwelling, presently home to twenty-five sleeping roommates. She closed the front door and glanced around their block. Newcomers spoke of countless deaths at the camps where they'd been before being sent to Tjideng. Could anywhere else be worse? Her mother had confessed last night that every day she saw sheet-covered bodies being carried out of homes— yesterday two from the house next door. Annika paused on the front stoop. "Please God, keep Phillip and my family safe. Amen," she whispered.

Rain splashed onto the shoulders of her light coat. She dragged her bicycle away from the sidewall. The muddy road in front of their house might as well be a freshly poured mixture of the cement and asphalt which they used to pave the roads. Or at least that's what the Dutch had used when they oversaw Batavia's streets. New potholes appeared daily on her route. The bike's rusty chain clicked and skipped over gears with each circle she struggled to pedal.

Every week, more Japanese – and fewer Indonesians – held posts at the camp's gate. Fewer vendors waited for early camp shoppers to buy produce or goods on Laan Trivelli, the street that led into Tjideng. Rumors must be true of the Japanese cutting off trade to nearby islands. The Dutch system of producing certain crops on designated islands had worked for centuries. Even the arrogant invaders should have seen the benefit of that system. Annika surmised that it was probably not the Japanese way to use someone else's system, successful or not.

Ahead sat an intersection once filled by Indonesian, Indo, European, and Chinese people traveling to work. She slowed the bike. Only Japanese soldiers, whether on bikes or in jeeps, cars, or trucks, filled the crossroad. She avoided them by taking a longer route via smaller roads. A tingle of apprehension kept her alert while she cycled alongside the Tjiliwung River. Fishy, sharp smells hung in the air. Flat boats being poled by Indonesian men jostled for the center. Women in batik sarongs washed laundry in the muddy water, but today no singing or chatter came from them. She turned the corner, then glided onto the hospital's driveway. At the rear double doors, the security man and a

Japanese soldier stood on opposite ends of the cement pad.

"Mevrouw Van Hoven. Glad to see you." Worry lines creased the Indonesian man's forehead. "Their colonel is asking for you."

Verdorie. Her throat went dry. Medals wanted to see her. Every night, she left in its assigned spot the clipboard which showed the number of deceased Japanese soldiers. Had she done something wrong? She followed the soldier into the corridor where Medals stood, his face contorted into a grimace. Hairs rose on her forearm. He looked angry enough to strike her.

"You go now." He thrust a thick envelope at her. "Take this."

Where to? A sinking feeling told her it wasn't good, but it would anger him worse to ask. Annika put the envelope in her satchel and followed another soldier outside to a waiting jeep. He motioned to her to climb into the passenger seat and then he jumped in after her. The driver sped out to the road. He veered around horse-drawn sados and honked to move through an intersection. A traffic policeman shouted at them. The farther they went, the more her fingers tightened on the seat.

Roadblocks sealed off several main streets. The driver checked his watch and careened around corners. What was the hurry? If someone needed quick medical assistance, wouldn't they have sent a doctor? Her stomach tightened as they passed by Mayor Bishop Square, Burgemesster Bisschopplein. On her right stood Nassau Church, where she'd married Phillip. She pressed her hand to her heart and studied her empty ring finger. It seemed like a lifetime ago they'd exchanged vows and rings. Phillip, dear Phillip, so handsome in his blue dress uniform—the uniform of the "enemy" army. She sucked in her breath. Had the Japanese learned that her husband was a lieutenant in the Dutch Army? Was she being hauled off for questioning? Would they believe that she didn't know anything?

The driver backtracked to an expensive neighborhood between Waterlooplein and Koningsplein. Formal gardens led to homes twice the size of Mansion Annika. The jeep turned onto a circular drive leading to an elegant, sprawling, one-story mansion which must have held a dozen bedrooms. Four rifle-wielding Japanese soldiers stood guard at the base of marble steps leading to the house. The jeep parked nearby. The driver spoke to the guards, and the soldier seated behind her hopped out and waved his gun for her to move.

At the top of the steps, ornate carved pillars fronted the entry onto an expansive terrace. Sweet-scented oleander, rare black orchids, and other flowers grew in a landscaped yard fit for a painting. Four double doors led from the wide veranda into the house. "Inside," the driver ordered in English.

Annika followed the two soldiers across polished marble floors. Heavily carved furniture and brass sculptures seemed dwarfed by the size of the twenty-foot-wide corridor.

The two men led her down a hallway and into an office nearly as big as her entire house at Tjideng. Light brown paneling lined the walls except at the far end, where leather-bound books occupied floor to ceiling shelves. In front of that wall and behind a ten-foot-wide mahogany desk sat a younger Japanese man in an officer's dress uniform. He looked up when they entered. Deep-set, thoughtful dark eyes set off the sharp contours of his face. Annika bowed, willing her body not to shake. Her white blouse remained stuck to her back. What could this man, with twice the decorations Medals had on his chest, want of her?

"Good day," he stated quietly in English. "Please be seated," He motioned to a nearby armchair, similar to the one in Pappie's office. "I understand you speak several languages."

She swallowed and walked to his end of the huge room. Did they want her to be a spy in exchange for her life? Lying wouldn't be wise. "Yes, Sir," Annika replied. "English, Malay, French, German, and Dutch."

"You should have received an envelope holding a syringe. I require a shot every day. I need you to bring the medicine here from the hospital and administer it."

Give him a shot? Every day! No. No. No. Not a good idea. From behind her, the soldier cleared his throat. Annika removed the envelope, opened the narrow metal box it held, and studied the unlabeled syringe. "What is your ailment?"

The soldier stepped forward. "Not your business. Obey General Yamamoto," he exclaimed.

If anything happened, she and her mother could both die. "I can't give you a shot, General." She shook her head. "I'm only a trainee nurse."

The general gave a curt, polite command to the soldiers who'd transported her. One left at a trot. Then, he turned and smiled at her, not fiendish or challenging, but friendly. "As you are the English-speaking interpreter, we will return to the hospital and get this straightened out." He put on a hat and ushered them all from the room.

A low-slung, black Mercedes now replaced the jeep. Annika descended the front stairs weak-kneed. She gripped the handrail as if her life balanced on the very point of a syringe needle.

Verdorie! Annika had been assigned to give daily shots to an enemy commander. Or else.

The Japanese general had met Tjikini Hospital's director, Dr. Modjo, and he'd vouched for Annika's ability to administer the medicine. After working four hours at the hospital, she'd been instructed to head to Koningsplein and to Major General Moichiro Yamamoto, who supposedly commanded the entire 16th Japanese Army. Whatever his position, she'd obey. Keeping him happy could keep her and Mamma alive. Days following the same routine turned into weeks.

Of late, he'd requested she bring his noontime meal from the kitchen after his shot. He often asked her to join him for rice and seafood, then kept her to converse during his meal. Despite her dislike of how fishy the food often smelled; she accepted helpings of what he offered. Obtaining a decent meal from him allowed her to offer Mamma her share of food back at camp.

The general's education at an American university gave him a full command of English. He quizzed her on her views of history and art, and expressed his positive perception that Americans accepted all cultures and races. She appreciated his respectful and pleasant nature, but nevertheless heaved a sigh of relief after each session. His continued good health fell squarely on her shoulders. Three months in, the trek to Waterlooplein and the spacious mansion began in its normal fashion after a deluge of rain. Her bike's old, worn tires wobbled through muddy sideroads. The leather satchel which held the syringe banged at her side. The heat made her sweat. Petrol fumes hung in the muggy air. One would have thought that if her patient was such a high and mighty general that they would've sent a jeep for her. Nope. Annika pedaled on.

A few blocks from the general's mansion, a horn blast sent her to the edge of the road. Enemy soldiers stared angrily at her from the jeep. One of them shouted in Japanese. The driver veered the rig in front of her and stopped.

Annika jumped off the bike, bowed low, and held out her identification. The habit of carrying her Mobile Nurse Card in her hand had paid off on two occasions during stops by other patrolling soldiers. This time, louder and angrier Japanese words blasted forth from a man who shouted near her bowed head. Her fingers tightened on the satchel against her hip while one set of boots walked around her, and the man closest to her yelled an order. Something was wrong. Very, very wrong. She froze in the bowed position and began a silent prayer to keep her and Mamma safe.

A rifle barrel whacked her knee from behind, pitching her forward until her kneecaps hit gravel. She thrust her hands out before face-planting. Keeping her head lowered, and bare shins on the rough ground, she pressed her chest to her thighs. Was this enough groveling to stay alive?

"Bow!" The ugly voice shouted. A saber rattled.

Please Lord, help me, she prayed. She dropped her brow to the ground and stretched her shaking arms out ahead, palms down, as if prostrated in prayer.

"Bow!" he shouted again, and the sole of a boot pushed onto the back of her head, driving her forehead into sharp stones. Searing pain hit as he pressed harder and rotated his foot. She bit her lip, knowing any sign of weakness produced more punishment. Would they lash her back? Or worse . . .

The weight lifted from her head. The saber rattled again. A different voice commented in Japanese from farther away, one laughed, and she heard boots stomp off and the engine start. She remained cowered on the ground, shaking.

The jeep roared off.

Shock and relief swept through her body, except at her throbbing, burning forehead. She rose on wobbly legs, shoved her bent nurse's ID card into her satchel, and removed a hankie. After dabbing at her hairline, she checked the white cloth. Splotches of mud and fresh blood soaked the thin material. Should she return to the hospital? No. It was only a flesh wound, and the general needed the medicine. They'd come looking for her if she didn't appear on time. If she slipped into the house, she could clean the cut, administer his shot, and go home. The shot! Did the glass syringe shatter as her bag hit the ground? She dug out the thin metal box and lifted the lid. "Thank the Lord!" she uttered. Nothing cracked.

Pedaling and holding the hankie in place took effort. A block away from the mansion, she stopped and squeezed her soft front tire. A thin slit gaped at the edge of the deflated rubber, now pressed flat on the road. The brute who'd assaulted her must've pierced the tire with his saber as a sick joke. Light-headedness set in as she walked the bicycle onto the circular driveway. "Stupid heat, stupid tire," she mumbled. One of the Japanese soldiers ran out, grabbed her bike, and squinted at her. He motioned for her to remove the cloth.

Another guard stepped forward. "How hurt?" he asked in English.

Shouldering guns or not, they'd been polite each time she'd appeared. Pappie had taught his children never to lie. "Did not bow correctly." She imitated her initial stance, then pointed to the ground. "To a jeep driver." Mud and dried blood covered the scrapes on her shins.

The first guard wheeled her bike away. The English speaking one signaled her to follow him, caught the attention of another soldier, and pointed outside to take his post. He directed her to the kitchen and removed a first aid kit from the shelf. He ran water in a glass and put it on the table. "Sit, drink," he instructed, then pulled a cloth from the drawer and ran water in the sink.

Annika sank onto a stool, took several gulps of water, and removed the blood-stained hankie. The wet cloth he handed her felt warm against her tender skin. She swabbed at the cut.

The guard stepped out and returned carrying an oval mirror on a stand. He set it in front of her. "Bad soldiers do this. General you help is good man."

She nodded and found tweezers in the first aid kit, then adjusted the mirror. Mud splattered her flushed cheeks. Blood dotted her temple. From under a two-inch section of raggedly torn skin at her hairline she extracted embedded bits of gravel. No way could she get it all with the tools she had, but a couple of fragments wouldn't kill her. She removed a thimble full of grit and doused the gap using witch hazel astringent. "Ouch." Not as bad as the sting from a paper wasp, but it hurt.

The guard grimaced, then straightened when a Japanese cook in a white uniform entered the kitchen. The two men spoke briefly before the cook pulled a platter of crispy coated fish fillets from the oven, scooped rice to sit beside it, and set two bowls on a tray alongside four chopsticks.

Both men stared at the Band-Aid tin she'd removed from the medicine kit. She cut a butterfly shape from the middle of one strip, removed the thin crinoline covering the adhesive, pinched her ragged skin together, and applied the bandage. She did two more. If the trick she'd recently learned with the new product worked, she might prevent an ugly scar. Dr. Modjo could suture her later if stitches were necessary. She pulled her hair over her handiwork and reached for the general's lunch tray.

The guard shook his head. "I carry today."

"Thank you." Every inch of her felt numb. Annika trailed behind him to the office.

The general looked up from writing and spoke to the guard in Japanese. The soldier replied, his voice angry.

"Are you okay? Should we take you to the hospital?" the general asked her.

Relief shot through her at his genuine concern. "I'll be fine."

"I abhor the treatment you endured," he stated, his eyebrows pulled down in anger. "Can you identify the men responsible?"

Annika shook her head. "No, I never saw their faces."

"I'll provide a letter so no soldier will hurt you again." He wrote on a piece of stationery, then used an etched seal and red ink to stamp it.

Annika took the paper he offered, put it in her satchel, and administered his shot. "Thank you." She bowed to leave.

"Not today. You need food and a rest." He drew out her stay by sending for a fresh pot of tea served alongside manju, a steamed bun filled with sweet red bean paste. By the end of the meal, she felt exhausted, but from what the general had told her about his culture, politeness was mandated. She glanced around, fearful she'd be too tired to get to Tjideng if she didn't leave soon. The need to sterilize the syringe got her excused.

The corridor leading to the veranda outside seemed to stretch a mile. The bike needed to be walked to town to get the tire repaired. Her foot caught on a carpet and she stumbled. "Buck up and think," Annika mumbled under her breath. Where's a bicycle shop? She leaned against a six-foot-tall carved lion sculpture. No shop came to mind. She shouldered open the double doors and then trudged down the steps. A new black bicycle sat parked below. She looked at the guards.

The man who'd shown her the medical kit smiled. "Yours broke."

"Domo arigato gozaimasu." She had learned a few Japanese phrases. This one – "Thanks very much" – came in particularly handy.

He nodded and pointed to the wing holding the general's office.

She waved goodbye to the guards and pedaled back toward the hospital on the smooth-riding bicycle, similar to the one she'd left at Mansion Annika. One problem was now solved, but another bothered her. Word circulated in camp about an incoming commander who'd caused horrible suffering to interned prisoners at previous locations. Could one

Japanese general protect her and Mamma throughout the endless war?

A group of occupying soldiers marching in a long row, ten men wide, blocked her way as she passed the Sociëteit Concordia Building in Waterlooplein. She tucked the new bike close to a row of shrubs and waited. The white marble pillars at the entrance shone in the afternoon sun. Memories flooded her mind of walking into her first military ball between those pillars on Phillip's arm, wearing her beautiful diaphanous dress, and proud of Oma Elodie's jewelry. A smile came to her lips while she recalled the romantic prelude to love they'd shared while dancing. An ache began in the back of her throat at the thought of losing him.

"You! Girl!" The command, bellowed in accented English, startled her back to reality. She'd let her guard down.

The leader's finger pointed at her. He signaled for her to approach with a flick of his hand.

Annika produced the letter from General Yamamoto and her Red Cross card, bowed in front of him, and waited to be struck.

CHAPTER 15

JANUARY 1944

Angry soldiers who ordered nerve-wracking stops on the streets continued to plague Annika, but they never harmed her again. She watched the latest jeep speed off, hopped back on her bike, and pedaled. After eighteen months of their occupation, she ought to be used to the ugly routine. She wasn't. Cold sweats broke out each time she bowed and handed over the general's letter. Whatever he'd penned a few months back deterred the Japanese soldiers. For now.

Medals had discontinued nursing classes at Tjikini Hospital. They'd carted away textbooks in Dutch and converted the classroom to an office for the Japanese doctors. Worse, a discreet but definite barrier rose between any Indo doctors and nurses and the Indonesian staff. Annika's nightly prayers included the Dutch and European doctors who'd taught her at the onset of her training, as those elderly men were now POWs. Would the same fate befall the Indo doctors? She prayed it wouldn't.

Her routine of administering the general's daily shot continued. Afterward, she'd leave his mansion on Koningsplein and bicycle back to camp. There, she'd check on Mamma and head to the make-shift hospital, or infirmary, for Tjideng patients. Nurses were scarce and beds were crammed side by side, which barely allowed room for elderly Dutch doctors to treat the hundreds of women, children, and old men still being trucked into their camp each day. As the foodstuffs continually dwindled, more and more of the four-thousand-plus hungry souls currently crowded into Tjideng filled the available beds. They suffered from malnutrition, malaria, dysentery, and other neglect-related ailments.

Annika arrived at the camp hospital one stormy February afternoon and proceeded to listen to lungs and hearts using the stethoscope from Pappie. Rain blew through the slatted windows.

"Mevrouw Van Hoven," called one of the oldest men from his hospital cot. He slipped her a carved wooden ring. "I make these to pass the time," he whispered. "Not worth anything, but you've spoken lovingly of your husband and I thought you'd appreciate wearing one. Yours has an imaginary sapphire on the top." He lay back on the pillow. "I told my wife about the promise between you and your husband. She thought it was a very romantic story. We've been married fifty-three years."

Annika clutched the ring to her heart. Lord willing, she'd see Phillip again. "How blessed you both are." She slid his gift onto her ring finger and brushed her thumb over the polished wood. He'd carved a burled knot into a faceted stone. "It's beautiful. I pray each night to see Phillip again. Thank you for your special gift." She leaned over and kissed his weathered cheek. "If you need me after you're released, you'll find me at the house across from Ogan Field."

His face crinkled as he gave her a warm smile. "I'll be fine, thanks to your care."

Her next task was to assist a weary-eyed Dutch doctor who had gnarled, shaking hands. Together they completed an appendectomy. He instructed her to make sutures when he didn't trust his own skill. Walking home after the grueling session, she saw a group of women huddled around a table beside a house. A young girl stood as lookout. Annika slowed her pace.

"I learned of goena-goena from a baboe who worked as an upstairs maid," one boasted in Dutch. "I don't think its bad witchcraft." She handed the woman opposite her a ten-inch piece of twine. "Wrap the ends of this string around your pointer fingers, stretch it tight, hold it over the wooden stick, and close your eyes. The way it sways will tell if your husband still lives or not."

Annika shook her head. Desperate times meant desperation—silly and harmless unless it bred hysteria. She rubbed her wooden ring. She'd know if she'd lost Phillip. The past Friday marked their two-year wedding anniversary and she'd felt his presence in her heart stronger than ever. Or was it wishful thinking? A rain squall pelted her as she rounded the last corner.

Mamma stood in the doorway and raised her face to the dark sky. "Praise be to God. You're still safe." She patted Annika's cheek. "Long day. You must be tired. Need a cup of tea and a dry towel?"

"Sounds lovely." They walked to the kitchen and she sat on a rickety chair. Mamma handed her a thin towel, then pulled a wet tea ball from her cup and placed it into a clean one, determined to get a third or fourth brew from the spent leaves.

Annika removed her jacket and blotted rain from her hair. At least the tea water would be warm. No money remained in her shoe soles and only two pieces of jewelry still lay hidden in the toes of her ballet shoes. She blew on the barely-flavored hot water. "I translate frequently between the Japanese doctors and Dr. Modjo. He'll sell me typhoid vaccines for a small fee. If I added a small charge to each shot, we'd be able to buy tea."

Mamma's lips twisted and relaxed while she considered the idea.

"We wouldn't charge anyone who's destitute," Annika added. "I've seen a few who must've squirreled away money."

"Of course we'd charge accordingly." Mamma's old smile appeared for a fleeting moment. "Pappie always said you were of strong character, Annika. He took pride in how you made the best of situations when challenges arose. The shots are a perfect example." She leaned against the counter. "I don't see a moral dilemma to charge the wealthy ones in camp an extra kwartje or two. Twenty-five or fifty cents won't break them. Tomorrow, I will subtly spread the word and compile a list."

"If any of them need simple nursing help, I'll make time in the evening. I trust you to determine their financial situations. You've always been good at sizing up people, for clothing and for character." Annika sipped her watery water. It bore only the faintest hint of tea. Things couldn't get any worse.

∽

"They're sending me back to Japan in early April," the general told Annika a month later.

Her heart sank. She'd soon lose her only Japanese ally. "Thank you for alerting me, General. I bet you'll be glad to return home." She administered his shot and waited for him to invite her to lunch.

His mouth turned down. "I've done my best during the occupation. Apparently, I'm needed elsewhere." He looked out the window. "There's worse news for you. Tjideng Camp will soon be run by untrained, unvetted officers." When he turned, concern marred his face. "One is particularly known to be cruel and merciless, especially during a full moon if the reports are accurate." He put his hand on a stack of letters sitting on his polished desk. His fingers gripped the top sheet and pulled the paper into a tight ball. "However, I just learned that Indos are allowed to leave Tjideng. That mandate should've gotten to me sooner. You are not as pale as the others. Can you prove any Indonesian blood in your heritage?"

Annika blinked. Did several generations back count? Her empty stomach churned. She'd live in the jungle to escape the unjustified, regular beatings by the Japanese guards. With Mamma's bad heart, she'd been taking the abuse for the both of them. Leaving the horrible captors couldn't happen soon enough. "Yes. A direct male relative of Mamma married an Indonesian woman. Why?"

His hands relaxed. "Get paperwork showing your Indonesian ancestry. Have it sent to me and I'll verify the record. Holding such proof, you are free to leave the prison camp. Time is of the essence. Do you have a place to live?"

They'd live anywhere besides the camp. "We do. Thank you. I will visit the Civil Registry today and put in a request."

"Have it sent to this address." He wrote on a slip of paper and handed it to her.

"Thank you. I'll see you tomorrow," Annika said, and walked to the door.

"Good luck on your task," he called.

A canal full of luck might get her out of Tjideng. What about Phillip, Pappie, her brothers, and Emily? Who'd help them? "Mamma and I appreciate your help," she said, then departed and pedaled her bike through town. She parked it against a statue on the grounds of the government building. At the entry stood a Japanese guard, who scanned the "leave her alone" letter from the general and then stepped aside for her to enter.

Behind a counter stood an Indonesian soldier. A huge map of Java covered the wall behind him. She stepped closer and spotted Tjideng Ghetto written in Malayan. Other camp names dotted the map in red ink. Maybe she could learn the whereabouts of Phillip and her family. Annika spoke in Malay. "Good day. Is there a way to verify which POW camp my family members are in? My female cousin was transferred from Tjideng and my husband, father, and brothers are spread out."

"No," he snapped. The disdain in his scowl resembled that of Medals. "The Japanese maintain that information. We handle only our records."

But what of Dutch births and deaths? Lineage had always been scrupulously recorded. Had they burned those? "I see," she stammered. "I'm of Indonesian descent and I'd like a copy of my ancestry." She'd purposely left out her reason for needing it. "Is this the correct office to fulfill that request?"

His dark eyes studied her, as if determining whether or not to assist her. His glance stopped on her satchel bearing the red cross. "Yes, this is the correct office." He rummaged through a file drawer below the counter and then handed her a form. Name as many ancestors as you can."

She filled in the blanks and returned the paper to him. His thick, black eyebrows raised. He tapped on the general's name, which she had listed as the person who was to receive the documents she was requesting. "It will still take time," he said.

Waiting took patience, and day by day hers thinned to the zigzag threads of a spider's web.

~

LATE MARCH 1944

A monsoon flooded the streets of Tjideng with inches of water. The camp reeked from swelling cesspools of filth. Sick and starved residents took up every space at the ill-equipped Tjideng hospital. Annika knew that they lost as many patients as they saved. The sweet, elderly man who'd carved the ring had been discharged, though, and his recovery provided her with a glimmer of hope.

At the beginning of April, the Japanese Imperial Army took over all aspects of Tjideng and the General's warning came true. The camp's incoming commandant, Lieutenant Kenichi Sonei, took charge of the still-growing numbers of internees, now at more than five thousand. During a tedious process, they assigned each interned person an official prisoner-of-war, or POW number.

After processing, the prisoners were ordered to line up in rows and bow during Sonei's first tenko. The soldier who'd saved Foxy spotted Annika in the fourth row and motioned her to come forward. He fidgeted with his rifle while he introduced her to the cold-eyed new commander. He'd called Annika the "English-speaking Dutch girl they used as an interpreter." At least that's what she thought he'd said from the Japanese words she'd learned.

Hot afternoon sun beat down on the group. Annika waited for the sour-mouthed commander to refuse her help, and prayed he would, as every instinct told her to run for her life. Instead, he grunted and turned his back to her. A pair of guards yelled and waved their guns. The crowd went silent.

A different guard nudged her and tipped his chin in Sonei's direction. "You. Listen. Repeat to Dutch." She cleared her brain, intent on not making a mistake.

Sonei's speech began in broken English. He referred to all POWs as "Guests of the Emperor." Annika prayed no one snickered at the comment. A regiment of Japanese troops surrounded the perimeter of the group that overflowed into the side streets. The guards' dark eyes flicked between skinny and disheveled women, elderly men, and children. Holding rifles and swords, they poised their bodies to pounce on misbehavior. Thank the Lord, no one uttered a sound.

Next, Sonei decreed that vendors were not allowed to sell their wares to POWs. A central kitchen would be staffed by POW help for all food prep. No more home cooking. A mumble of protest rose from the group. Soldiers grunted and lifted their guns. The bayonets fastened to the barrels gleamed in the sun.

The crowd went still. Sonei puffed out his chest and then banished daily passes out of camp, except for anyone approved to work by the Japanese army. She translated and watched faces fall in the crowd. When asked about her bicycle trips by fellow prisoners, Mamma and Annika had only said she still worked at Tjikini Hospital. They'd kept quiet about the Japanese general's shot. But still, the other prisoners might consider her now to be a traitor. Survival for her and Mamma pushed the thought into a dark corner.

Sonei yelled his last decree. Anyone who broke a rule got severe punishment or death.

Gasps broke the silence.

He nodded to the soldiers, who then surrounded the residents. They shouldered their rifles, broke the prisoners into groups, and shooed them back to their lodging. Sonei marched toward the Camp Commander's building.

"He's dead serious," Mamma said in English. They'd walked past the nuns' quarters. No singing eased the tense mood of the shuffling POWs. "I assume you'll still be able to access emergency supplies from the outside."

"As long as I'm needed for translation, but I'll have to be careful." Bone weary, Annika entered the small house, currently holding thirty-one. The previous night's rainfall continued to splatter onto the floor from leaks in the roof. The outside faucet only dripped water even with the tap fully open. The toilet flushed maybe a quarter of the time. No one repaired anything.

A loud rap sounded from the open door. Two soldiers entered, "All money, jewelry. Now!"

Mamma rummaged through the pocket on her apron and extracted a few dubbeltjes coins. "That's it." She handed the twenty or thirty cents over and leaned against a kitchen counter, her head lowered.

Annika stood beside her mother until the rest of the occupants turned over their valuables. It took an hour before the street emptied of soldiers. "We'll be thrashed if we're caught using anything from our footwear stash," she whispered.

Mamma clasped Annika's hands. "Wie boter op zijn hoofd heeft, moet uit de zon blijven." *He who has butter on his head, should stay out of the sun.* The first gleam of defiance since they'd entered Tjideng shown in her mother's eyes. "I don't plan to get caught."

"Nor do I." Annika pictured a thick slice of Kokkie's bread spread with homemade butter. Her stomach growled. "It's my turn to retrieve the food for the household. Let's hope it's more than the usual stingy amount of tapioca gruel and stale bread." Something told her they'd be lucky to have any food at all if they remained as prisoners in Tjideng Ghetto.

Food rations shrank to a small portion of tapioca gruel per day. The ever-growing wave of unease increased after the Japanese moved in the fences to diminish the housing area, now a thousand yards by a thousand yards for nearly ten thousand internees.

A second fence rose a few yards outside of the first. They'd affixed platted bamboo matting, or gedek, to the first fence, making it impossible to see through or have any contact with the outside world. It still didn't stop the smallest children from sliding under the fences to trade clothes for fresh fruit or whatever they could barter.

The Japanese soldiers forced the young boys to work long shifts in the fields and required the same of the elderly men. Women continued to tend gardens, sewed clothes, unloaded supplies, and knitted socks for soldiers. Desperate mothers instructed younger children to collect snails and catch geckos. They'd boil them at an overflow steam vent at the back of the cook house and eat them for protein. Each household got a few lumps of coal to make tea. If a soldier smelled food cooking or found food in the house, they'd punish the entire household.

Annika woke one morning from a restless night. Her thoughts had centered on how lucky they'd been to escape punishment the prior day. First light spilled through broken shutters in the bedroom window. She tiptoed over the cement floor of the hallway and glanced at the cramped space in front of the kitchen sink. The newest woman resident slept in a tightly curled ball. She'd endangered all of them when she'd dared to trade a pencil stub for a banana and been caught. Thankfully she had been two houses away when she was apprehended, so the soldiers hadn't traced her back to their dwelling. Dried blood from her shaved scalp created dark splotches on her head scarf. The subsequent beating cost her one broken tooth. Mamma had watched it fly from her mouth after tenko, when the thrashings and head shaving took place in front of the entire camp. Merciless commander Sonei took every opportunity to set an example and extract any remaining shreds of dignity from his prisoners.

The woman could've been her or Mamma, they all took whatever food they could. Annika quelled the urge to run out the front door, scramble under the two camp fences, dash across the railroad tracks, and run to the warm ocean. She'd never leave Mamma, but she desperately wanted to escape. Rain drizzled on her shoulders as she stepped outside and pulled her now worn-out jacket from her satchel. It was still enough to keep her dry on the ride to Tjikini Hospital. Today she'd retrieve the last shot to administer to the general.

Her stomach rumbled. Last night, she'd greedily eaten half the thin crust of bread given to her by kitchen worker who, luckily, wanted a vaccine. Mamma had gobbled the other half.

Hunger inched into their lives in slow increments, as opposed to the continuous lack of medicine they endured since the first day they'd established the camp infirmary. Treatable diseases routinely turned deadly. First the elderly, then all ages arrived in debilitated condition. Annika glanced at garbage piled in the street. Sanitation and vaccines could have prevented most of the ailments that she tried to treat.

Looking back did no good.

As her hand touched the bicycle, thumps and pings broke the stillness and signaled the hustle of morning chores. Soon she'd see children foraging for anything edible that walked, slithered, or crawled to augment their meager rations. What had their lives come to?

Annika couldn't recall pedaling to Tjikini Hospital or on to Koningsplein. She muttered a greeting to the guards at the general's mansion and plodded along the hall to his office. Open boxes sat on the floor and on the chairs. He turned from the file cabinet in front of the window. "Thank you for being my nurse." He bowed to her. "I leave tonight." Compassion shone in his handsome face. He handed her a thick manilla envelope. "I drove to the records office and demanded they research your heritage. You can leave Tjideng Camp any time."

She bowed low, then stood and met his dark eyes. "Thank you for your help. I will never forget your kindness. Given the chance, I will tell of your respectful and refined manner."

"Thank you for delivering my shot every day. I will speak of your compassion and intelligence." He showed his even, white teeth in a quick smile. "I hope there are honorable Japanese soldiers in your future, Mevrouw Van Hoven." His face became serious. "You are an amazing young woman, and your husband and family should be proud of you. May this war end soon, and may you be reunited with your loved ones. Until then, prepare for the worst. The Allies occupy Hollandia in Papua and Morotai, Halmahera. Batavia is a stronghold and a key port. I'm afraid your city will be bombed soon."

Bombed! Annika's body shuddered. "I appreciate the warning. We will plan accordingly. Safe travels to you, General." She administered the final dose of medicine, which she assumed was insulin, and left the mansion. Angst at his final words overshadowed the reprieve from the responsibility of his daily shot. The horror of Nazi bombing raids on European cities flashed in her brain from the old newsreels she'd seen at the movies. She shook her head of the thoughts, just in time to avoid a double-parked truck.

Koningsplein buzzed with frenzied activity by soldiers and a few Indonesians.

She pedaled directly to camp and maneuvered to avoid jeeps and sados filled with soldiers. Outside Tjideng's gates a woman sat strapped to a chair, her head dropped to her chest. Annika greeted her but got no response. She pedaled on and dodged children and mud pools smelling of human waste. No one sang anymore in the nuns' building. She finally parked the bike at their house and dashed inside. "Mamma?"

"Coming," her mother's strained voice replied. She rose from beside six other women, all knitting brownish-green socks while seated on the wall surrounding the patio. "You're early. Everything okay?"

"Why is the woman roped in the chair outside the gate?" Annika asked.

Mamma dropped one of her bamboo knitting needles. "They caught her this morning carrying an egg. She'll remain outside for forty-eight hours. No food, no water, no breaks."

Bile rose in Annika's throat. "No wonder she didn't answer me."

A train rattled by on the tracks outside the double fences. It belched the black smoke that settled on laundry hung to dry. Annika pulled Mamma across the street to where they might have privacy. "We can leave." She patted her satchel. "The general obtained the necessary documentation to prove our Indonesian ancestry. Food's disappearing and punishments are more violent. I think we should get out of here immediately."

Mamma hugged her. Little remained of her formerly ample bosom. "I'd about given up on seeing the outside world ever again," she said. "That general you met is one of the few Japanese I'll praise. I wondered how Trinka got to leave."

"Trinka's gone?"

"Yes. Left with barely a goodbye. Her niece appeared at noon to collect her. In ten minutes, I can be ready. We'll go to Mansion Annika first."

"Okay. I'll grab our clothes from the bedroom." She ran her palm down her best skirt, soft from laundering and splotched by faded stains.

"I'll only take a few belongings," Mamma said. "No telling what we'll find at home. We may end up at Pappie's stable." She tugged Annika's sleeve. "Your Oma Elodie criticized Frederick and I for not being more authoritarian in dealings with our servants. I am glad we ignored her."

Annika squeezed her mother's hand. "I'm glad, too. Hopefully, the staff has returned home and weathered the onslaught of soldiers and limited food." She'd heard of Indonesian servants brutalized by the invaders because of their association with the Dutch. She'd not passed the rumor to Mamma. "Please God," she prayed under her breath while she packed their meager items from the kitchen, "let Oudje and the others be alive and welcoming."

CHAPTER 16

EARLY APRIL 1944

Their sado's skinny horse clopped at a slow pace. Annika's fingers tightened on the buggy's frame. What would they find at home after being interned for over three years? She rose off the plank seat and craned her neck to see around The English Club and onto Boxlaan. The red tile roof and white stucco of Mansion Annika's upper story stood out against a bright blue sky. She placed a hand over her eye to block the sun. Laundry flapped in the breeze behind the garage. "The house survived, and someone hung out clothes to dry in the usual spot." Annika turned sideways and hugged her mother. "That's a good sign."

"Many of the Indonesians treated the invading

Japanese as saviors." Mamma wrung her hands. "I didn't relay all the stories I heard at Tjideng. We may be turned away."

"I know. Pappie's insistence we treat the servants fairly may be our saving grace," she contended. "If strangers took over Mansion Annika, I'll find Phillip's aunt. Tante Suze's house number is Rudy's birth month and day."

Mamma patted her knee. "You are my rock. Anytime the seas are rough, I can hold fast to you, knowing we'll weather the storm."

Unfortunately, the rock sat in the middle of Annika's belly—a cold, hard ball of fright. Her brothers had played indoor soccer several times and made the servants nervous. No doubt they'd done other disrespectful things. Would they find a place to stay if they weren't welcome here? She'd seen Tante Suze once in all the time since her wedding. At the time, Suze had brought her dark-skinned Indo mother-in-law to the hospital and they'd barely whispered greetings to one another. Annika had understood Suze's concern. All the Indonesian and Indo people she knew feared they'd be beaten or thrown into a POW camp if the Japanese soldiers saw them with Europeans. Hatred of the Dutch grew as Allied forces fought their way through the Pacific Islands. Talk had recently circulated about Allied ships being not far from Batavia's harbor.

"Turn into number eight, please," Annika instructed the sado driver in Malay. Overgrown grass and unkept shrubs fronted stately Mansion Annika. An opened door led to the empty garage. She finger-combed her hair and readied her Mobile Nurse Card in case Japanese soldiers occupied their home. "We may need to continue our trip. Please wait?" she asked their driver.

"Of course," he said in Malay, and halted the horse opposite the front door.

"Stay put, Mamma." Annika walked up their stairs. She knocked and the front door swung open. No grandfather clock in the entry. The living room and dining room no longer held furniture. The piano remained, but no paintings, end tables, lamps, or rugs. "Hello." Her voice quavered. "Hello. Anyone home?" she called louder.

"Annika?" Oudje trotted from the kitchen. "My sweet girl!" She brushed Annika's cheek. "You survived. My prayers were answered." Oudje pulled her into a soul-warming, tight hug. Annika felt bones where soft flesh should be.

"Oudje, I'm so glad to see you. Let me bring in Mamma. We got released from Tjideng POW Camp. Is it safe to stay here?"

"Of course, of course. I'll tell Kokkie. Everyone's been worried." She pecked Annika on each cheek. "Ahmad and Budi took their families to relatives in the countryside. We returned here shortly after. We haven't seen them for over two years." She wiped her eyes. "Japanese soldiers took all the men, and Kokki's little son, Ardi. We don't know if they're in the army or laborers. We hid Kokki's girls, Ratih and Legi. They've grown since you've seen them."

"I'm sorry about Ardi and the men," Annika said. "About all of this. We prayed for you all and hope the rest of our family is alive in POW camps. I've got to tell Mamma that you're safe." She ran down the front stairs and pulled Mamma from the seat. "The women are fine! It's okay for us to stay." She paid the driver, grabbed their luggage, and returned inside. Everything would be okay at Mansion Annika.

Still, a shiver of doubt hit.

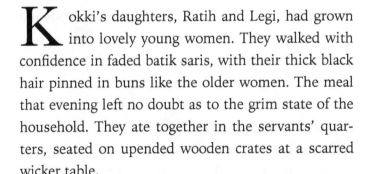

Kokki's daughters, Ratih and Legi, had grown into lovely young women. They walked with confidence in faded batik saris, with their thick black hair pinned in buns like the older women. The meal that evening left no doubt as to the grim state of the household. They ate together in the servants' quarters, seated on upended wooden crates at a scarred wicker table.

For the celebratory meal, each of them received a

dollop of rice the size of two sugar cubes, a table-spoon of vegetables, and a one-inch square of fried tofu. Ratih and Legi dished the portions onto chipped plates and handed them out.

Annika smiled. "Kokkie, thank you for sharing your delicious smelling food. It's the best meal we've eaten since we left here. We have a bit of money for supplies, and I can earn more by nursing."

"Money isn't the issue," Kokkie confided. "Those soldiers are hoarding rice and other staples. They created a shortage by taking our men from the fields at planting time." She patted Mamma's arm. "We're expecting a famine. Your vegetable garden allows us to trade for what's left in town. But we must barter for everything we used to buy."

Mamma nodded. "We've learned to bargain, also. You were wise to tend the garden so well," she praised. "I'm afraid we must dig deeper in the ground, though. Annika learned Batavia may be bombed by Allied airplanes. Tomorrow, we should take turns digging a trench where we can run to take cover." She glanced around the room, then pointed at the hanging pot rack over the small kitchen sink. "If we hear air-raid sirens, a wok or a pan could work as a helmet. I noticed they left several old pans in the main kitchen, too. Pappie read me a passage from a World War I story which mentioned trench warfare and the ineffective cloth or leather headgear issued to soldiers." Mamma rubbed her empty ring finger and brushed a tear from her eye. "These are only my thoughts. If you have a better idea, please say so."

Kokkie shook her head. "No. We all will help. The Japanese soldiers removed everything of value they could cart away. We thought they'd want to live here. Seems they didn't appreciate how far Mansion Annika is from town. We saw them pointing north and scowling."

"Lucky for us." Annika smiled. "Did they leave any beds?"

"No. There's a pile of old mats in the storage room, and I aired them out," Oudje stated proudly. "We've each slept on a sizable stack. I'll divide them and put some into your bedrooms."

Annika glanced around the servants' quarters, seeing for the first time the small bedrooms and sparse communal cooking area the families shared. A lump formed in her throat. Years and years ago, when Mamma and Pappie went out for the evening, she and her brothers had often visited Kokkie back here, in hopes of receiving some delicious home cooked Indonesian food, but Annika had never paid attention to their living conditions, especially as compared to the large and comfortable mansion her own family occupied. "You never moved into the main house?"

"Of course not," Kokkie answered. "It wasn't our

place to take over your home. We prayed you'd return." She touched Mamma's hand. "We had no idea where to look for you. The phone's shut off and the Japanese terrified us when they stole the furnishings."

"You were smart not to come looking for us. The Japanese are brutal captors," Mamma said, and gently patted Oudje's shoulder. "We prayed that you'd all made it to safety in the car."

"Your prayers were answered for a short time." Oudje went to a cabinet drawer and removed a battered envelope. "This came a few months after you left. No mail since then. I knew which of your boys wrote it." She wiped a tear from her wrinkled cheek and handed it to Mamma.

"Rudy's scrawl!" Mamma ripped open the envelope, examined the single sheet, and held it to her chest. "Rudy made it into the RAF. He thought he'd be flying bombers out of England by the time this reached us. Dear Lord, I hope he returned after each trip."

"His dream came true," Annika said. Over a cup of weak hibiscus tea after the meal, they answered questions about Tjideng Camp. Later in the evening, they all rummaged through the old toys, mismatched chairs and other odds and ends which remained in the storage room. Oudje and Kokkie spoke of days with little food and shared the same worries about their own loved ones as she and Mamma had for

Pappie and Phillip and Rudy and Claude and Emily and Uncle Bajetto.

When they'd quit for the night, Mamma stopped Annika in the hallway. "You are welcome to put your sleeping mat in my room," she offered. "The big, empty room will seem strange after sleeping noses to toes at the camp."

"I'd like that. My room is bare. They even stole the painting of Maggy." She pinched the skin of her throat. "I hope our animals are still safe, but it would be dangerous to check."

Mamma cleared her throat. "Dr. Subroto's skills will be needed by the Japanese. I'd bet they're fine."

"I'll keep them in my nightly prayers," Annika pledged. "That's all I can do." In bed that night, she whispered to Mamma. "Should we dig out any of the jars we buried out in the shrubbery?"

"No," her mother murmured. "We'll need every bit we can scrape together when the war ends. Frederick and I started over after the Great Depression. This time it'll be worse. Before we were taken to Tjideng, after you'd already buried the rest in the garden, I found a couple of less valuable brooches on clothing and hid them in the light fixture in my closet. The Swiss army knife Frederick carried was in there too." She muffled a sob. "The invaders never found them. I retrieved them tonight. Get some sleep, Annika. We're home again."

When they woke, women's voices and the sound

of shovels thudding into dirt sounded through the open doors of Mamma's balcony. Annika stepped out into sunshine. Ratih and Legi stood on each side of a wide section of ground at the edge of the property. They'd removed grass in preparation to dig the six-foot trench. "Great job!" Annika called, and leaned on the iron railing. Both young women grinned and waved.

Annika threw on shorts, grabbed a shovel, and joined them within minutes. An hour later, she paused to catch her breath in the heat. The memory surfaced of her first sight of Phillip walking across their lawn, and how he'd stopped and looked up, like he was guessing what someone would see from Mamma's balcony. She glanced at the tall grass on the tennis court next door, and cricket field across the street, where Pappie once played. Would he ever play his favorite sports again? Hopefully somewhere. Annika stuck her foot on the edge of the shovel, pushed it deep into the growing trench, and threw the dirt onto the lawn. The women all did the same for another four hours, taking turns at the back-breaking work. Even Mamma and Oudje insisted on helping.

That night, after a meager dinner, Annika excused herself while Mamma and the other women had weak hibiscus tea. She entered her parents' room and stepped onto the balcony. Tears ran down her cheeks while she brushed embedded dirt from the carved "Mansion Annika" letters in the dusty cement. "Dear Lord," she prayed silently, "show me to carry the present only, with a calm and peaceful mind. And please, oh please, protect all our loved ones from harm."

For the next week or so, Annika rode her bike into town to trade cucumbers and tomatoes for tempeh and eggs. Word spread to Indonesian vendors that in exchange for food, she'd competently set bones and stitch cuts. Most nights she'd return carrying enough to keep the six of them from going to bed hungry.

Her bartering ended on an early morning in late April of 1944.

Air raid sirens pierced the morning quiet with their shrill, high-pitched, overlapping blasts.

"Airplanes! Run!" Kokkie shouted from the first floor.

Annika jumped from her thin mat, ran with Mamma downstairs, and pushed her out the back door. "Head to the trench. I'll grab pans." She rushed into the kitchen and unhooked metal pots and woks.

Kokkie ran in carrying several pots. "Is your mother safe?"

"Yes. Headed outside," Annika answered.

"Good. The girls took Oudje to safety."

They ran to the trench and dropped the pots and pans on the grass. Oudje and Mamma crouched at the bottom, their backs muddy. Annika held Kokkie's hand until she'd descended. Ratih and Legi tossed in the pots and dropped in next. Annika put her feet over the edge and scooted down the wall on her butt. Damp earth stuck to her thin shorts.

"Cover your heads, I hear planes!" Ratih yelled.

They huddled together and waited. Annika's fingers ached from her grip on the metal rim of her wok.

Airplane after airplane buzzed over. Explosions boomed in the distance. Annika flinched at each blast, and prayed for the people of Tjideng Camp and for the hospital staff. She also prayed that the Allies knew they were only scared Batavia residents living across from cricket fields. The echoing blows from landing bombs grew louder and rose to a deafening roar. They'd be hit next.

Dusk cast eerie shadows over the group of women crouched in the pit. Drizzling rain brought rivulets of mud onto Annika's bare feet. She checked her watch. It had been thirty minutes since the last bomb dropped. She leaned her sweaty back into the slick earthen wall. "I think we can go inside. They can't locate targets in the dark."

Kokkie's daughters scrambled out first, leaned over the edge, and held out their hands. They firmly grasped Mamma's wrists, and Annika gently pushed from behind. They repeated the effort for Oudje. "If we're lucky, the walls won't crumble like the stale bread we got in camp," Annika said, trying to lighten the tension. No one had the energy to laugh. By the time she and Kokkie had climbed up to the wet grass, an inky black sky and flickering stars formed a backdrop for the trilling and chirping cacophony of night bugs. An owl hooted from the left. A loud scraping sound came from the right, maybe a stag beetle. They all tromped toward the house.

"Wait." Mamma tugged Annika's sleeve at the steps to the back veranda. The other tired, muddy women kicked off their shoes and headed to the servants' quarters. One of them struck a match and used a candle to light their way.

As the light grew dim, hairs raised on Annika's forearms. Something else bothered Mamma.

"I think its best if we leave Mansion Annika," Mamma stated quietly. "Pedaling into town after today is dangerous for you. The vegetable garden can't support all of us, and worst of all, our presence here may endanger the others."

The thick, muggy, night air pressed into Annika. She slumped onto a step. Another loss. Tears wet her cheeks. "How will they survive?"

"We'll give them half of the jewelry from my bedroom," Mamma said. "We can't let the Japanese find us here and punish them. I know Frederick would agree."

Pappie would agree. Dangerous to ride into town or not, it was the right thing for her to do to protect their servants and find her and Mamma shelter that didn't put anyone else's life in jeopardy, either from a shortage of food or from brutal soldiers. Annika touched her muddy fingers to Mamma's arm. "You're right. Noblesse oblige. I'll bicycle into town at first light tomorrow and find Tante Suze's house. The Japanese will be busy assessing damage." She straightened her posture to look competent, but inside she cringed. Where would they go if Suze had moved? "I'll bet Phillip's aunt can help me find work, too."

Mamma wiped her face using the back of her hand. "While you're gone, I'll get busy. I saw my stash of batik ends and pieces and my old sewing machine in the storage room. If the old Singer still can stitch fabric, I'll sew sarongs for us to wear. We'll let our skin darken more in the sun and speak Malay if we meet anyone."

Annika nodded. They needed to manage one more day, one more week, one more month. Three years ago she never would have thought that hiding her European ancestry might keep them alive.

Would it?

～

The morning they left Oudje and the other women, Annika's already battered heart felt slammed one more time. "We'll see you again," she'd promised, knowing it would take a miracle for them all to get back together.

Oudje handed her a slip of paper. "This is my sister's address in the northern part of Batavia. If we have to leave Mansion Annika, that's where I will go. I am glad Phillip's aunt has a place for you in her home."

Annika nodded and hugged Oudje. "I'll write. We'll keep in touch." She moved her suitcase, along with Mamma's, out to the veranda. Ratih had flagged down a sado as it left the English Club, and the horse clopped onto their driveway. She and Mamma climbed aboard and waved goodbye until they could no longer see their friends. Neither of them spoke on the way to the Tjikini neighborhood. Annika pointed out Tante's tidy home to the driver. Flowers bloomed on either side of the walkway. They set their bags on the cobblestone sidewalk.

"I'm so happy to have you here." Tante Suze, wearing a loose, pale green sarong, awaited them at the bottom step of the porch. She hugged Annika and her mother. "Let me look at you, Johanna." She patted Mamma's thin arm. "We're all skinny and battle weary," she touched her own gray hair, "but we're survivors. Welcome to my home."

Annika retied her hair with a ribbon she'd found at Mansion Annika. They'd all aged ten years in the last three. "We truly appreciate your hospitality."

"Family is a blessing," Tante said to Mamma. "Annika's visit yesterday was a pleasant surprise. My Indo boarders are all interned now. The Japs did a final sweep of our homes about four months ago. I had a Japanese nanny as a child. She taught me her language. The soldiers needed me early on to interpret documents, so they don't bother me now. I prepared a bedroom at the end of the hall for you to share. Leave your things in the entry for now and join me in a cup of tea?"

"Sounds lovely," Mamma's voice once again held the refinement which Annika had missed over the last years.

They moved their dwindling pile of belongings inside. Tante Suze ushered them into a compact living room. A loveseat and two overstuffed chairs upholstered in rose-toned floral fabric fit the space perfectly. Framed family photos and pencil sketches hung on the walls. A wheeled wooden cart held a porcelain tea service delicately painted in tulips.

"Please sit." Tante lifted a tea pot and poured the dark, aromatic brew into three cups.

Annika licked her lips and Mamma did the same. They settled into comfy chairs.

Tante passed the cups to their waiting hands, then eased onto the loveseat. "Knowing Japanese,

I've kept my ears sharp," she began. "I initially avoided internment because my husband's bedridden, darker-skinned mother lived here when the Japanese first invaded. Her infirmity protected us both, because she wasn't able to make the move to the camp and needed me to stay to take care of her. Her Indo husband had been a respected public administrator and he received the tea you're drinking as a gift. I use the little that remains for special occasions. They're both now in God's hands, bless their souls. Any word from your family?"

"Only an outdated letter from Rudy." Mamma lowered her eyes to her lap. "In the second year of captivity, we each got a postcard to send to our husbands. Nothing arrived back from Pappie, Phillip, or Claude before we left. The Lord only knows where our men are."

"Phillip's a survivor. I only met Frederick, Rudy, and Claude once at the wedding. I pray nightly for their safe return." She put her hand to her heart. "Please, if you can, tell me about life in Tjideng Ghetto Camp. I need to hear truth, not rumors."

Mamma took a sip of tea, then placed her cup and saucer on the end table. "Fresh tea. So unbelievably delicious. In the end we reused leaves five or six times when we had them. The Japanese allowed us to make tea, but we couldn't afford to buy or barter for what little was available. Annika picked hibiscus leaves to brew. Even those became scarce. Detention in Tjideng began as a tolerable experience under civil rule. Gradually, the slight overcrowding changed to scarce food and harsh punishments for minor infractions. A monstrous Japanese military commander came to Tjideng just before we left. Horrible Kenichi Sonei arrived the first of April. He beat women to the ground and ordered their heads shaved if they couldn't bow low enough during twice-a-day tenko, or if they didn't place their fingers in the exactly correct spots along the seams of their garments. Other infractions equaled worse punishment." Mamma's fingers clenched the handle of her teacup. She took two sips.

"How awful." Tante Suze's pinched expression reflected her distress.

"Tjideng took more than freedom," Mamma said quietly. "Being in that horrible camp eroded our souls to mere shadows clamoring to survive."

Annika reclined in her chair and settled into the cushions supporting her back. Mamma seldom shared negative thoughts. It might be good for her mother to voice her bad memories. Drinking the strong tea brought soothing relief, hopefully having the same effect on them all. Annika inhaled the wonderful, calming scent and felt her cheeks grow warm.

"If anyone missed tenko, or got caught stealing a crumb of bread, or committed any petty crimes, Sonei tied them in a chair and placed it outside the entrance gate for forty-eight hours straight," Mamma added. "No break from the blazing sun, and no water or food. During a full moon he'd order the entire camp, including the sick, to attend tenko. He'd make us bow over and over, then find a minor infraction and cut food rations for a day or two. By the time we left, we subsisted on a half cup of tapioca gruel."

"No rice? No vegetables or meat? Gruel doesn't constitute a meal."

A mantle clock struck the half hour.

Mamma's teacup rattled as she placed it on the saucer. "That was the full ration for the day. But those days are behind us." Her voice wavered.

Tante gasped. "Dear Lord. I've seen the Japs hauling trucks filled with bags of rice. They purposely starved you."

"We heard they hoarded food supplies." Mamma scowled. "Annika snuck in eggs and tofu. Her nursing knowledge and English allowed access to the outside. More sickly women, children, and elderly people arrived daily from jungle camps. I'm certain food rations aren't any better now."

Tante leaned forward. "I've heard gossip about Sonei's tortures and how hard the interned children are worked."

"Believe it. They remove boys as young as ten, leaving heartbroken mothers. There's no place for the toddlers to play except in the streets. During heavy rain the sewage flows freely from septic tanks built for hundreds of people but now servicing close to ten thousand. Annika treated patients in a makeshift infirmary near the camp for beriberi, dysentery, malaria, and malnutrition, besides festering cuts, broken bones, and worse."

Tante Suze paled, her eyes distraught. She smoothed her sarong. "I'm so sorry. Your accounts are more atrocious than what I'd heard." Her voice had softened to barely a whisper.

Annika cleared her throat. The truth needed to be told. "The sleeping mats shrunk to twelve inches wide. We slept on our sides," she confided. "At the camp infirmary, I assisted doctors in surgeries I'd never seen performed at Tjikini Hospital during my training. The scalpels are dull, and the equipment is old and shoddy, but the elderly surgeons taught me what they knew." She drew a deep breath and recalled memories she'd sworn to forget. "If a prisoner escaped, they would search house to house and tear everything apart. The soldiers would grab us by the collar and shake us. I kicked them hard. They quit shaking me. I could have been killed twenty times for fighting back. The camp guards were horrible."

"Annika never told me about that atrocity," Mamma said. "She is my rock, remaining brave and clever, even translating for the Japanese who spoke English. Her skills gave us higher standing. I speak English but couldn't handle the strain of dealing with their angry, impatient soldiers. They made her administer a shot each day to a Japanese general, who became an ally. He'd attended university in America. After months of discussions about the Roman Empire, architecture, and art, he alerted us to the new rule about leaving the camp." She smiled at Annika and spoke directly to her. "I'd bet you're glad of the education we provided."

"Yes. And the sayings I've learned," Annika interjected. "Oma Elodie often repeated one, "De molen gaat niet om met wind die voorbij is. *The windmill doesn't care for the wind that's gone past.* When things got tough, I tried to move forward by treating everyone with dignity. One of our wedding hymns included the line, "show me to carry the present only, with a calm and peaceful mind."

"You are wise beyond your years, Annika." Tante Suze's round face wrinkled with smile lines. "I've heard the Malay term tempo doeloe, about returning to the life before the war, spoken with longing by a few Dutch. The olden days only benefitted a privileged few. I witnessed how my Indo father-in-law fought for respect. Phillip's a lucky man to have won your heart."

Annika shrugged. "There wasn't much of a contest. I vowed he'd be my husband the first time I set eyes on him."

They all chuckled. Annika hadn't heard that happy sound from Mamma in ages.

"It's good that you are a determined girl." Tante smiled. She then turned a sober face to Mamma. "I'm sorry about your horrible confinement. Please help yourself to whatever food or clothing I have." Her hand swept in a circle around the room, "or anything else. I can't begin to imagine what you've been thru, and I won't inquire about the camp again." She showed them to their room and fixed them a light meal of stir-fried vegetables before they retired for the evening.

That night, in the comfort of a small, real bed, Annika went through her muscle groups from her toes to her neck, releasing built up tension. They'd found safety. Nothing else mattered, as long as Phillip and her family survived. The Allies were closing in on the Japanese. Deep, slow breaths carried the perfumed smell of sweet oleander in through the open window.

Flowers bloomed, even in strife. Was that a faint rose scent?

What flower was Phillip smelling tonight?

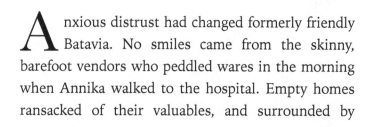

Anxious distrust had changed formerly friendly Batavia. No smiles came from the skinny, barefoot vendors who peddled wares in the morning when Annika walked to the hospital. Empty homes ransacked of their valuables, and surrounded by neglected, overgrown gardens lined the streets. Japanese soldiers shouted orders to anyone unfortunate enough to cross their path.

Elderly Indonesian men in ragged clothing and women in threadbare sarongs scurried across roads with bowed heads. Annika stuck to less heavily-travelled routes. She ducked into alleys or hid behind hedges to avoid being questioned. The letter she carried from the general was barely legible, and with him gone, it probably wouldn't protect her anyway. Nothing ensured their safety.

But that didn't stop Annika. Evenings, she nursed people in the neighborhood, and Mamma sewed clothing to earn a few coins or trade for what little fresh food was still available.

At the end of 1944, as supplies became scarce in the city, the Japanese were no longer the disciplined, smug soldiers. Gas supplies must've run low. They darted on their bikes, not in straight lines, but looking more like frenzied rabbits.

"The predator had become the prey," Annika thought as she walked home from stitching a laceration on a toddler. She entered the living room and stopped. Tante Suze and her mother sat side-by-side on the loveseat. Tante held a letter and Mamma scribbled on a note pad. Her grave expression brought tense alarm to Annika.

Tante Suze waved the battered envelope. "Phillip's father, my brother Louis, wrote an alarming reply to my last letter. He and his dear wife, Julia, have separated but remain cordial. She's nearly blind, and in dire need of cataract surgery."

Not a death. Annika flopped into a chair and her limbs went slack. "Do they still live in Bandoeng?"

"Yes," Suze said. "I know you've only met them once." She wrung her hands. "Nurses are in short supply. Louis asked if you'd travel there by train to help care for Julia after surgery?"

If the war ended soon, would she be closer to Phillip and Pappie or farther away? She dismissed the selfish thought. "Of course I'll help." She cleared her throat. "Mamma, we will go together?"

"Yes. I'm thinking tomorrow," her mother answered. "The train leaves at five in the morning. Suze double-checked. We should reach Bandoeng by nine."

Another relief. She couldn't separate from her mother now. "Then I'll start packing." Annika walked to their room. She threw her things into the battered suitcase and laid out a batik sarong and scarf to cover her head. The Japanese might not want their translator leaving Batavia and many guards recognized her from Tjikini Hospital and Tjideng camp.

In the morning, she took a sponge bath, then slid into the blue and white tube-shaped sarong Mamma had sewn. A shaft of dawn's first light brightened the color to a brilliant sapphire hue. A hitch formed in her throat. Her treasured ring from Phillip lay hidden under a floorboard in the storage room of Mansion Annika. She sank onto the bed and cradled her head in her hands. The ring didn't matter, but their promise did. She must see him again, feel his muscled arms around her, and return his sensual kisses. Otherwise, why continue struggling?

"Annika?" Mamma returned from the bathroom, dressed in a black and white sarong. "Are you okay? Are you sick?"

"I'm sick of war," Annika groaned.

"As am I." Mamma patted her back. "I believe it's nearly over. Meantime, family needs us in Bandoeng. Tante Suze packed us lunch. She's worried of a train delay out in the middle of nowhere. I'm glad we still have flat-soled sandals for walking to the train station."

Annika lifted her beat-up suitcase and satchel and carried them out of the bedroom. She draped and folded the scarf on her head to conceal as much of her face as possible. Her fingers touched the pink ridge at her hairline.

The bumpy scar on her forehead proved a train delay was nothing compared to enraged enemy soldiers.

∽

The Japanese rushed through the streets, panic on their faces. No one gave Annika and Mamma a second glance en route to Koningsplein Station to catch the train to Bandoeng, nor after they'd boarded alongside other Indo and Indonesian travelers who'd stood at the same platform. Smoke from the train puffed over the beautiful Art Deco arches in the station.

Annika took a couple of deep, slow breaths and then chose a seat on the outside wall of the train car. Mamma plopped down beside her. Too soon, Batavia and the Java Sea faded from view as they headed inland. After half an hour, Mamma's head dropped to her chest and she slept.

Annika folded her hands in her lap. If their men were released and came looking for her and Mamma in Batavia, the women at Mansion Annika would send them to Tante Suze. And one thing she'd learned was that worry never helped. She glanced out the window. Their belching, coal-fired train chugged past many idle rice fields. The next harvest would be scant. She tensed each time the train rumbled over old squeaky bridges made of a shoddy bamboo and wood mixture. Tiny shacks built too close to the rails shuddered. At stations, people who wore conical, straw hats hovered in anticipation. They held over-flowing baskets, crying children, and cackling, scrawny chickens. All vied for space on the crowded train's semi-open cars. After a long flat stretch, the train climbed hilly terrain. Suddenly, the brakes screeched, and their car jolted to a halt.

Annika gripped the seat edge. "Why'd we stop?" She checked her watch. "We're already an hour behind schedule."

Mamma shrugged. "Cow on the road?"

Other passengers chatted nervously. A conductor entered. "Quiet please!" he shouted in Malay. "The bridge ahead was destroyed by a bombing raid last night. You can either cross the ravine and wait on the other side for the return train to Bandoeng or stay put and be taken back to Batavia." He strode down the aisle, jumped to the next car, and repeated his news.

"Stay here, Mamma." Annika waited her turn to reach the stairs. She dropped to the ground and trotted to the edge of the deep ravine. Broken, tangled tracks no longer crossed the thousand feet or so to the other side. Splintered boards littered the rocky slope, some still smoldering. The steep angle of descent to the bottom ended at a shallow river strewn with boulders. She rubbed the back of her neck. Thank goodness for sturdy sandals. Hot sun brought beads of perspiration to her upper lip. Mamma had never enjoyed sports, and three years of malnourishment took away stamina, even in a younger, fitter person.

The decision to proceed or not should be her

mother's. Annika returned to the train, waited until other passengers had clambered off, then walked back to her seat.

"How steep?" Mamma asked.

"Fine for a goat," Annika said. "We'd need to traverse a treacherous downhill slope and cross a river. The steep climb to the other side looks close to three hundred feet."

Mamma adjusted the strap of her cloth shoulder bag, sewn in a patchwork array from scraps of material. She'd bartered away her leather one. "I'm ready." She jostled her suitcase to the exit, turned around, and climbed down the rickety metal stairs.

Black clouds hung low in the sky to the south.

Annika followed her. "We'd better beat the rain or climbing will be impossible." She lugged her own heavier suitcase off the train and moved her trusty medical satchel to her back. They approached the rim together and stood side by side. If they fell, they wouldn't stop until they hit a rock below. "Put your suitcase to the outside hand, Mamma. We'll hold hands and do this together. Let go of your suitcase and push your butt to the ground if you think you're going to fall."

"Okay. This is one of the more daring things I've done. Frederick would be proud."

"He's always been proud of you." Mamma's bright smile dispelled any remaining doubt in Annika. Her mother would keep up if it killed her.

And it nearly did. Skidding and stumbling, they wove through rocks all the way to the bottom.

Other Indonesian and Indo travelers fanned out alongside the slope. Many of the others were halfway up the far bank ninety minutes later when the two of them finally reached the river. Annika pointed to a flat boulder. "Want to sit for a minute and dip our feet in the water?"

"Resting sounds good. Removing my sandals takes too much effort." Mamma's weary grin still shone with accomplishment.

"Fair enough." Annika gazed into the muddy river. "No telling what we'd catch or what would catch on our toes."

Climbing out took over three hot hours in the sun. On the final fifty feet, Annika carried both suitcases. Sweat dripped into her eyes. She lowered her head and trudged the last few steps, her shoulders bent forward to thwart a tumble. She heaved the bags onto a gravel strewn bank ten feet from the train tracks. "Made it." She stretched her cramped fingers. "There better be a train soon. You could cut this muggy air with a knife."

Mamma pulled a ragged hankie from her bag and mopped her face. She perched on her suitcase. "I'm not certain a rain shower wouldn't be welcome."

A distant whistle blew. Cheers rose from the forty or so travelers who'd completed the trek. "A heavenly horn," Annika joked. They waited behind the rest of the people to climb the train's metal stairs. "I never thought a wooden seat would be so alluring." She sank onto the bare plank, her body exhausted.

Two hours later the train crested a hill. Ahead, at the base of rock-faced mountains, lay the sprawling city of Bandoeng. She and Mamma lugged their suitcases off the train. The station they entered buzzed in activity. Annika pulled the return envelope from her father-in-law's letter out of her satchel.

Sado drivers waited in a line running for half a block along the tracks. She showed the first one the envelope. "Take us here, please." In a few minutes, their buggy stopped in front of a neat bungalow. Annika counted out their fare and unloaded their cases. A tall man on a bicycle wheeled in behind the departing buggy. His handsome profile bore a strong resemblance to Phillip. Longing tugged at her heart. She missed her husband every hour of every day.

"Annika, Johanna!" he exclaimed. "So glad to see you."

"Meneer Van Hoven, pleasant to see you again," Annika said, while her mother kissed him on both cheeks.

"Tut. Tut. Call me Vader, like my other children." His eyes were the dark brown color of Phillip's. "Julia will be relieved you're here. I managed to get her into a hospital room, but the doctors hesitate to operate. Japanese rules, I guess."

Temporarily, if Annika's nightly prayers came true.

~

After a sparse lunch with Vader, Annika headed to Julia's room in the hospital. She checked in on her, then walked to the nurse's station. A woman wearing a stethoscope looped around her neck hurried to the desk.

"Good day," Annika began. She propped her elbow on the counter so that the red cross patch on her blouse showed. "I'm the nurse available to assist Mevrouw Julia van Hoven's recovery. The surgery can be scheduled without a worry for her after care. She's my mother-in-law."

The slim Indo nurse pushed back a lock of black hair and began shuffling through a stack of papers on her desk. She didn't make eye contact. "We're short-staffed. I'll try to send in a doctor. Please wait in her room."

Odd, at Tjikini Hospital, the nurse would have checked the surgery schedule and given her a day and time. A bad feeling grew to worse as hours of waiting by Julia's bedside stretched to evening. Finally, an Indonesian doctor entered the room.

He glanced at Annika, then to the sleeping Julia, who's complexion was nearly as pale as the sheet she lay upon. He lifted the clipboard at the foot of the bed and scanned the intake document. "Is she pure Dutch?"

"I'm not certain. Does that matter?"

"It does. We can't operate on her."

"We're related. My family is Indo and I have papers to prove it. I'll stay by Julia's side for the first few days." She paused to gather her courage. Failure meant blindness for Julia. "For the remaining week of her incapacity and thereafter, I'd voluntarily work here in three-hour shifts. I trained extensively at Batavia's Tjikini Hospital and as a field nurse assisting during operations at the Tjideng POW Camp. I can provide you references for either location."

Julia woke up and smiled. "She's very trustworthy, doctor."

The doctor's gaze flicked over Annika. He stepped to Julia's bed and examined her eyes. "Severe cataracts causing vision loss." He scraped his fingers through his black hair. "If I got caught, we'd all be hauled out of here."

"Nurse needed!" A woman's voice called in Malay from the hallway. No one answered. The wall clock ticked. She shouted again in a shrill voice.

"Okay. I agree to your terms and trust your experience. I'll do the surgery tonight at the shift change. Scrub up in two hours to assist me."

Annika nodded. Probably not a good idea to mention she'd never assisted during eye surgery.

"Thank you. I'll be ready." She watched him rush out, then slumped onto the edge of Julia's bed.

Warm fingers touched her arm. "Annika, you are so brave and assured. My son's a lucky man."

"Pray for both of us, Julia. I've never even watched during eye surgery."

Julia squeezed her arm. "I have the utmost confidence all will go well. I've had no energy the last few weeks worrying about this. Bless you for coming to Bandoeng." She dozed off again and Annika napped as best she could in the chair, knowing she'd need to be alert for tonight.

That evening's operation on Julia fascinated Annika. The doctor's long, slim fingers precisely guided a specialized surgical knife to remove her cataracts. He finished and turned to her. "Excellent job. I'm glad you'll be assisting our staff. Go home and sleep in your bed tonight. After we discharge her, she'll need to lay perfectly still for ten days. Can you manage?"

Annika raised her chin. "Of course. Thank you for helping a kind lady." Returning to the house after dark, she contemplated the surgeon's instructions to keep Julia's head perfectly still. Some kind of wooden brace?

A freshly installed roadblock barred traffic to their street. At the bottom of the barrier sat a row of sandbags. Annika lifted one and grunted at the thirty or so pounds. She scanned the empty street and hefted another. Julia wouldn't be able to move with these placed at either side of her head.

Adrenaline kicked in and she picked up her pace, her ears on alert. The sandbags she'd removed banged against her shins. If she got caught stealing from the Japanese military, she'd be executed.

CHAPTER 17

BANDOENG, EARLY OCTOBER 1945

The war had officially ended in August, but the Japanese continued to drive Indonesian Republican pemuda, the young extremist nationalist fighters, out of Bandoeng. Under the terms of the Japanese surrender, the Japanese were to hand governmental control of Bandoeng to the British. Nothing had gone as planned and the city hadn't been safe.

"Finally! Allies are nearby! The fighting will end," whispered the excited Indonesian doctor who'd helped Julia. He passed Annika in the hallway of the Bandoeng hospital.

The news he'd just relayed was the best news ever. Allies! Goosebumps rose on her arms. She opened her mouth to speak, then ducked her head to avoid the narrowed eyes of a Japanese soldier who rounded the corner on his hourly patrol. The anger of the Japanese toward the city's residents seemed to swell with each new day.

Shouting in Japanese came from the entry.

Annika stopped walking. The soldier spun on his heel and ran out the front doors. She backtracked to the doctor. After Julia's successful cataract surgery, he'd frequently requested Annika's assistance on operations, and he'd taught her new techniques. "Thank you for sharing the great news. I'm at the end of my shift, so I'll head home. Japanese soldiers hauled Julia's husband off to a POW camp the day she left the hospital. I won't leave her and Mamma alone and defenseless, just in case."

"Of course. The deadly skirmishes between the Japanese and the Indonesian pemuda have us all on edge. Go home to your family," he said. "I'll be sorry to see you leave our hospital. You've been a great help. I'll pray tonight for you and your husband to be reunited soon."

"If I don't see you again, thank you for all that you've taught me," Annika said, and waved goodnight.

"Be careful, there may still be fighting for a while," the doctor cautioned her.

Fortunately, things on the streets did seem calmer. The following day Annika returned to the hospital and began her shift by recording the temperature of patients in the post-surgery ward. She sterilized the thermometer and turned to leave. A rumble of noise grew louder outside. She dashed to the open window. "Please, let it be the Allies," she said under her breath.

The jeeps and large trucks carrying non-Japanese soldiers flew the red, white, and blue British Union Jack. Annika clapped her hands, stepped into the hallway, and walked through the front doors.

A blond-haired man jumped from a jeep and ran to where she stood. "Do you speak English?"

Smiling British soldiers finally had taken charge of Bandoeng! "I do." Annika nodded. "We're free of Japanese rule?"

"Yes. Spread the word, we're hoping to post the whereabouts of POWs in three days at the train station." He ran back to his comrades.

Annika clutched her heart. Finally, she'd find Phillip and her family. "Thank you!" she yelled.

The next three days seemed endless, as did waiting in line for their turn to read the huge sheets of paper tacked all along the train station's outer wall. Women ahead of them searched, cried, and prayed out loud. Some left bawling.

"We're next," Mamma said. They split up and ran their fingers over columns of names. Mamma tapped a line of print. "Claude survived. He's in a POW camp near Hiroshima, Japan. He'll be shipped directly to Holland."

"Dear Lord." Annika gasped. "That's where the American's dropped one of their atomic bombs." She clenched her teeth at the slip. "Claude's always been lucky," she added hastily. Doctors at the hospital had mentioned accounts of the horrible casualties from burns and radiation sickness—another detail she wouldn't tell Mamma. Annika continued searching names. "Emily's alive and in Sumatra!" She moved to another sheet. "Phillip's father is at a nearby camp!"

"I found Frederick!" Mamma shrieked. Her hands flew to the sky. "Thanks be to God, I found Frederick. He's in Kanchanaburi, near Burma."

"That's wonderful!" Annika hugged Mamma. She bit her lip. Only two more sheets of printed names remained. Her finger touched the bottom of the next page. "He's alive!" Joyous relief shuddered through her. Her heart felt ready to burst with excitement. "My Phillip's alive and in Nakhon Pathom, Thailand." She spun on one foot and clapped. "We can travel together to Thailand."

Her mother scanned the last sheet, her face grim. "No word about Rudy."

"Mamma, if Rudy's in England, he's not a POW. Don't give up on our flyer."

"No, I'll never give up on him." Mamma nodded and the two of them returned to Julia's house.

Determined to get on the next boat to Bangkok, Annika set out at five the next morning to reach the correct building where transport would be arranged. She'd left Mamma with Julia, the two of them hashing out the best way to get Emily a letter.

Thin, haggard women formed a line around the block behind Annika, all ready to work with British soldiers and be reunited with their POW husbands or others whom they'd lost track of during internment. At eight, she reached the desk. "Good morning," she said in English. "My in-laws want to return to Holland and my mother and I need passage to Thailand to reunite with our husbands."

A young soldier with kind eyes and a clipped English accent answered her. "Let's see what we can do, miss." He shuffled through several stacks of papers. "Hmm. Sumatra, Bali. Boy, those bloody Japs had camps all over." He continued scanning papers. "Sorry we didn't get here sooner. We've heard you endured horrible things."

"We did, and many poor souls didn't survive," Annika said. Worry inched up her spine. Would she ever get to Phillip? "Thank you for coming to our aid."

The man smiled. "It's our privilege." He put two papers side by side, then rose and checked a sheet posted on the back wall. He trotted back to Annika. "Success! There's space for your in-laws on a boat leaving for Holland next week. The day after tomorrow I can book you and your mum on a train to the port, and then get you both passage on a

British boat bound for Staffordshire. It makes a stop in Bangkok, Thailand. I will write out the name of the hotel for free lodging. The Americans are coordinating the further process to get everyone reunited. Will this trip work?"

"Yes! The sooner we get to Thailand, the better," Annika rejoiced.

"I don't want to give you false hopes. It may be weeks before you are reunited with your husbands, due to attacks on prisoners coming out of the camps."

Her stomach tightened. "What attacks?"

"The Japanese trained the Indonesians for battle and assured them of independence for Indonesia. Many of the young men are hell-bent to eliminate the Dutch, whom they see as enemies wanting to reestablish their control. There are renegade Japanese and Indonesians killing innocent people in the fight for who's going to rule these islands."

Not on purpose. That couldn't be. Annika pulled her satchel to her chest and clutched it tight. Phillip and Dr. Subroto had warned about unrest, not murder. And she'd thought leaving Bandoeng would get her out of a war zone. "Bangkok should be safe. We'll wait there for word of their release and I'll offer my nursing skills."

Concern marred his handsome features. "Okay. We've heard the men leaving the POW camps are in bad shape. You won't have a problem keeping busy as a nurse. Be careful though, it's a little unmonitored right now."

"Unmonitored doesn't worry me," she assured him.

"I believe you. Stop by tomorrow afternoon and I'll have all the tickets ready for pick up under your name. Nice to make your acquaintance, Mrs. Van Hoven. Good luck finding your lieutenant."

She'd soon fulfill her promise to cross an ocean to find Phillip. Annika stuck out her hand and they shook. "Thank you again for your help."

"You are very welcome, ma'am." He smiled, then greeted the next woman in line.

Annika pushed out all thoughts of malnourished men, women, and children being attacked after they left a camp. Surely that would be under control by now. Nothing would ruin the thought of her seeing Phillip. She walked with the lightest step she'd felt in years. Soon she'd reunite with her dear, sweet husband to continue the love story they'd only begun. She could count on her fingers how many nights they'd spent together as a married couple. Regardless, over the last four years her love had grown stronger. A new thought struck like a blow. Might his have weakened?

BANGKOK THAILAND OCTOBER 1945

The boat trip from Bandoeng to Thailand had been uneventful. Annika and Mamma were now thrilled to only be a brief train trip from their husbands. They'd been assigned a room in a decent hotel, and Annika had begun volunteering her nursing skills in Bangkok to pass the time until they got notification of Phillip and Pappie's release.

Annika signed out from another nursing shift. This day had started with a great opportunity from a pilot she'd vaccinated in the medical tent. Maybe this afternoon she'd finally get exact dates from the Americans coordinating the prisoner releases. She stopped by the tent dedicated for reuniting families with the interned Dutch, Australian, and European soldiers and repeated the information to the American soldier currently staffing the desk.

He'd searched a file and provided wonderful news for Mamma. "I'm thrilled you know when my father will be released," she said to the soldier. "Having three days of notice beforehand means I can arrange for someone to accompany my mother when she travels to meet him."

"I'm sorry to verify that your husband's release may take a couple weeks," the soldier said. "Just in case things change, stay put in your Bangkok hotel until further notice." He focused again on his paperwork.

The news on Phillip was not what Annika had hoped for, but Mamma would be ecstatic. "I'll arrange for someone to go with my mother."

The American's blue eyes met hers. "I'd suggest a burly male escort." He continued to fill out a form. "There are still renegade Japs and young Indonesians in many areas. They're out for blood." He looked up and must have caught the shock on her face. "Just a precaution. Your mother's route hasn't seen any fighting recently. I can't share any other details."

He'd shared enough to put Annika on alert. "I'll get a local man through the hotel. Again, thanks to all of you." Her admiration for the Americans' thoughtfulness grew as she watched how meticulously he recorded information about both her and Mamma. "This must be a huge undertaking to reunite the thousands of families who spent the war in separate camps."

"I have to double check each entry. The Japs had their miserable camps all over the Pacific."

"So I've heard. Believe it or not," she continued, "as a nurse I ministered to a genteel and respectful Japanese general, Moichero Yamamoto, who studied in America. He helped Mamma and I leave Tjideng POW Camp. He also told me how accepting and generous Americans were. You are proving him right."

He smiled. "War is hell. There are good men on both sides." He laid down his fountain pen and handed her a sheaf of papers. "These documents are for your mother. A courier will deliver a notice to your hotel alerting you when to board the train taking you to meet your lieutenant. Shouldn't be too much longer."

"I'll never forget how the Americans came to our aid after the horrible attack on Pearl Harbor." Annika waved goodbye. She strode through town and skipped up the steps to their Bangkok hotel like a colt frolicking in fresh grass. Mamma sat in the lobby, waiting in her usual spot in a wicker chair by the window. "I have two pieces of great news," Annika perched on the end table beside her and handed off the travel documents. "Phillip probably won't be released for a couple of weeks. But in three days, you will travel to reunite with Pappie."

"Annika, bless you!" Mamma shrieked.

"Nope. Bless the Allies, in this case the Americans." She hugged her mother, then leaned close. "I also met an older British pilot today at the hospital. He remarked on my ring, so I explained that my treasured wedding set lay buried in the shrubbery of our home in Batavia. He can fly me there on a quick trip he'll be making tomorrow afternoon. We'll return to Thailand at dawn, so there's no danger I'll miss Phillip—even if he's miraculously released early. The pilot assured me I can borrow a jeep at the airfield."

"No. It's too dangerous," Mamma hissed. "I don't venture out during the day here because some of the people are unfriendly. And there's probably someone else occupying Mansion Annika. I can't imagine our staff still lives there with all the fighting. You'd be considered a burglar."

"I can always say I'm on an emergency medical call and use Marta's old address from next door. I'll carry my nursing satchel and a good flashlight."

"Flashlight? You're planning to go at night?" Mamma's eyes grew round.

"I'm hopeful a family lives in Mansion Annika. It's a beautiful home," Annika said. "It's not like I can knock on the door and tell them why I'm there."

Mamma sank into the chair cushion. "I know I can't stop you."

Annika stood. "I stole sandbags from the Japanese army for Julia's recovery. You said you'd need money in Holland. Pappie and you are depending on me to reclaim what is rightfully ours."

"I'm horrified of the risk, truth be told. The least I can do is insist you take Pappie's Swiss army knife. He'd want you to have it handy." She clutched Annika's wrist. "You must be careful, Annika. You can't leave me now. Not like this. We've been through so much together."

"I won't. Don't worry. Rudy and Claude taught me some stealth tricks." Annika knelt at her knee. "We're all going to be reunited in Holland. And we'll have Oma Elodie's jewelry."

"No jewelry is worth losing you."

～

Annika put her face near the glass window of the airplane as it made a gradual descent. Piloted by two Brits, their plane had flown from Bangkok nearly four hours ago and reached Batavia at sunset. Below lay the old crescent shaped Sunda Kelapa – Coconut of Sunda Harbor – which ran into an estuary of the Ciliwung River. Farther up, the bustling new Tandjoeng Priok Harbor supported all sorts of ships. The airplane circled and dropped in altitude. Her stomach did a flip flop. Flying in the cargo area of a bigger plane felt different than flying in a Piper Cub. She took a couple deep breaths and closed her eyes, thinking of another time she'd seen the harbor from the ground. The Buginese schooners below would be pulling against their mooring lines. It seemed like a lifetime ago that she and Phillip had stood and compared them. What would he think of her next adventure? She'd better not get caught. No husband wanted his wife to be a burglar!

The plane's wheels bumped onto the runway. Her body lurched. She gripped the metal bench and held tight while the wheels skidded to a stop. Annika followed the pilots out of out the airplane and onto the tarmac. "May I run inside and make a quick phone call?" she asked.

"Sure," the familiar pilot responded, and when she returned outside, he grinned. "Vehicle secured.

Be back before 0100 hours," he instructed, and tossed her keys to the nearby green army jeep. "The fighting's subsided for the time being, or I wouldn't have brought you. Nevertheless, be careful and don't take any chances. Get as close to your destination as you can while there's still daylight."

"Yes, Sir!" Annika climbed onto the seat, made certain the shifter was in neutral, stepped on the brake, and then turned the key. The engine rumbled. Next, she pressed the switch and pulled out the headlight beam knob by her left knee. All set. Thank the Lord, Phillip had shown her how to drive when he'd managed to borrow a jeep to take her to ballet classes the last few weeks he'd been in Batavia. How she'd loved learning to drive with him as a patient instructor.

Like he'd coached her back then, shifting was merely footwork. The jeep eased onto the pavement as she moved to second gear. Her backpack barely shifted on the passenger seat. On top of it sat the leather medical satchel, empty except for her stethoscope and the mobile nurse card tucked under the flap. If she got stopped, between the battered ID and her blouse with an official Red Cross emblem, she should be safe.

Few oncoming vehicles approached while she headed south. Batavia, once pristine, looked neglected. They'd heard radio broadcasts that British troops had tried to curtail looting. The result was a

few boarded-up windows, pock-marked brick buildings, and debris that littered business areas. From
the reports, they were all thankful that Java wasn't as
war-torn as Europe. Were Mamma's parents in
Holland okay? Those worries needed to be shelved
for later. Annika gripped the wheel and drove until a
crossroad looked familiar. The stable wasn't more
than a block away. If it looked abandoned, she'd wait
there until later.

She eased her foot off the gas pedal and spotted
the lane beside their old horse pastures. Scruffy,
knee-high weeds lined the dirt road, now gouged
with deep holes. Before the war, Henri had kept the
lane flat and the grass perfectly mowed. Those days
were long gone. At least her horses, Newt-newt, and
Foxy were safely at Dr. Subroto's clinic. The phone
call to the veterinarian, which she'd made from the
base, had set her mind at ease. The nervousness in
Dr. Subroto's voice had kept her from visiting them.
Gripping the wheel with her left hand, she down-
shifted with her right hand, and drove slowly up to
the stable. One barn door hung off a broken hinge.
No sign of people anywhere. She parked with the
jeep's front end pointing to the road and hopped out.

Six goats wandered to the fence in front of the
pasture where they used to keep Maggy and Penny.
Bells on their collars tinkled, adding rhythm to the
repetitive chirps of early night bugs.

The goats stuck their heads thru the wooden rails

and bleated. One knocked over an empty bucket. "I get it. You need water." Annika filled the bucket from the spigot, stuck the pail in their pasture, and pulled her flashlight and dark shirt from her backpack.

This was the easy part of the night. The last rays of daylight gave the dusty interior of the barn a spooky look. She inhaled the faint smell of manure. Would the stalls hold horses again soon? She wiped her clammy hands on the black cotton trousers she'd borrowed. It would never be their barn again, never again would it house their precious horses. No one really knew how the fighting between the Indonesians and the Dutch would turn out, especially with Holland being in debt from the war. From what she'd heard, all the families had suffered emotionally, physically, and financially.

She unbuttoned the sleeveless blouse she'd flown in and put on a long-sleeved, dark shirt. Mamma had tacked a Red Cross patch to the upper arm. With luck, she wouldn't need to talk her way out of trouble. She turned on the flashlight and checked her watch. Several more hours to wait until people should be in bed, unless they were night owls.

Petting the goats took up some of the time. Too easily she recalled the wonderful adventures she'd had here, accompanied by Maggy, Newt-newt, and Foxy. Pappie had taught her so much about riding and life. Rocks littered the arena footing. They'd kept it sandy and smooth so she and Maggy could fly over jumps without a thought about landing. She wiped moisture from her eye. Would Pappie ever see his beloved horses again? Different, good times must lay ahead for them all, but for now the memories brought comfort. No war could take those away. Her glance flicked to the dark woods beyond the pasture. Even non-horseman Phillip had enjoyed walks on the peaceful trail. Time slowed to a standstill.

Finally, at eleven o'clock, she climbed in the jeep and drove onto the main road.

Shuttered windows and untended shrubs fronted the once elegant and bustling English Sports Club. No uniformed man stood at the door. Not a single sado or taxi drove on the road; no late-night guests needed to return to their homes. That all worked for her plan. Annika scanned the area.

The jeep would fit onto a strip of overgrown grass alongside the pool's fence at the side of the club closest to their house. She slowly passed a darkened Mansion Annika and made a U-turn. Parked in the shadows of the club, she took a deep breath, shouldered the backpack, and grabbed her medical satchel. Except for ever present sounds from bugs, silence pervaded her old neighborhood.

Crouched low, she moved through their weedy, overgrown lawn. Towels hung from the wrought iron rail of Mamma's balcony. Oudje or Kokkie wouldn't allow that. A broken bicycle sat on the circular driveway, beside a pile of garbage.

Sloppy strangers occupied their former home.

She ducked inside the open garage and released the breath she'd been holding. The shovel they'd used to dig the trench stood against the near wall. She grabbed the handle and crept toward the house, where their apothecary jars should lay buried under two feet of dirt. She'd placed them directly below the ends of the two living room windows, now fitted with vertical bars for protection.

The hint of coal smoke and spices hung in the sultry night air. Her pulse pounded. Someone had cooked a meal recently. Someone who worried enough to install bars. Her body felt numb. Leaving now would be cowardly. The people inside could have the house, but not her family's money and jewelry, if she could help it.

Sliding the shovel into the damp earth, she repeatedly scooped out dirt and then tapped the bottom of the hole. A soft ping jolted her. She dropped to her knees. The ground felt cool through her thin trousers. Her hands pushed dirt from around the outside of the jar. She lifted it, then ran her finger around the unbroken seal. Success! She stuffed it in her backpack and dug out the other three. Now the biggest challenge. The storage room had one small window. With all the fighting, would it be barred, too?

She laid her backpack on the ground and returned to the garage. Their old, eight-foot-long ladder sat tipped against the wall. Without a car inside, carrying it out was easy. She gently propped the ladder against the wall under the second-floor storage room window, put the flashlight and Pappie's knife into her medical bag, and slung it over her shoulder. If the rungs held her weight, she should be okay. She slipped off her shoes.

Wood creaked as she climbed. Her fingers relaxed. No bars blocked the window. Putting one hand flat against the wall, she balanced on the top rung and folded back the wooden shutters. The wood banged against the window frame. Tingles of fear shot into her toes.

Verdorie! Someone could be sleeping in her room, the next one over. Frozen in place, she listened. She heard only the incessant, methodical rattling of the night bugs. Using her flashlight, she panned the storeroom. Not much had changed except she saw less stuff cluttering the space. She wiggled through the opening on her belly, folded at her waist and let her fingers touch the floor, and then scooched her butt through. Her bare feet slapped onto the dirty wooden planks. Crouched, she waited and listened. Nothing. She crept forward and shone the flashlight beam.

Claude's hidey-hole had been near the back wall. With the blade of Pappie's knife, she pried the corners of several boards. On the third try, the plank lifted. A thin layer of dust covered the jar. She pulled it out, broke the seal and fished out her sapphire ring and wedding band. She replaced the lid and shoved the jar in her bag. Jewelry clinked against glass. Her fingers trembled as she slipped her wedding set on, fisted her hand, and pressed the ring to her heart. Warmth crept into her soul, the likes of which she hadn't felt since the night Phillip had made the trip to see her in the cargo plane. She was so close to having Phillip back. So very, very close. Soon they'd be together to continue their sapphire promise of loyalty, trust, truth, and love. Please Lord, let him survive, she prayed. Her eyes misted, and she wiped them with her sleeve and swung the flashlight toward the outer wall.

The panel where she'd tucked the family papers still had one corner slightly ajar. Wedging the flat knife blade under the edge allowed her to pry it back from the wall. She slipped out the packets of papers and photos, then tucked them into her leather satchel beside the jar.

A door closed in the hallway.

Had they heard her? Goosebumps rose on her arms. In two strides she'd made it to the window. With the satchel hanging from her neck heavy against her chest, she put one leg out the window, rolled onto her belly, put the other leg out, and bent her body over the sill. Her feet dangled in thin air. She bit her lip, gripped the windowsill's edge, and brought her legs to the outside wall of the house. By inching her foot to the left, her big toe finally hit wood. She swung the bulky satchel to her back and moved her foot onto a rung. After she'd slid her toes to find the center of the board, she backed down the creaky wooden rungs and dropped to cool grass.

A dull light shone from her room. A bedside lamp? Were they looking outside? Her heart thundered in her chest. She grabbed the backpack and ran toward the jeep with the glass jars clattering. Sharp gravel scraped her bare feet. Verdorie! She'd left her favorite sandals on the lawn! Too late. In one move she'd leapt in and thrown the two bags on the passenger seat. Her fingers shook as she stuck in the key. The motor failed to turn over on the first try. A light shone from her parents' room.

"No!" she hissed, and pumped the gas, then turned the key again.

The engine rumbled to life. She sped past the English Club without looking back. A jeep and a truck were the only vehicles on the road as she headed north. Her shoulders relaxed after she turned from the main road into the airfield parking lot. Safe!

The pilot stood near the space where the jeep had been parked. He thew her a broad smile. "Mission accomplished?"

She pulled the two bags onto her lap, then swung her dirty feet out. "Yes, thank you. A good soldier wouldn't have left her shoes behind at the first sign of danger."

"I'd say you're pretty damned gutsy, shoes or not," he chuckled.

She patted the backpack. "Footwear is a minor sacrifice. I can't wait to give these to Mamma."

"Glad you're back early. We're scheduled to take off in ten minutes, and no telling who'll come looking for you." The pilot took the heavier bag. "I bet you have many stories to tell, Mrs. Van Hoven."

"Anyone who survived this war has stories. Mine will have a happy ending when I see my dear Phillip."

"He's a lucky man to have a courageous wife."

Courageous or dumb? Caught burglars got shot.

CHAPTER 18

What was wrong with her? Annika wiped her brow and forced her weary arm to grasp the handrail of the stairs leading into the Bangkok hotel. She'd remained in their room after Mamma had left over a week ago to be reunited with Pappie. Each long shift spent nursing POWs who'd been starved, overworked, and tortured made her more nervous while she waited for news of Phillip's release. Maybe that was why she felt so awful and bloated.

If Phillip was sick, would there be someone to help him? She dragged her feet up the last steps and onto the hotel's veranda. The slightly drier heat of Thailand must be affecting her more than the muggy heat of Batavia, or maybe she'd put in too many hours at the field hospital. The uncertainty of Phillip's release date didn't help. No matter. She'd need to elevate her feet before dinner. The swelling in her ankles looked worse. She stepped into the lobby.

"Mevrouw Van Hoven," The desk clerk called. "A letter arrived for you."

"Thank you." She took the battered envelope, plopped onto the nearest wicker chair, and then clutched the letter to her heart. Meneer and Mevrouw Frederick Wolter appeared in the sender's area. Warmth rose in her chest. Her parents were reunited. She ripped open the thin flap.

Dearest Annika,

Pappie is malnourished, but his spirits are fine. The escort you secured for my travel to Kanchanaburi proved to be invaluable. I spent one night at a hotel before we all got word the militia prisoners would be released. There wasn't a dry eye when us older women flocked to meet our bedraggled husbands. I have so much news to tell you from Pappie. For some of the war, Phillip lived in a prison camp in Thailand and Pappie was in Burma. The Japs merged the two camps together, so Pappie came to Thailand for most of the duration. Both men labored in the grueling task to build a bridge over the Mae Khlung River. Some call it the River Kwai. Nonetheless, thousands of men perished.

Enough sadness.

Here's the good news. I met someone who confirmed that Rudy is alive! He's in London. Hopefully, we'll see him soon. Pappie and I had a long talk. I want to see my parents in Holland, and he feels Batavia won't offer us another fresh start. A contact of Pappie's arranged for our passage on a

ship to Amsterdam, where we'll stay with Oma and Opa.
I've put their last known address at the bottom of the page.
We contacted Dr. Subroto, who will bring our trunks to the
Batavia Harbor. He had to sell a couple of Pappie's imported
horses, but he verified that all the other animals are fine.
Pappie can't believe you stole into our old house at night to
retrieve our valuables. He acted outraged, but I saw pride in
his eyes when I patted the patchwork on my purse concealing
the money and jewels. I'm glad you sent them with me, as I'd
bet the ship for Europe will have set sail by the time you
receive this letter. We'll need money in Holland, which you
provided.

Annika sank farther into the chair. Rudy was
okay! That was great news. But her parents were out
to sea and headed to Holland. Would she see them
soon? If something happened to Phillip she'd be
totally alone. A tear dropped onto the page. She
blotted the smeared ink and continued reading.

Pappie wanted you to know what a kind and loyal man
you married. Your father was only a sergeant in the militia,
so after being moved to a different camp, he was relieved to
hear that First Lieutenant Phillip van Hoven would
command them. If Pappie asked Phillip for favors to aid the
sickest prisoners, Phillip did everything in his power to help.
You know Pappie, and his mantra to first feed the ones who
cannot feed themselves. Anyway, our two men developed a
close and loyal friendship. Your Phillip contracted malaria,
so every few weeks he gets sick. I know you'll be the best
nurse he could ever ask for.

I've told Pappie how you got us through the hell years at Tjideng by your cleverness, your positive outlook, and your faith.

Keep that faith and we'll celebrate as a family at Oma and Opa's in Holland.

We both send all our love,

Mamma and Pappie

Annika folded the letter and slipped it into the envelope. More tears wet her skirt. She swiped them away. No mention of Phillip missing her or doing everything in his power to reunite. She squeezed the sheet of paper. Did men not discuss these emotions as women did, or had he regretted marrying her? Maybe the malaria had progressed to later stages of mental confusion. No, that couldn't have happened. She stared out the open doors and onto the busy street.

"Annika Wolter?" the vaguely familiar male voice called out.

Annika flinched, and Mamma's letter fell to her lap. That voice belonged to Herman, the mean-mouthed business associate of Pappie's. A twist of fate or bad luck? Regardless, another affirmation from him of her ugliness wasn't what she needed to hear. She stuck her chin in the air. "I'm Mevrouw Van Hoven now." She waved the hand bearing her precious wedding rings.

"Yes, yes," he chortled. "Belated congratulations. I lived in Paris at that time. I'd heard Frederick's beautiful daughter married a handsome, rising lieutenant."

"What? Wait. You always called me ugly." She'd blurted the accusation without thinking.

His jovial smile changed to a dropped-jaw face of alarm. "Oh dear. You didn't know I was teasing? I am so sorry. I don't have children. You struck me as this perfect little princess. A lovely, talented, and athletic child any parent would cherish. Every adult admired your spirit." He knelt beside her. "I never knew my words hurt you. Will you accept my apology for being a lout?"

Annika strained to take a deep breath. Lout didn't begin to cover the hurt he'd inflicted. But with all she'd been through since then, it seemed so insignificant. "I will."

"Thank you," he said. "Did your family move to Thailand?"

"No. I'm waiting for my husband to be released from his POW camp. Mamma and Pappie are on their way to Holland. Hopefully, my brothers are as well. Does business bring you to Bangkok?"

"I'm not as connected as I once was." He smoothed the fine jacket he was wearing. It would have paid for many months of food in Batavia or Bandoeng. Judging by his belly, he hadn't missed too many meals. "I'm a liaison officer here in Thailand." He tapped his plump cheek. "Say, I'm invited to a party at a Siamese prince's palace on Saturday. It will be a lavish affair for Dutch, British, and French businesspeople to celebrate the war's end. I'd be honored to take you as my guest."

A party. Annika placed the envelope in her bag and sat in ladylike fashion—hands folded, and legs crossed at the ankles. "I'd enjoy an evening out." She glanced at her scarred leather shoes. Her paltry wardrobe consisted of nursing clothes and the well-worn batik sarong Mamma had turned into a sheath that now fit snugly. She shook her head. "Sorry, I'll need to decline. I don't own anything suitable to wear. I wouldn't want to embarrass you."

He patted her hand and rose. "I know a seamstress here in town. After dinner tonight, we will visit her. She'll have a dress made for you by Saturday."

Only a fool would turn down the opportunity. "Sounds lovely." They arranged to meet later that evening and Annika let Herman handle all the details. Whatever he'd paid the seamstress, she'd complied with his request. Two days after the late-night fitting, Annika twirled in her silk party dress. The material gave the hint of a pinkish glow. It draped over her body, flowed to her ankle, and grazed her new, open-toed white sandals. She descended the stairs with confidence.

Herman met her in the lobby wearing a well-cut black tuxedo. "You're lovely, Annika. As always." He escorted her to a waiting car. They travelled for nearly an hour out of Bangkok, then entered an estate with spectacular formal gardens. Trees shorn into pom-pom-shaped tops, spraying fountains, and blooming flowers lined the winding driveway. A white, three-story palace festooned by red and gold-trimmed windows was topped by stacked layers of reddish roof tiles tipped in gold. Fifteen-foot-tall marble columns supported the entryway. Gargoyle animals twice the size of the lions they resembled sat on each side. In front of them stood live guards to ensure that no one entered or exited the palace—they'd staged the affair outside in several dozen tents.

Herman's hired car parked behind a row of Bentleys and Mercedes. He hopped out first. "I have a few people to speak with. I've never known you to be shy, and there may be folks here you recognize. Let's say we meet back in two hours?"

Her stomach tightened as she got out. "Perfect." Annika smiled and he walked away, his posture loose. She took a champagne flute from a strolling waiter and watched Herman.

He approached a man in a blue uniform embellished by a chest full of medals and a gold-rimmed monocle that dangled from a chain. The man smiled broadly to Herman, and the two of them began animated conversation.

Women in dazzling ball gowns or intricately decorated sarongs gathered in clusters of two or three. Men strode about the lawn wearing traditionally embroidered garments or tuxedos. Annika sipped the cool, bubbly drink and recalled her wedding reception and Pappie's French vintage. How star struck by Phillip she'd been, and what a wonderful wedding night they'd shared.

It seemed like a lifetime ago. She walked away from the palace. A peacock displayed his indigo and emerald plumage, which brightened the backdrop. That bird would never become a feather duster. He pecked at the edge of clear glass covering a huge, in-ground swimming pool. Beneath the glass, twinkling lights illuminated flowers that floated in the water.

Annika wandered amongst the white tents. Inside them, tables held overflowing platters of food. She'd been starved for over three years, but none of the lavishly garnished delicacies perked her appetite. Strange, she'd dreamed of unlimited portions of food while at Tjideng and now the thought of gorging herself held no appeal.

A waiter offered her plump steamed shrimp laid out in a conical pattern atop a silver tray. She took two and placed them on her napkin.

The perfume of flowering jasmine competed against aromas of roasted meat, spices, and sweet desserts set out in other scallop-edged tents. A wooden dance floor covered part of the perfectly trimmed lawn. Scattered beyond it sat chairs and round tables covered by brightly colored brocade cloths. Waiters in crisp white formal jackets passed trays laden with wine, champagne, and liquors. She nibbled the shrimp and found a chocolate tart in the dessert tent, then strolled past clusters of guests speaking in a variety of languages.

At the far end of the pool the polished wooden dance floor glowed as two men carrying torches lit an array of candles. The assembled band struck up a waltz, and couples took to the floor. She swayed to the music, and imagined she was waltzing in Phillip's arms. Please, oh please, grant the two of us another dance. She lifted her eyes to a dazzling night sky. Somewhere out there, he saw the same stars.

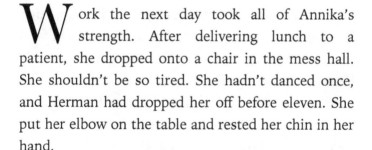

Work the next day took all of Annika's strength. After delivering lunch to a patient, she dropped onto a chair in the mess hall. She shouldn't be so tired. She hadn't danced once, and Herman had dropped her off before eleven. She put her elbow on the table and rested her chin in her hand.

"Annika," said an American medic. "I believe you may have beriberi. I've been watching you and noticed telltale signs. He raised his fingers as he rattled off her issues. "Difficulty walking, lethargy, swollen limbs, and loss of appetite. I can treat you immediately."

"Oh dear." Annika rubbed her temple. "I'll take whatever will get rid of it. I've experienced pins and needles in my fingers and shortness of breath for a few days. I feel incompetent to not have recognized the symptoms."

He patted her shoulder. "That's not uncommon." He left for a moment and returned with a syringe, swabbed her arm, and administered a shot. "You should feel much better in a few days."

Annika woke the next morning and touched her achy face. Tightly stretched skin pushed against her eye sockets. She threw her legs over the bed and grabbed the hotel's hand mirror. "Good Lord," she cried. Her face resembled a fully-inflated puffer fish. Verdorie! A drug reaction. She cradled her head in her hands and glanced at her still swollen legs and ankles. No wonder she'd had to let all the darts out of her skirt. Beriberi often caused water retention.

An envelope shot under the closed door.

She stumbled across the floor, saw her name, and ripped it open. Her hands shook while unfolding the thin paper.

Lieutenant Phillip van Hoven. POW of Nakhon Pathom. One relative may board the train leaving Bangkok at 09:30 for travel and reunion. All riders will remain seated in the train. Released men will traverse the aisles. Please stay seated to accommodate the large number of freed prisoners.

Annika checked her watch. A little over an hour to dress and get to the station. No amount of time could disguise her bloat. She pulled on the silk party dress and slipped her pudgy feet into the new sandals, then walked to join the throng of women in line for the train. She took a seat on the aisle end of a bench in the last open car. The train chugged through grassland and rice paddies and screeched to a stop on a side rail. Haggard men with carved cheekbones and little flesh on their frames waited at the station. Women opened compacts with tiny mirrors. Some added rouge or pinched their cheeks. Nervous energy and hope swirled through their car. Annika pulled strands of hair to lay along her puffed cheeks and chin.

"All aboard!" yelled the conductor. A loud cheer rose from the men and they scrambled single file up the ladder of the car behind the engine. Laughter and cheers came from the cars in front of theirs. Finally, the first men stepped into their aisle. Squeals erupted in the front row. Two men pulled smiling women to their feet. More couples reunited in the next hour, including the husband of the woman seated beside her. She touched Annika's shoulder as she slid by. "Your lieutenant will be here, don't you worry."

Annika sat quietly, watching the faces of men passing her. No Phillip. She refolded her hands in her lap, her memories turning back the pages of time from their wedding to their engagement party, and to their first sado ride to the harbor to study the boats.

She wasn't sleek and elegant, but she'd weathered the storm like the Buginese schooner they'd seen so long ago at the pier. Would that be good enough for Phillip?

A smaller group of emaciated men entered. The last five women sat at attention. The men stalked between benches, desperation etched in their faces. Several shouted to loved ones. Three left the train keeping their hands on their wives' waists. A final man ducked his head to enter. He walked the aisle with the stride of an athlete, not an old zakenman. Annika clutched the bench. Thin, haggard, and still handsome—it was Phillip! Her voice stuck in her throat. His clothes were threadbare, his shorts patched. He'd pinned the sapphire tie tac to his lapel. Her breath came in gasps. He remembered, he still loved her.

She looked up and brushed aside the hair which hid her bloated face.

He passed her row.

No! Phillip deserved the best and here she sat, unrecognizable with puffed cheeks and slits for eyes.

He turned and approached from the opposite end. His eyes flicked over her. She couldn't talk, couldn't move. No noises came out of her throat. He dodged a man who grabbed his wife in the row ahead. A wrapped chocolate bar stuck out of his pocket. Annika smiled and felt relief course through her veins.

He turned again, his eyes lowered and his lips tight as he prepared to exit the car. When he reached her seat, she scooted to the edge, slipped her hand in his pocket, and removed the chocolate bar. She peered up again, her pulse racing at the sight of her darling man, her sweetheart. "Liefje!" she sobbed.

"Oh my God!" he exclaimed. "Annika!"

"Yes."

He pulled her to her feet and pressed her into his chest, close enough to feel his thumping heart. "Oh, Annika, my love. I've missed you more than you'll ever know. I ran like a demon when I heard the Red Cross was handing out chocolate bars. I had to have one for my sweet, beautiful wife."

She crushed her face into him and clenched the thin material of his shirt. He smelled of lye soap and shaving cream. "No, I look terrible. I got beriberi," she fought to keep her voice from cracking. "The medicine caused this bloating. I'm so sorry." Her tears wet his shirt collar.

"Annika, never apologize. I'll love you forever, no matter what. You'll always be beautiful in my eyes." His fingers combed through her hair. "You dazzled me during your first ballet performance, you captured my heart wearing a ball gown. Most of all though, at my lowest when I frantically worried about your safety, neither of those images came to mind." He stroked her back, his hands warm and comforting in their strength. "The confident, capable

Annika I admired jumped her beloved mare over a huge obstacle. That Annika waited for me. That clear memory of you sailing over those rails kept me going days and nights, through all the horrors." He lifted her chin. "You're my courageous and beautiful wife whom I've longed to see again with all my heart. My special meisje." His dark, gold-flecked eyes warmed deep into her soul.

The sparks she'd seen in Phillip's beautiful eyes nearly four years ago hadn't diminished. Thank the Lord, no. They'd intensified to brilliant flames, and Annika knew why after her own years spent yearning, and praying, and hoping that he'd survived. Her liefje, her handsome lieutenant whom she'd loved from the very start. Wrapped in his strong arms, she knew that they'd face challenges together. They'd both carry battle scars for life, but they'd beaten the war. His warm lips and sensual kisses told her a wonderful new world lay ahead. True peace healed her tortured heart. From this day forward, during their second romance, they'd continue to honor their sapphire promise of loyalty, trust, truth, and most of all, unfailing love.

～

And so, this part of the love story concludes with their joyous reunion. Sally hopes you enjoyed reading Annika and Phillip's story as much as she enjoyed blending incidents from her friend Iris's life with fictional sequences to give readers a sense of the time period and its challenges. **For a free download of an overview of the continuation of their life together,** please go to www. sallybrandle.com **To book a free zoom book club appearance** with Sally Brandle, visit the Events tab on her website. Please know that **reviews are gold** to an author, and the time taken to write one is appreciated.

If you enjoyed Annika's story, you may also enjoy Sally's contemporary romantic suspense stories from her **Love Thrives in Emma Springs Series.**

REFERENCES

A selection of the websites that the author used to authenticate historical details in the story:

- From Dirk Teuween: photos and information (the Netherlands) http://www.indonesia-dutchcolonialheritage.nl/indexaims/dirkteeuwenaims.pdf
- The wedding song: https://www.youtube.com/watch?v=QDMVzoXnm7E

From Internet searches:

- https://theindoproject.org/murder-of-indies-dutch-is-genocide/
- https://myindoworld.com/?doing_wp_cron=1615720133.2954289913177490234375

- The Forgotten Women of the War in the East: https://www.bbc.com/news/magazine-29665232#:~:text=By%20far%20the%20largest%20group,to%20starvation%2C%20exhaustion%20and%20disease.

- http://factsanddetails.com/indonesia/History_and_Religion/sub6_1c/entry-3954.html

- https://jhna.org/articles/dutch-batavia-exposing-hierarchy-dutch-colonial-city/

- https://uwm.edu/wp-content/uploads/sites/231/2016/01/2008KehoeArticle.pdf

- https://www.thejakartapost.com/news/2015/10/05/two-centuries-slavery-indonesian-soil.html

- https://apjjf.org/-Elizabeth-Van-Kampen/3002/article.html

- https://www.britannica.com/place/Indonesia/Toward-independence

- "Dutch Colonial Nostalgia across Decolonization" by Paul Bijl, University of Amsterdam https://www.journalofdutchliterature.org/index.php/jdl/article/download/40/40#:~:text=The%20words%20'tempo%20doeloe'%20denote,'%2C%20meaning%20they%20are%20indolent.

- https://en.wikipedia.org/

wiki/Japanese_occupation_of_the_Dutch_
East_Indies

- Tjideng : http://members.iinet.net.au/
  ~vanderkp/tjideng.html
- https://www.britannica.com/place/
  Indonesia/Toward-independence
- Hybrid Identities https://escholarship.org/
  uc/item/70h3s06r, Montclair, Sani
- Indo culture today: http://scholarworks.
  csun.edu/bitstream/handle/10211.3/
  118333/Stern-Jamie-thesis-
  2014.pdf?sequence=1

Many photos were graciously provided by NIOD.
https://www.niod.nl/

**Map.derivative work: Emok (talk) World2Hires_-
filled_mercator.svg: Emok   Image:Pacific_Area_-
_The_Imperial_Powers_1939_-_Map.jpg

WORD TRANSLATION TABLE

- Mamma: (Dutch) Mother/Mom
- Pappie: (Dutch) Father/Dad
- verdorie: (Dutch) damn
- Opa: (Dutch) grandfather
- zakenman: (Dutch) businessman
- Djati (Dutch) teak
- Oma: (Dutch) grandmother
- schatje: (Dutch) little treasure
- Georgette: (French) translucent silk fabric
- kleuters: (Dutch) toddler
- gymnasium: (Dutch) university prep high school
- Goede Morgen: (Dutch) good morning
- Sociëteit (Dutch) Society or private club
- Sint Nikolaas: (Dutch) Saint Nicholas

- Meneer: (Dutch) Sir
- Mevrouw: (Dutch) Mrs.
- Juffrouw (Dutch) Miss
- Nonna (Malay) Miss
- Kembang sepatu: (Malay) hibiscus flower
- gado-gado: (Malay) mix-mix, steamed vegetables and peanut sauce
- laan: (Dutch) avenue-Boxlaan is Box Avenue
- baboe: (Dutch) nanny
- kokkie: (Dutch) cook
- kapot: (Dutch) broken
- meisje: (Dutch) girl
- liefje: (Dutch) darling or sweetheart
- Noir: (French) black or raven
- merdi: (French) good luck-specifically in ballet
- kwartje: (Dutch) twenty-five cents
- dubbeltjes: (Dutch) ten cents
- tenko: (Japanese) Roll call
- Tempo doeloe: (Malay) the olden days
- sado: (French) small two wheeled, horse-drawn buggy. The driver and passenger sit back-to-back
- Indo: a person of mixed Indonesian and European descent
- beriberi: thiamine deficiency/starvation disease

- French Indochina: Modern day Vietnam, Laos, Cambodia
- KNIL: (Dutch) "Koninklijk Nederlands Indisch Legeror", Royal Dutch East Indian Army
- ML (Dutch) Military Aviation Division

1. In real-time, Iris (Annika) was indeed fifteen and a half when she first saw her future (twenty-three-year-old) husband. He wasn't aware of her age, due to her maturity and her accelerated high school graduation, until well after he'd begun to fall in love. Her parents put restrictions on their dating. How would you, or your parents, have handled this scenario?

2. The family credo of noblesse oblige figured prominently in Annika's story. Have your read other books which featured a similar expectation? Do you think noblesse oblige is still relevant today with many countries continuing to have a monarchy?

3. Annika came from a socially prominent Dutch colonial family, while other characters are Indonesian, such as the servants and the veterinarian, or

Indos, of mixed ancestry. In what ways is this distinction relevant to the story?

4. This book differs from many WWII books in that it spends a good portion of the story during the protagonist's life prior to the war. How did her family life, her relationship with animals, and her healing skills aid in her war-time survival?

5. One of Annika and Phillip's wedding songs in the story features the line, "Show me to carry the present only, with a calm and peaceful mind." Are there any song lyrics or poetic lines that guide you in tough times?

6. During Annika's childhood, D.E.I. equated to the colonial Dutch East India. In the present day, DEI is an acronym for Diversity, Equity, and Inclusion.

"Diversity is the presence of differences within a given setting. Equity is the process of ensuring that processes and programs are impartial, fair and provide equal possible outcomes for every individual. Inclusion is the practice of ensuring that people feel a sense of belonging in the workplace." *

Where did you see instances in the book which would hint at the brewing revolution of 1949 and the reasons behind it?

7. In the epilogue available free on Sally's website, the author lays out the next thirty or so years of Annika's life. Were you curious about what happened to the characters after the war? Did their lives turn out differently than you imagined?"

8. Research sites were named in the References section of the book. Did you go to any of them, and if so, what did you learn?

*https://builtin.com/diversity-inclusion/what-does-dei-mean-in-the-workplace

The Hitman's Mistake

Love Thrives in Emma Springs Book 1

A woman pursued by mobsters. The FBI agent protecting her. While they escape killers...they can't escape falling in love.

Torn By Vengeance

Love Thrives in Emma Springs Book 2

Look over your shoulder, he's watching. Corrin Patten is solidly on a path to make partner in a prestigious Seattle law firm when an ominous threat from her past turns deadly.

The Targeted Pawn

Love Thrives in Emma Springs Book 3

Threats forced her to flee Seattle. Honor binds him to Montana. A second chance at love tethers them together.

Purchase links for Sally's *Love Thrives in Emma Springs*
contemporary romantic suspense series:

- *The Hitman's Mistake*:
  www.amazon.com/dp/B07DM795GP/
- *Torn by Vengeance:*
  www.amazon.com/dp/B07P1D33K1/
- *The Targeted Pawn*:
  www.amazon.com/dp/1647160707/

ABOUT THE AUTHOR

Multiple-award winning author Sally Brandle weaves slow-burning romance into edgy suspense, motivating readers to trust their instincts. Growing up as a tomboy alongside brothers prepared her to work in a male-centric industry, raise sons, and create action-packed stories featuring strong women. She thrives on creating unintentional heroines who conquer their vulnerabilities and partner with heroes to outwit cunning villains. Penning Iris's story presented a challenge to stay true to her life while portraying the colonial aspect of *Sapphire Promise* in a sensitive manner. Research and consultations with a variety of experts is her way of checking facts. Her rescued Tuxedo cat, Shepherd dog, and Blue Heeler are her companions during long spells of writing or bouts of tormenting weeds in her garden. Afternoons she often spends riding on the wind with her thirty-one years young Quarter Horse. Find Sally on:

- Website: http://www.sallybrandle.com
  (EVENTS tab-offers for free Book Club
  zoom appearances)

- Facebook: https://www.facebook.com/profile.php?id=100012840931763
- Twitter: https://twitter.com/sallybrandle
- Pinterest: https://www.pinterest.com/sallybrandle/
- Instagram: https://www.instagram.com/sallybrandle2018/
- Goodreads: https://www.goodreads.com/author/show/18116238.Sally_Brandle
- Blog link: https://smpauthors.wordpress.com/author/sallygfrog/

Sixty-One Years of Love and Devotion

Iris, our heroine, and Sally